The Language of Negotiation

The Language of Negotiation

A Handbook of Practical Strategies
for Improving Communication

Joan Mulholland

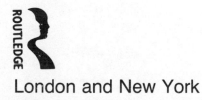

London and New York

First published 1991
by Routledge
11 New Fetter Lane, London EC4P 4EE

Simultaneously published in the USA and Canada
by Routledge
a division of Routledge, Chapman and Hall, Inc.
29 West 35th Street, New York, NY 10001

© 1991 Joan Mulholland

Typeset in 10/12pt Garamond Linotronic 300 by
Florencetype Ltd, Kewstoke, Avon

Printed in Great Britain by T.J. Press (Padstow) Ltd, Padstow, Cornwall.

British Library Cataloguing in Publication Data
Mulholland, Joan *1939–*
    The language of negotiation: a handbook of practical
    strategies for improving communication.
    1. Negotiation
    I. Title
    158.5

    ISBN 0–415–06040–0

*Library of Congress Cataloging-in-Publication Data
has been applied for*

93 – 3041 mc

For Margaret Phillips: a friend indeed.

Contents

PART V WRAP-UP – LANGUAGE AFTER THE EVENT

Introduction

Begin at the beginning, the King said, gravely, and go on till you come to the end: then stop.

(Lewis Carroll)

GENERAL

Negotiation as a social activity ranges from such examples as discussion of the daily distribution of work within an office, through an inter-firm disagreement over an ambiguous contractual detail, to organising a massive sales campaign aimed at an overseas market. Every negotiation is constituted of language, is a set of social behaviours enacted within the domain of language. Every utterance made and every text written within a negotiation is an act with repercussions on the outcome. While such acts cannot solve some of the problems of business, such as high interest rates or declines in sales, they can solve the problems of misunderstanding which arise from language use and can always improve the conduct of a negotiation. Therefore it is important for negotiators to recognise the power of language and to understand its potentialities as a negotiating instrument. With this knowledge they can radically improve the effectiveness of their negotiating skills. A fuller awareness of how language functions in communication can lead to several useful outcomes: in general terms it allows for greater creativity at both personal and institutional levels, and in specific terms it improves the quality of a participant's contributions to a particular negotiation, and assists in the accurate reading of others' negotiating strategies.

Competence in negotiation cannot be achieved by following a list of rules or using any one particular set of tactics, but rather it comes about when people acquire a sensitivity to the factors in language that affect negotiation, when they develop a personal repertoire of skills based on this sensitivity, and can adapt those skills in a flexible manner to suit the needs of a particular negotiation. The process to be undergone begins in acquiring cognitive awareness and continues by self-monitoring, and skilled practice.

This book is intended to be of assistance in this process to all those in business and professional life whose work involves negotiation. The material presented is distilled from recent developments in language pragmatics, and in rhetoric and communication studies, and is adapted for practical purposes. It requires no preliminary study of language on the part of its readers. It assumes only that readers are experienced language users, who recognise the value of an increased knowledge of their present usage and wish to improve their contributions to future negotiating activity.

There has been much recent research into discourse, exploring the characteristics of language as a social instrument, the differing values of spoken and written language forms, and the strategies available for interaction. Useful findings have been produced on the acts of speaking and writing as powerful social events. Sites of difficulty in encounters, particularly cross-cultural ones, have been examined. The most appropriate findings of these research enterprises have been selected and synthesised here, in order to assist those whose practical task it is to negotiate as part of their working lives.

The book first deals with preparation for a negotiation, then with the various elements of the negotiation proper, in order that they can be influenced and managed efficiently, and it ends with an account of the follow-up actions which complete the event.

READERSHIP

The book is intended for any individual or representative who has to negotiate with others, either within an organisation, or between organisations. It could be of particular use to those in graduate schools of business or management. The material is presented in a form which should be useful for people in business, industry, commerce, government service and the professions.

GOALS

The goals of this book are:

1 to provide an increased cognitive awareness of language as a negotiating instrument;
2 to provide such insights into the strategies of negotiation as will enable readers to increase the effectiveness of their own contributions; to improve their reading of the situation by enhancing their ability to predict and analyse the discursive behaviour of others; and so ultimately to manage and control the complex processes of communication;
3 to provide for this increase in skill without denying the importance of the individual qualities of negotiators, and this will be achieved by: (a) focusing on the general functional possibilities of language and discourse

rather than insisting on the use of specific behaviours; (b) providing information which enables readers to codify and assess their own strategies and thus improve their use; and (c) enriching readers' abilities to design their own interactive strategies;

4 to provide ideas and suggestions that can help readers to achieve the end result of production efficiency, customer satisfaction, the full utilisation of human resources, the best corporate interaction, financial and social rewards, and personal satisfaction.

METHOD

The book is written as a resource guide to the language of negotiating activity. Each chapter provides information on the factors to consider with respect to the various parts of the negotiating discourse. Examples are provided where necessary to show the value of enhanced language use; and practical exercises give opportunities for the reader to consider his or her own practice in the light of the ideas which are offered.

Chapters 1 and 2 discuss the complex of factors and forces that constitute negotiating language, presenting material on the roles of culture and discourse in language use, and on the qualities of language that are particularly influential in communication.

The later chapters deal with some of the specific aspects of negotiating. Chapter 3 focuses on spoken negotiation, examining the strategic and tactical elements of speaking, taking turns, listening, and topic use. Chapter 4 deals with two particular aspects of the interpersonal side of negotiating language: (a) ways of achieving a fair degree of cooperation and agreement, even in adversarial negotiations; and (b) ways of dealing with cross-cultural encounters. Chapter 5 addresses the problems involved in media interviewing. Chapter 6 deals with one specific kind of speech interaction which can be problematic: using the phone. Chapter 7 focuses on written negotiation, offering some techniques for composing ideas in written form and designing a useful text. Chapter 8 provides a set of important negotiating acts, suggesting some methods of ensuring their efficiency. Chapter 9 investigates the important follow-up acts of remembering and recording, without which a negotiation's outcome could founder.

TO OPTIMISE THE BOOK'S VALUE

In Chapters 1 and 2, allow the ideas to stimulate your awareness of language, in general terms, as a powerful element in negotiation activities.

In Chapters 3 to 7 where different aspects of the process of negotiation are dealt with, go steadily through the material. Any item in the process might suggest a train of thought which would otherwise be neglected. Try to increase your repertoire of behaviours in all aspects of the interaction process.

In Chapter 8, on specific speech actions, note any observations which arise as a result of reading the section, with the aim of alerting yourself to your own negotiating behaviours, and those of the people you negotiate with, as you develop the habit of speech-analysis.

It is particularly recommended that after considering the aspects of negotiating language dealt with, you determine which you have the 'best ear' for, and build on these as your own individual skills.

Using Chapter 9 as a guide, make sure that you round off the negotiation properly, and that you both store it in memory and are able to recall its features when necessary.

Because language is used all day and every day, it is often taken for granted, and its powers left unexamined except where serious problems with its use arise. Negotiators may have their attention focused on the more cognitive or material aspects of an issue they are discussing, and neglect the fundamental role language is playing in the representation of these aspects. Yet if the language used is inadequate for its purposes, or the representation is at fault, the whole interaction may falter or fail. Successful negotiators do not take language for granted in the difficult and complex world of human interaction.

ACKNOWLEDGEMENTS

Thanks are due to all those scholars whose work in the field of language pragmatics has inspired the materials in this book; many of their names appear in the reference list at the end. I should like to thank the reviewers of the manuscript for their helpful suggestions. To those students of spoken discourse who have patiently borne with early versions of this material in class, my thanks and appreciation. In particular, I would like to thank those senior executives who shared their expertise in negotiation so generously in my advanced communication classes; their contributions have helped to keep this book alert to the practical implications of language research. My thanks are also due to Rebecca Pelan for help well beyond the call of friendship in preparing the manuscript.

Part I

Preparation – the power of language

Chapter 1

Language and culture

This section raises issues concerning the three factors, language, culture and discourse, that constitute negotiation. Though language, culture and discourse interlock to form negotiation, they are separated here for analytic convenience.

READER WORK   Consider the ideas discussed here in relation to your own negotiating experience as speaker and hearer.
(PRACTICE sections are provided to assist in this process.)
GOAL   To increase awareness of the factors that impact on negotiation.

LANGUAGE

The functions of language are deeply embedded in human behaviour and there is little in our lives as social beings in which language does not play an important part.

The aspects of language that are of relevance to negotiation are:

1 its role in creating meaning out of the world for social use;
2 the means language adopts in order to realise meaning;
3 its dependence on history and culture;
4 its work as a socially bonding device.

LANGUAGE'S ROLE IN CREATING MEANING

The most important capacity that language has is its power to realise or actualise some speaker's or writer's idea, impression, attitude or emotion. Our understanding of the world is not merely expressed in words; it actually comes into existence, is realised through them. That is, language does not work by putting into words some previously existing event in the world, the information about which is then communicated to the hearer. Rather, language works to make some of the phenomena of the world into 'events', while ignoring others. By 'events' here is meant not only happenings of a physical kind but also (and more importantly) ideas, values and opinions. Language, as it were, imposes digital distinctions on the world, isolating aspects from the great mass of undifferentiated phenomena, making 'events' of them, registering them in words, and supplying them with meaning. What gets registered as an 'event' depends on the purposes of the speaker, who may wish to direct attention towards some things and away from others. A useful image for this aspect of language is to see it as a map of the world, giving some details of the terrain while omitting others. It is a very helpful instrument by which to understand the world, but it does not give us the world in all its detail.

When the 'event' is realised through speech or writing, language acts to share the speaker's interpretation with others. If the language chosen for the realisation is forceful enough, or the interpretation is reiterated often enough, or the 'event' is socially appropriate enough for hearers to accept it, then the speaker's version of that 'event' becomes social currency, and eventually part of a common understanding. Through language a community's sense of the world is created, modified and developed, and the versions of it which are frequently spoken become institutionalised. Other versions which are omitted from language use become weakened, and matters rarely talked about are perceived as unacceptable or 'unreal'. So language (a) creates meaning from the world, and (b) offers up that meaning for social understanding and acceptance.

Example

This can be done in at least three ways. First, new objects can be registered through language – for example, a *modem*. When a situation arose in which computers had to be linked by telephone, a modulator–demodulator was invented to adapt the data to this transmission and reception system. A name 'modem' was given to it, for easier social use, and it is now a widely disseminated notion. Its full technical meaning, however, is not so widely understood. This example is one of many which could remind us that we all use words for which we have only a hazy meaning, a fact which leaves us open to manipulation by those with a better understanding of them (for example by the sales representatives who insist we need a new modem), and to exploitation (for example by politicians who can use vagueness to bring about an alteration in meaning by incorporating different aspects of potential meaning as it suits them).

Second, new perceptions can be registered through language – for example, the recognition of *pre-teens* as a specific period in youth. It was always the case that a child grew from being a baby to a child, through ages ten, eleven and twelve, and into its teen years. Recently, however, marketing agencies have specified pre-teen children as an age group, inserted between the group 'children' and the group 'teenagers'. Those involved in sales of goods found it useful, and so accepted it; the children themselves found it attractive because it gave them a more important social presence;

and so it has become a common awareness. Society is not always certain, however, which children are in the pre-teen group, or what features distinguish its members from children and teenagers (since children are notorious for their different rates of development). As a 'fuzzy' category, it lends itself to manipulation by those who have an interest in so doing.

Third, current perceptions can be altered through language use – for example, a term like *old-fashioned*, which once meant 'of long standing, tried and true, and still valued', as social values change can gradually be brought to mean 'outworn, unacceptable, no longer valued, and out of date'. Or speakers can use a phrase in association with others whose meanings society already dislikes, so that it gradually acquires the same valuation. Another possibility is illustrated by the phrase 'the black problem', where the very selection of 'black' and 'problem', and their juxtaposition to represent some happening in the world, makes a judgment which would differ markedly if instead the phrase used were 'the white problem', or some other word were substituted for 'problem'. Another technique to achieve a change in perception, less favoured (and often less successful), is to use argument against or on behalf of an idea. This often fails because it is overt and so allows the hearers to understand what is going on, and hence permits them either to defend the current view, or at least to resist the argument.

Practice

Ask yourself which terms are currently in favour for the important matters in your various negotiations. A standard set might be 'tried and true', 'standard methods', 'well-honed skills' or 'it's good because we know where we are with it'. Who instigated them? For what purpose? Could the perception they realise be changed? Have any such terms changed during the negotiation process, and to what effect? Would it be useful for you to seek to change any of the terms, for example to 'a welcome change', 'creative originality', 'more efficient methods', 'more up-to-date'? (Remember that everyone is suspicious of change and the readjustment of ideas that it will require.) Would it be useful to resuscitate any terms not currently favoured? Does one participant favour a particular set? Would there be negotiating value in your copying this usage? (We like to talk with people who share our perceptions.) What are your own favourite terms? Has using them ever been a help or a hindrance?

THE MEANS BY WHICH LANGUAGE WORKS

When we create communicated events from the happenings of the world, language can work at two levels to give socially accepted meaning to these happenings.

On one level, a speaker can make a careful choice of words or grammar to realise the happening (to suit his or her purposes), or can mention it alongside events already recorded in speech, thereby giving it the same social value that those events have, and creating an association of ideas in the mind of the hearer.

However, meaning can be affected in this way only because the very act of speech is a profoundly significant happening. On this deeper level, any utterance (or act of writing) in our communication with one another, however apparently trivial it may seem, can form the basis for our sense of some aspect of the world and its happenings. We acquire less meaning in directly experienced, unmediated ways than people often understand. It follows then that every utterance has the power to affect our perception of the world. Every utterance is a *speech act* with three aspects: it is a locution, that is, an uttering of recognisable sounds and rhythms; it has illocutionary force or discursive power, compounded of what can be estimated of the speaker's intentions and its material content; and it has perlocutionary effect, that is, it has some interactive significance and social meaning (see pp. 88–9, and 94).

Speech is not transitory in value though it may be brief; it is central to our shared understanding of the world and also to the processes of interaction. Every time speakers speak they provide information about their subject matter, and simultaneously reveal such things as their sense of self, the roles they are adopting (and expecting others to adopt), their perceptions of the interaction, their expectations of the other participants' behaviours, and their anticipation of its outcome. Therefore, any speech event has potentially serious social consequences. Speech is irreversible: once something is said, it cannot be unsaid. It may be an opinion – 'I think Smith lacks administrative skill', – or a fact – 'We offered 17 per cent interest on the loan.' The first may offend, the second will form a commitment, and in both cases, the speakers will be held to their words.

Example

During an inter-organisational negotiation a speaker says: 'I am the managing director.' In so doing, several things occur, and several different kinds of meaning are actualised.

First, referential information is supplied. This can happen because the words have common values for the speaker and hearers who all have perceptions of what a 'managing director' is. But while they may share elements of understanding, there is also the possibility of interpretive differences. To one hearer it could mean 'The speaker is in charge of the company's contribution to the negotiation', or 'The speaker is knowledgeable about the matters in hand', or 'The speaker is a policy maker and does not deal in detail', or 'The speaker is the principal not an agent', or any combination of these.

Second, the social event of the sentence's being spoken, becoming an element within the interaction, brings another kind of meaning. The speaker has some purpose in saying it and so making it part of the negotiation. The hearer will certainly assume this. The sentence may be intended by the speaker, or read by the hearer, as a clarification, a statement of position, a boast, or a way of preventing embarrassment (which might occur if the speaker's highranking role were not understood). Each reading can give rise to different social consequences which in turn impact on the negotiation and change its nature. Consider the following examples.

1 If read as a clarification, the hearer may understand that the speaker (a) thinks clarifying participants' ranks is good for a negotiation, or wants it as an element in this negotiation, or (b) generally likes clarity, or (c) may want something clarified by others. In the short term, it may cause others to tell their rank (and this would have an effect on relationships, which would become more strongly influenced by the concept of rank), and in the longer term it could lead to the negotiation becoming one in which clarification is a major component, occupying much of the participants' time.

2 If read as a statement of position, the hearer could understand that the speaker wants the negotiation to be one where positions are taken up and declared, and this might have the effect of making the negotiation more adversarial than it would otherwise have been.

3 The hearer may perceive it to be a boast, and in the short term produce an anti-boast response (a snub), and in the long term may hear other contributions by this speaker as arrogant, and so develop a position of antagonism.

4 If taken as a means of preventing embarrassment, the hearer might indicate that it was in fact useful ('Oh I see, I was going to ask if as an agent you had to seek approval for any decision reached today'). This response, however, contains the implication that the hearer did not recognise the high status of the speaker; some managing directors might find this annoying, with consequences for their future attitudes in the negotiation.

The sentence may also, of course, be presented to appear as a combination of all these things, so as to allow the speaker to avoid being called to account on one particular meaning by claiming that another was intended. It is rare for any speech act to have only one meaning and only one purpose. The skill of speaking lies in producing subtlety of combinations.

It is this capacity of language to form speech events that gives it its greatest social power. Speech events are the most important vehicle for the construction, understanding and maintenance of our sense of reality. Much of everyday life consists of the use of spoken interaction for these ends. It is of course done implicitly for the most part, by the presuppositions and assumptions of what is said, though it is possible to speak in terms which act explicitly to define some aspect of the world. In a negotiation, everything said or written, however seemingly trivial, including any preliminaries and any future matters linked to it, makes that negotiation what it is; and everything that the participants bring to it of their previous experiences of negotiation and of every other kind of communication also makes a contribution.

Example

In a casual exchange during a break in negotiation, one senior participant said to a junior colleague, 'That was a most unproductive session.' From this *explicit* comment, the colleague will (a) understand that for the speaker a negotiation should be productive, (b) understand that for the speaker this particular negotiation was so far a failure, and (c) therefore guess at what outcome would be regarded by the senior as productive. The junior may hold a different valuation, and have found it a useful negotiation because ideas were exchanged and joint goals were set; if the senior sees this as 'unproductive', then he or she must have a different sense of the meeting. In that the senior has authority over the junior, the junior could find it useful to adjust his or her sense of what a negotiation should be. Alternatively, if the senior had said, 'We really must get through more points at our next meeting', this *implicitly* suggests that (a) this one a poor meeting, and (b) getting through points is what meetings are about. If the junior then adapted his or her conduct accordingly, this brief and apparently casual speech event could then set the agenda for both speakers' future discussions, their thinking about future meetings, and their behaviour at them.

Practice

Can you recall from a recent negotiation a word or phrase that had a strong impact on you? Or can you recall a speech act whose illocutionary force markedly affected you? Examine which features of the circumstances might explain this force, and ask what was the nature of the impact and its consequences. Try to recall one of your own speech acts which caused a problem, or which in hindsight you regret. Examine its features for the cause of the difficulty.

THE DEPENDENCE OF LANGUAGE ON HISTORY

By 'history' here is meant both the long-term development of language through general community use over time, and the shorter-term personal experience of language use by individuals. Meaning accrues to words and phrases from their previous occurrences, and as their associations change so too do their meanings. Since experiences of language vary, a negotiation can involve the use of words which are differently understood by the participants, and so cause misunderstanding.

Example

In one company the phrase 'position paper' (that is, a paper in which a personal opinion is argued in some detail) is in constant use by those who wish to demonstrate their ambition to rise in the company. As a result, in that company a position paper is recognised as a mark of self-aggrandisement. On this understanding, if a member of that firm hears the phrase from someone in another company, where it is a standard requirement that everyone produces papers before meetings, then there could be serious communication problems, with neither party aware of the cause.

Experiential history also affects the value given to the kind of speech act itself, for example *declare*, *accuse* or *dismiss*, since its social meaning also depends on previous experience of similar acts, so *accuse* can be a rare and powerful act in one context, but frequent and little regarded in another.

Example

A new member of a negotiating team who uses the speech act of *irony* may find it goes unrecognised if those present are unaccustomed to (a) the use of irony in negotiations, or (b) the member's particular contributions, which could have told them that he favours irony as a device. Similarly, an emotional outburst can cause problems since the other participants may be unable to read its value if they do not know that this is a favoured persuasive strategy of the speaker, and they may read it as an embarrassing breakdown of productive interaction.

Practice

What happened last time someone used a term to you whose meaning you did not know for certain? Were you able to ask for clarification? If not, why not? What consequences were there? Can you recall an occasion when a particular kind of speech act, perhaps an out of place assertion, a joke, or a personal revelation, caused problems? What can you learn from analysing it? What happened last time you yourself used a term which caused problems? How do you know it happened? What consequences were there?

LANGUAGE AS SOCIAL BONDING

In the previous three sections the focus has been on the power of language to create meanings out of the happenings of the world. This assumes that language is primarily referential. It is certainly true that there will be language of this kind in any speech event, and in such purposeful encounters as negotiations people usually 'speak about' things; but it is also true that even in a critical stage of a negotiation there may be some speech activity which has another, non-referential, value. This occurs because language realises not only events but also social relations, and, further, it acts to organise the interactive conduct and to regulate the process of every social interaction. There is a need, for example, to establish the nature of the bond that will obtain between the speaker and hearer during an interaction. At the start of a negotiation, non-referential language is used to set the kind and degree of relations, and at any stage there may be a need to check whether the relations set previously are still valid. As people gather for a meeting this is usually done through 'chat', for example discussing the weather, or the news of the day, or sharing personal problems. Although the speech used does appear to be 'about' something, it is usually quite clear that the topic is not the main focus, but rather a vehicle for social bonding. For example, the weather is a favoured social device for establishing a relatively open bond; the news, with its potentiality for the expression of opposing views, is favoured for clarifying opinions and attitudes, and so assessing the kind of bond that will be possible before engaging with the matters to be negotiated; the sharing of personal problems is an indication of a close relationship (or a wish to increase the degree of bonding).

This non-referential language does other work also: for instance, it can be used to set up the roles to be taken by the participants. Words may be exchanged at any time in a negotiation whose purpose is to set or change the relative status of the participants and to establish who will have power and what kind of power, for example who has valuable knowledge to offer, who has a major responsibility for legal affairs, and so on. Non-referential language can also act to set the tone of the negotiation as urgent or relaxed, serious or jocular, routine or unusual. While important at the start of a meeting, it has, on occasions, a function to fill throughout, because changes in bond, role and tone can be sought at any point. Persuading participants to become more urgent, or to assume a greater degree of formality, if neither of these qualities has been present in the past, may take effort. It would be a mistake, therefore, to hear this kind of language as irrelevant or trivial, or as an aside to the major business of the encounter. To do so is to fail to recognise the work such language does, and its social significance for the very nature of interaction.

Practice

Have you experienced any problems with the establishment of bond, role and tone? How and when were they set in the last important negotiation you were involved in? Can you recall any occasion when these elements changed during the encounter? How was it done? Note the signals that are used by people to indicate that they wish for change. Try to recall how someone you respect as a negotiator sets or changes social elements in the interaction. Recall occasions when a signal was ignored, and what the consequences were.

CULTURE

In this context the term 'culture' is used to mean the cultural community that shares a language. The language which they share has qualities that affect the way they perceive the world. It enables them to hold certain perceptions of the world while effectively inhibiting them from considering others. The language can be as broad as English or as narrow as journalese. This can occur because, in some sense, a language is the master and not the servant of those who use it. Its power resides in two aspects: its body of words, that is, its vocabulary, and the ways in which words can be combined, that is, its grammar. It is able to have a strong influence on perception because of the routine nature of so much language usage – conversations are repetitive, and so are meetings, news broadcasts, soap operas and business negotiations. These constant repetitions of language influence us to accept that way of looking at the world. It is possible to be different, but it involves cognitive effort, and for our hearers it may be seen as problematic or be misheard or questioned.

When the vocabulary of a given language in general community use is examined, it can be seen that although it has immense resources to realise many aspects of the world, there are noticeable absences. This occurs because each language has a limited set of structures and words in frequent use in which the ideas of its community are registered and realised. The regular vocabulary usage influences how the categorisation of the world is effected, and the routine grammatical preferences influence the logic by which that categorisation is understood. They each favour a particular way of looking at things, and this differs from the way of looking of someone using a different language, because each language has its own normalised modes of categorising and ordering. For example, some perceptions about things cannot easily be accessed by an English speaker but would be commonplace for a Japanese one. This not only affects the digitalisation of the world into events but also determines how those events are ranked and evaluated. No two languages present identical views of the world as their most favoured; each is rather like a pair of spectacles with more or less warped lenses, and produces different astigmatisms. Negotiation is, obviously, something that can be affected by these differences in perception.

When words are frequently used by the majority of the community, they become part of the common repertoire. The ideas they realise form the basis of everyday thinking. When no word is immediately available from the common stock to use for an idea, that idea is hard to express, can be hard to perceive, and ultimately is neglected.

It is always possible, of course, that the language itself can be changed, new words can be created (as with the *modem* and *pre-teen* examples mentioned above), and old words can cease to be used, so that altered perceptions can be brought into awareness. However, in all human inter-action there is an important general principle – that of using least effort; this decrees that speakers and hearers work no harder than they need to in order to understand and to be understood. This is why language that is familiar and in frequent use can create the dominant understanding. During a negotiation, this holds true also. It should be recognised that those elements which are not put into familiar words, or into easily understood phrases, may not be easily grasped. If it is important that a new or unusual idea should be remembered, then it should be emphasised, reiterated, and some attempt should be made to link it to some commonly understood terms. Words in frequent use acquire associations and lead to instant attitudinal responses. So the majority of the community respond to a particular word and its idea with similar attitudes, for example disliking 'spiders' or worrying about 'delays'. Experiments have shown that we adopt attitudes to almost every word that is used, whether it is 'snakes', 'wood', 'books', 'youth', 'democracy', or the terms used in negotiation, such as 'settle', 'clarify', 'compromise', 'contract', 'terms' or 'agree'.

Practice

Consider the most important words that could occur in your next negotiation, and examine your response to them. Would it be shared by those who matter? Should you (or can you) alter any potential usage, select a better word or omit a word with misleading associations, to achieve a more satisfactory outcome? What indications have your fellow negotiators given of their attitudes to particular words?

As to grammar, it has been said that

> the grammar of each language is not merely a reproducing instrument for voicing ideas, but is rather itself the shaper of ideas, the program and guide for the individual's mental activity, for his analysis of impressions, for his synthesis of his mental stock in trade. The formulation of ideas is not an independent process, strictly rational in the old sense, but it is part of a particular grammar and differs, from slightly to greatly, between grammars.

(Whorf 1956)

In this view, the impact of grammar on activities is least important in practical contexts like engineering, but most important in such speech activities as negotiation. We shall deal with the particular grammatical strategies that English lends itself to in Chapter 2 (pp. 30–2). But for an example here, it is worth considering the grammatical pattern of the standard English statement, which is subject, verb, object, as in, for example, 'Bill handed round the report.' What this means at a fundamental level of understanding is that such sentences as this set a pattern: 'An actor does an action and there is an end result.' To the extent that this pattern recurs (as it does extremely often), English speakers come to have a predilection in statements for representing the actors involved in 'events', naming the actions performed, and seeing actions as things done by actors which lead to results. This becomes the 'natural' way to see actions. It is, however, not the only way; Moslems see persons less as actors than entities subject to the actions of Allah.

Chapter 2

Language and discourse

DISCOURSE

Negotiation is a discursive practice in society, of which the two major elements are social interaction and communication about matters. Several broad aspects deserve attention before moving on to a detailed account.

First, every discourse is a social event in itself; it is not just a commentary on or an accompaniment to some other kind of event. Every discursive act is an act of power: speaking or writing always has an effect. Producing the right speech at the right time can empower the speaker; producing the wrong speech can undermine the speaker's power, render his or her future utterances fragile, and can lead to them being ignored and his or her aims being thwarted. Learning to read this discursive information is crucial for an understanding of the activity of negotiation.

Second, the production of discourses in society is controlled, organised and distributed by a certain number of socially determined procedures. Discourses are, for example, affected by the conventions of:

(a) **exclusion**, whereby certain people cannot easily speak to certain others (for example, a mail-room clerk in a large company would not normally represent the company at an international meeting);
(b) **prohibition**, whereby certain topics are deemed inappropiate in certain contexts (for example the expression of political views in a meeting to negotiate the timetabling of work allocations);
(c) **decorum**, whereby certain speech behaviours are thought improper (for example rude personal remarks at almost any formal occasion).

In each case, the control of discourse is not absolute, but if an exception occurs, it will be recognised as such, and treated as unusual, or inappropriate. So, for example, the community's general sense of the exclusion procedure would find the clerk's representation so peculiar that this would strongly influence their understanding of the meaning of his discourse – so much so that they might not 'hear' his subject matter while seeking for a meaning for his presence. So also the expression of strong views at a timetabling meeting could be not only time-consuming but also disruptive, causing responses which could impact on future discursive acts by that speaker. And one who makes a derogatory remark out of place will be seen as an inadequate communicator who ignores socially accepted practices, and this might affect his or her working future, etc.

Example

At a timetabling meeting to determine workloads, one participant raised an objection to his allocation based on his need to finish an urgent administrative task, another argued that he had arranged a long weekend holiday and so would be unavailable, a woman participant raised a difficulty with child care at the time in question. Any member of the group could find one or more of these topics inappropriate, and form a negative reaction to the person raising it.

Practice

Can you think of instances when the rules of exclusion, prohibition and decorum have been broken? What effect did they have in the short term and in the longer term? Could you postulate any other social conventions of this kind that operate in a specific kind of negotiation with which you are familiar?

Negotiators with a natural gift for communication automatically use their knowledge of such discourse factors to evaluate particular situations. Others need to develop the habit of systematically exploring the factors to assist in their evaluation. Any element of the discursive context in which language is used can be of significance in reading its meaning. Evidence for its interpretation could include:

(a) the speaker's own general sense of what discourse is, and of what negotiation is as a discursive act;
(b) his or her expectations of a given negotiation and how it should proceed;
(c) any preliminary interactions (such as letters, arrangments made by phone, the exchange of papers);
(d) any previous experience or knowledge of the interactive habits of the other negotiators;
(e) the traditional sense of interactions of this kind likely to be in the minds of the other parties;
(f) the range of possible roles available to the parties;
(g) the roles likely to be adopted;
(h) whatever estimate can be made of the parties' emotional, social, and psychological baggage.

The social aspects of discourse, then, act to influence the range and kind of language use available on any occasion. No speaker is free to use the whole range or to say just anything whenever he or she speaks, but must understand the limited choice of language use imposed by convention as the appropriate behaviour for particular discursive events. Each discourse type has its own conventions and practices, its own codes, styles and strategies. These set the terms for each of its speech acts so that any act which occurs is measured in these terms (rather than in terms of the language as a whole), and so is interpreted as, for instance, acceptable, odd, boringly obvious, or highlighted.

Example

If a senior negotiator breaks the prohibition convention and launches into an emotional story of a personal event, this would be evaluated as breaking the convention (and the others would question his or her reasons, motives, purposes) and as the speech of a senior, with social and discursive power unavailable to others. The meaning of the story as a discursive event would arise from an understanding of these (and other) factors.

Most people understand the difference between a negotiation and, say, a dinner party, and make different judgments of the speech that occurs at each: the same fact-filled speech would be an informative action at the first, and a boring contribution at the other.

People perform well in each instance because they can use their previous experience of the social uses of language to understand each new occasion, to see the signs that tell what kind of event it is, judge the discourse conventions, and so produce good examples of discourse themselves and make good evaluations of others' language use. Every participant present could, however, have a different understanding of a negotiating act, and the discourse expectations of all parties may need to be addressed either beforehand or as the occasion proceeds.

Practice

Consider an instance where your own expectations of a negotiation turned out to be inappropriate. What caused your expectations, and why did things occur differently? Did any particular negotiator dictate the nature of the meeting? Can you remember an instance of negotiation about the very nature of the discursive event that was to occur, such as 'Now then, what shall we do today?' What was the strategy that won the day and dictated the kind of event it would be?

The inevitable consequence of these features of discourse is that speech is not just informative about some subject, but influential as a discursive act and a social event. It is not only such obviously persuasive speakers as advertisers and political rhetoricians who influence their hearers, but every speaker who ever speaks, and in their every utterance, however brief.

Example

As people settle into their seats after a coffee break, one negotiator says, 'And now we come to the most important phase of our discussion.' In so doing he or she is attempting to persuade the other parties that the next stage is 'the most important', and this may not be altogether acceptable to the others. However, it will be hard to resist because the judgment of 'importance' is so relative that it is hard to query, and it is difficult to do in a practical sense, because such acts happen at speed (the average speaker produces some 150 words a minute in relatively informal interactions; speech is very much a micro-level activity), and it might also be missed because the attention of the other parties might well be on more apparently substantive matters. Yet such an act as this does two things: it contains a judgment which if not resisted will give a value to some aspect of the occasion and this may have lasting consequences; and it acts to end one part of the negotiation and to start another. (Compare it with these alternatives which might have been used: 'Well now, if we've finished this stage, I suppose we should move on', or 'Well now, the last thing we have to do today is . . .', or 'Can we now move on?') In the original example, if any of the other participants did not agree with one or other of the statement's values, they would have to decide whether they wanted to express disagreement with the ending of a phase, or the value given to the next phase, or both. They would then have to find a form of words which did exactly what they wanted and no more. It might be hard to sound clear, and yet sounding unclear would be taken as a sign of a poor negotiator. Negotiators need to develop a rhetorical sensitivity to such discursive practices, and to acquire a knowledge of the range of tactics to deal with them. We will suggest some specific tactics later in this book.

Practice

Consider a recent instance of a major negotiation in which you were involved. Try to remember the ways in which the discussion (its movement from phase to phase, its priorities, etc.) progressed; who were the major agents of change? How did the others react to them? What tactics were used? What role did you yourself take? What tactics might have achieved a better outcome?

LANGUAGE IN ACTION

Language is the instrument by which meaning is realised and by which effective social interaction can be created and sustained. In this section, two of the most important general ways in which the use of language can influence negotiation will be considered:

1 the persuasive power of metaphor generation, and
2 the functioning of language as paradigm and syntagm.

The first allows us to explore one of the most crucial, all-pervasive, but often unobserved, ways in which 'ordinary' language acts to form the groundwork of a discourse, and so to influence the whole nature of a discursive event. The choice of a metaphor sets up the terms of reference by which the fundamental meaning of the interaction will be understood.

The second allows us to consider the important implications for discursive power that follow once one recognises that language is not a neutral tool, but that whenever one encodes something of the world into language one is fitting it into a systematic code, which works to produce meaning both paradigmatically (by choice of one item from a set of similar ones) and syntagmatically (by arranging the choices into sentence patterns). This can influence how it works to represent both propositional content (the happenings of the world when they become the subject matter of speech) and interpersonal content (the attitudes, roles, tone, and so on, of relationships).

THE POWER OF METAPHOR

Many of our expressions are metaphorical – the philosophy of our forefathers lies hidden in them.

Many of the concepts by which we live and work are abstract, for example, *work* itself, *collaboration*, *group*, *agreement*, *power* and *institution*, and when we try to explore our understanding of them in more concrete terms we seek the assistance of metaphors. Most of the time people do not think out detailed theoretical accounts of such concepts; instead we use as guidance the standard, conventional metaphors through which our social group or culture perceive them. We share our understanding with others by speaking in terms of the metaphors, and so consolidate the meaning. Further, when we act upon the understanding that metaphors provide, they give us an organisation of experience which affects how we interpret the actions of others, and which also influences our own acts, by providing us with a ready-made set of behaviours to follow. Only on rare occasions do we consider whether this conventional understanding might be inadequate; and if we find it so we have to work hard both to think through to a non-metaphorical meaning, and even harder to find a form of words to render it meaningful to others. Therefore, metaphor is important, since in its frequency of use it solidifies a whole set of perceptions about a concept, which then dictate how we use it, how we understand its meaning, and how we behave with respect to it. Its frequency of use also makes the metaphor seem 'natural' or 'inevitable' as the meaning of the concept; though it may be only a partial truth about it, and not even the most useful one on a particular occasion.

The recognition that metaphors have this kind of power, and that their use is of significance in practice, may enable communicators on appropriate occasions deliberately to influence the discussion of a concept by either selecting one that is particularly suited to their goals from the range of standard metaphors, or inventing a new one to achieve their desired effect. Equally they may be able to recognise when others are using a metaphor which might be detrimental to a successful outcome, and reject it, or substitute another.

> The one who chooses the metaphor sets the agenda, and by that choice can persuade others.

How a metaphor works

There are two ways of seeing how the use of a standard metaphor acts to structure the understanding of a concept and its related activities:

1 Examine the implications behind the metaphor.

Example

Take the standard metaphor,

> We have to find a bridge across these troubled waters.

This implies the following notions which should each be assessed for suitability to the concept being communicated, and the negotiation in which it takes place:

- There is an area of turbulence and trouble.
- It is a 'naturally' occurring trouble (not man-made).
- It is a 'body' of trouble (not a two-sided problem, a dilemma).
- Examining the trouble in detail will not be necessary or helpful.
- It is important only to pass over the trouble, get beyond it, leave it untouched.
- Activities which metaphorically resemble 'building' will be required to solve the problem.

Or take the standard metaphor,

> 'This is absolutely the bottom line.'

This implies the following notions:

- The elements of something add up to a total.

- The total is what matters.
- The total is a matter of profit and loss, a statement of clear oppositions, of black and white with no grey shading possible.
- It is a material total, without non-material elements (like values, or attitudes).
- It is a conclusion of a particular kind: a result and not a summation, a climax, a finalisation or a termination.
- The activities required will resemble those involved in adding up, sub-tracting and totalling items of relevance, and will not include such acts as making provisos, allowing exceptions, or leaving some factors to be finalised elsewhere or at another time.

Practice

What are your preferred metaphors for the important concepts you frequently use at work? What might you use instead? What values would another metaphor bring? Look at the letters you write, your reports and notes. What are the preferred metaphors of your colleagues and those with whom you must deal? What are the implications of their preferences?

2 Examine the value of a metaphor which has been used in a negotiation.

Example

A participant who was arguing a case used a standard set of metaphors for 'argument' itself. The one chosen was seeing argument as if it were a war. This involved the use of terms like 'winning' and 'losing' or 'defending' and 'attacking' arguments, 'targeting' opponents' weak spots, or having 'impregnable' or 'indefensible' positions. The use of this metaphor acts to structure the argument activity itself as warlike: we see ourselves as winning and losing arguments, and we see those we argue with as opponents to conquer, or be conquered by. The influence of the metaphor can even extend to reporting on the event later. The constant use of this metaphor during a negotiation would have a strong effect on how the participants conducted the arguments and responded to winning or losing them. The sheer familiarity of using this metaphor in such circumstances can make it very difficult to realise that 'war' and 'argument' are in fact different things, and need not be linked, and that there are other ways of understanding arguments. In the above instance, the metaphor could mean that flexibility in negotiating was rendered less viable (it could be seen as 'defensive'), and it could have distracted negotiators from focusing on other aspects of their argument (those to which the metaphor does not easily apply). In some circumstances it may have been counter-productive, for example where the goal of the negotiation required cooperation and mutual understanding or where the desired outcome was an acceptable result for both parties with no loss of face, or where a compromise was the only possible solution and the negotiation was concerned only with how best this might be achieved. In war, compromise with the enemy is perceived as treachery, so compromise in an argument–war could be seen as a poor outcome, whereas if the war metaphor had not been so influential it could be seen as good. In war we take sides, and only one side can win; in negotiation all parties (*not* 'sides') must achieve as good an outcome as they can.

It is necessary to be alert to the metaphors which others use, since these will be selected to assist in the achievement of their own purposes or the failure of yours. If such a metaphor is noticed, you have two options.

1 Consider changing the metaphor

Assess the value for you of the main metaphor being used in the negotiation. What does this metaphor highlight, and what does it ignore or leave unexplored? Would it be useful to change the metaphor; would it change for the better the negotiation process and outcome?

2 Consider creating a new metaphor

As well as using the standard metaphors, it may be possible to set up and use a newly minted one. There are several ways to do this.

(a) Note the set of metaphors that spring most easily to your mind with respect to the idea for which you need to create a new metaphor. What useful implications are entailed by them? Can you think of a metaphor which has only these implications and none which would be inappropriate? What metaphors are comparable to the one that came to mind? Would they be more useful? What metaphors form a contrast with the one that came to mind? Would they be of use?

   For example, in a matter of business a typical metaphor might be that of movement towards an object – pursuing (goals), getting there (good outcomes), reaching (targets). What is the value of thinking of business as a movement? Is there any way in which thinking like this could disadvantage you in the matter? Could the *kind* of movement be usefully specified? For example, 'rushing to conclusions' can be used to devalue a speech act. In the metaphor of movement, the goal is understood to be 'out there' somewhere; would it be more useful to see the goal as something already 'here', requiring only to be recognised?

(b) Recall metaphors that appeal to you. (If they appeal it may be because they have been associated with success in the past, or because you feel comfortable with their use, or because they represent well the stance you want to take; any of these could support you psychologically in your negotiating activity.) Would they or some adaptation of them be of use in the present case?

(c) Note the goals of your negotiation. Do they suggest any metaphors which might assist your achievement of them?

(d) Recall occasions when you have had success in negotiation. Were there any metaphors that were used then (by yourself or others) that could be used to advantage in the present case?

As an example of a newly minted metaphor, there is the report of an Iranian student who heard the expression 'the solution of my problems' and understood it to be metaphorical. He imagined a liquid containing the problems, which were either dissolved or in precipitated form. In the liquid were catalysts constantly dissolving and precipitating out the problems. The value of this as a metaphor is that it suggests that problems do not disappear or are finally solved, but that they are always present though not perhaps always in solid form. The metaphor enables us to recognise that problems that we thought were solved can recur ('come to the surface again'), and that recurrence may not be failure on our part, but rather an inevitability given the nature of problems. The goal for a problem-solving approach that accepts this view is to find a catalyst that will make one problem dissolve without making another one precipitate out. This metaphor may well be an efficient and economical resource in problem-solving.

(Material in this section has been drawn from Lakoff and Johnson 1980.)

PARADIGM AND SYNTAGM

Words and grammar form a code or system by which events are realised through language. The code consists of the language 'tokens', that is adjectives, nouns and noun phrases, verbal mood and voice, clause types, and so on, with which we build our sentences. In English, as in any other language, there is only a finite set of these tokens by which we can record our sense of the whole complex world of our experience.

Behind each language token there is a mental construct in the user's mind which is his or her version of a happening in the world, and behind the mental construct is the happening itself existing as part of the world. We have been calling these mental constructs 'events'. Problems can arise at each point for someone reading (that is, interpreting) the language. First, the happening represented may not be familiar to the reader (as when an original or idiosyncratic idea is expressed, or a technical matter is mentioned to a lay reader). Secondly, the mental construct in the speaker's mind may differ from that in the reader's mind (as when an unclear word is used, such as 'box', which can be a small object for storing discs, or a large object for holding crates for transport). Thirdly, the token used may simply be misheard, and so evoke a quite different mental construct in the reader's mind.

The coding system works to allow a speaker to make two different kinds of choice: paradigmatic and syntagmatic. As a happening becomes a mental construct in the user's mind it is given a name and catalogued along with others perceived to be similar in some way. A *paradigm* is the name given to a catalogue of this kind, a set of language tokens for similar events. Every token of language belongs to some paradigm or another. *Syntagms* are the grammatical or structural patterns in which tokens are strung together to form sentences, paragraphs, etc. In the mind is a set of possible structures from which to choose on a given occasion.

Paradigms

A paradigm is a set of units from which a speaker makes a choice of one unit to say. The set is made up of members which share characteristics, so, for example, the letters of the alphabet form a paradigm set, and so do the personal pronouns (I, you, he/she/it, we, you, they). These are closed sets, that is they are not easily extendable (though at present there are attempts to create a new pronoun, *s/he*, which is meeting a lot of resistance). Other paradigms are not so clear-cut or definable. For example, there is a paradigm of terms for 'legal documents', including 'contract', 'settlement', 'act', 'law', 'record' and 'deposition'. There is a paradigm of terms for discursive interaction, including 'chat', 'meeting', 'discussion', 'negotiation' and 'encounter'.

In choosing an item from a paradigm a speaker is selecting a meaning. The meaning comes about in two ways: the particular item chosen has meaning as a realisation of an event, but also has a meaning which derives from the speaker's awareness of the other possible choices. Equally, hearers understand or make meaningful the word they hear, by fitting it into their own paradigm set, seeing it as a choice with specific meaning, and they enrich it by adding to it the 'negative' meaning of the words in the set which were not chosen. For example, a hearer hears, 'I have just bought a new car.' 'Car' here will be understood to have the meaning of four-wheeled motor vehicle of a certain size, but it should be remembered that the token also belongs to a paradigm, and was chosen from a set which might include 'car', 'Volvo', 'station wagon' or 'set of wheels'. The hearer knows this, and understands part of the meaning to be that the speaker has given a non-specific word where specifics were possible, for example has not given the make ('Volvo'), or size ('station wagon'), or expressed attitude ('set of wheels'). The hearer will then work out what extra meaning to give to the choice: whether the speaker is not interested in such details, or ignorant of them, or wanting the hearer to ask for details and so establish the car as the topic and the speaker as the centre of attention, or something else.

The ability to make a paradigm analysis can allow a more flexible approach to understanding language and using it as a realisation of events, and enables the analyst to understand the underlying meanings that might otherwise be difficult to see, or to think of alternative realisations, and understand why the particular choice was made.

Consider for example, the paradigm of marketing terms for eggs: 'standard', 'large', 'extra-large' and 'jumbo'. Thinking of the paradigmatic possibilities might show that these terms have been imposed on what is in reality a continuum of egg sizes, and that additions to or reductions in the categories of the paradigm might therefore be possible. It might also lead to questions about the basis of the categorisation. This could lead to a comparison with similar objects and it could be seen that other related paradigms operate with different terms, for example the marketing of fruit is done by named variety, and meat sells by both size and named variety. The basis for the paradigm of eggs is size, rather than, for example, health qualities, age, location of source, kind of hen, housing quality or feed quality. These others are all quite possible and useful distinctions (and indeed the housing-quality and feed-quality categorisations have been picked up by some selling agents who use the terms 'free range' and 'corn-fed'). So paradigm analysis may open up questions and suggest alternative strategies of realisation, assisting the analyst to get below the surface of 'natural' seeming categories, to see their presuppositions, and so to understand them more fully, or to think of alternatives, and perhaps devise ways of having them accepted.

Example

If a negotiator rings up to make an appointment to meet, and says, 'I think it would be good if we could have a chat about the matter', the language used shows that he or she has made several important paradigm decisions.

1 The choice of 'chat' has features which distinguish it from others in its paradigm of 'interactions', for example it is relatively informal or casual. The hearer knows of the alternative choices and thus is able to read the significance of this choice as opposed to, say, 'discussion'.
2 In choosing to say 'I think' the speaker is in one sense speaking redundantly since he or she presumably 'thinks' everything that is said. The paradigm choice was (at the very least) between saying 'I think' or nothing. The value of 'I think' therefore must have meaning when measured against the possibility of a zero alternative, and this needs to be worked out. One part of its contribution to meaning may be to express a general degree of tentativeness, which allows the hearer to resist without loss of face to the speaker, and this could have useful interrelational or bonding significance.
3 In choosing to say 'it would be good', the speaker is not using the other members of the paradigm of evaluations – 'useful', 'important', or 'helpful'. What distinguishes 'good' from these is a non-specificity about the kind of value, and possibly a down-playing of the value compared with the other choices. By doing this the speaker may intend not so much to

specify the nature of the meeting, but to do bonding work, by leaving the type of meeting tentative and open to negotiation.

4 The choice of the phrase 'if we could' down-plays something different – the power of the request being made by the speaker – since by indicating that the meeting might not be possible, the phrase allows the hearer to reject the idea, by replying 'I can't', and this again would mean little loss of face for either party.

There are other possibilities of meaning for the speech. It could, if offered by a very senior person to a new junior he or she rarely meets, be a signal of trouble.

Practice

Consider the differences in meaning between these possible variants of the sentence used above:

- *We must arrange a meeting soon about this matter.*
- *We must have a chat about this matter.*
- *The senior partner thinks we ought to have a chat soon about the matter.*
- *It is important that we have a chat.*
- *It would be most helpful to have a chat if you could manage it.*

What others could you suggest, and what meaning would they have?

Syntagms

A syntagm is the combination of paradigmatic choices to form sequential phrases, sentences, paragraphs and documents. Taking the sentence as the standard example, it can be seen as consisting of a series of slots (which are dictated by the rules of grammar), so that when producing a statement, 'subject + verb + object' is the basic syntagm or structure, while 'article + adjective + noun' is the basic noun phrase syntagm. Each slot (for example 'subject' or 'adjective') is then filled by a suitable paradigm choice. Knowing some grammar or remembering how to do sentence parsing from schooldays helps to see how sentences work in this way, but it is not essential to the process; most people have a feel for the way sentences could be divided into 'sense units' even if they have no term to name each unit. As a guide, ask which elements of the sentence could belong together as a selection from a paradigm. Take the simple sentence: 'Mary and I went out and bought a car.' This could be analysed in several ways, each of which has value.

(a)   / Mary / and / I / went / out / and / bought / a / car

where every token is seen as separate, and could be changed for another in its paradigm to realise the same event, thus:

/ My wife / came / in / with / me / when / buying / the / Volvo

(b)   / Mary and I / went out / and / bought / a car

where fewer elements are seen as separate, but each still has value and is a member of a paradigm set from which others could have been chosen, thus:

/ We / came into town / to / purchase / our sedan

(c)   / Mary and I went out / and bought a car/

where even fewer elements are separated but each could still be seen as a member of a paradigm set, thus:

/ We came into town / to purchase our sedan

Whichever sense units are used to analyse the sentence, something can be learned by thinking of the paradigms that are revealed, and the choices not made, which will enhance the understanding of the full meaning of the choices actually expressed. Such an analysis is worth doing on key passages in negotiation; seen in this way they can be very revealing.

Example

Suppose the following sentence to be worth a syntagmatic analysis:

I / think / it / would be / good / if / we / could have / a chat /

The syntagm could have been produced as follows:

It / would be / good / to have / a chat /

Looking at it in this way, it can be noted that in the second case, the personal element 'I' is missing, as is the tentativeness of 'think', and the bonding expressed in 'we'. Any reader will respond in a subconscious way to such differences as these, but can raise the level of consciousness by acquiring the ability to do a syntagmatic analysis. Then a reader can locate with more precision the kind and degree of difference and so read with more exactitude what is being said and done, and therefore can more easily recognise sites of difficulty, repair communicational damage, and so on.

Practice

Perform a paradigmatic and a syntagmatic analysis on a recent contribution of your own which caused problems. Do the same for a contribution by someone else which was an important factor in influencing a negotiation.

We understand language not by working out a kind of dictionary definition for each word we hear, but by subconsciously comparing and contrasting it with others of the same paradigm and attributing value to the particular member chosen.

LANGUAGE STRATEGIES

At this point, enough general information on the powers of language, culture and discourse has been supplied that we can now offer a set of particular negotiating strategies which should be of use for any speech act.

The strategies are listed according to their functions: those in the first set act to realise propositional content (events); those in the second set act to realise interpersonal content (such as bond, role, tone). (There is a third set of strategies, which act to organise the text that is spoken or written so that it has coherence, development, continuity, emphasis, etc. These are more appropriately dealt with in the sections on speaking and writing.)

REALISING EVENTS

Paradigm choices

Choosing words

In their word choice, speakers can use:

1 those which are in general everyday usage;
2 those in the ordinary vocabulary of negotiation as a speech variety;
3 those in the specialised language of a particular group who may be negotiating – barristers, members of the advertising department of a company, managers, trade unionists, etc.;
4 those in the language of a particular kind of negotiating activity – writing letters, instructing juniors, drafting contracts, etc.

In the situations of 1 and 2 a word may be used which is 'overlexicalised', that is, it more properly belongs to situations 3 or 4, and is too advanced, or specialised for its context. The effect may be to present the speaker as arrogant, or careless of his or her audience's needs, or just as one who has a specialised vocabulary and knowledge. In the situations of 3 and 4 the words used can be 'underlexicalised', that is, be terms which properly belong to the more ordinary situations of 1 or 2, and are less specialised than might be expected. These will be noticeable. For example, they might suggest ignorance of the specialised term, or that it is being deliberately rejected in order to conceal, or not to commit the speaker to, some precise position, or to defamiliarise the event for the experienced hearers so that they concentrate on its meaning. Euphemisms can be used to facilitate the mention of awkward matters, but be wary lest they are misunderstood:

using a euphemism is a substitution process, and the connection may not be as clear to an audience as it is to the speaker.

Naming a particular happening separates it out from the mass of experience, and realises it. In so doing it produces a categorisation of reality; so, for example, a negotiation outcome could be named as 'agreement', 'compromise', 'consensus', 'folly' or 'success'.

Changing the name of a matter already singled out can change its meaning, and hence the agenda, and even the whole focus of the negotiation. So, for example, in a transaction between an estate agent and purchaser, 'down payment' could be restated as 'initial investment'; 'proposal' as 'offer'; and 'second mortgage' as 'additional financing', and these changes might influence the success of the deal.

Choose carefully what names to give to matters, and do not automatically accept the names used by others unless they suit your own purposes.

Evaluations of words can vary during an encounter, for example when someone senior offers a negative opinion about a word use. This will then be accepted as part of its meaning by the others for the duration. Or after a certain term has been used for some time in interaction, people might express reservations about some elements of its meaning, and recommend that one element in particular be taken as its central meaning. From that point the term will be understood in that way.

Be alert to the nuances of the words you need to use while negotiating.

Using nouns

The nouns used may be specific, realising a particular event or person, or may be generic, realising a group or number of events. The breadth of meaning in a generic term can cover up details or exceptions which might not suit your case, as in *lawyers have found it so*, which leaves unclear how many lawyers, and which ones.

Use a generic term to suit your purposes.

For example, rather than saying 'John Smith of Smith, Smith & Brown', say 'lawyers', 'the law', or 'solicitors'.

Complex noun phrases may be used, which bind several events, ideas, and opinions together, and this may persuade hearers to accept the whole set as one without investigating any one of its elements. For example, if someone were to refer to 'a rather dull but well-organised conference committee meeting', hearers may accept quite readily that it was dull and it was a conference committee meeting, and therefore the more debatable view that it was well-organised may slip through into acceptance without being noticed. To object to one item, a hearer has first to separate the items, notice the objectionable one, isolate it, and then speak about it in such a way as to indicate that it is only that item that is problematic, and that the others are acceptable. This involves a lot of cognitive activity, which the principle of least effort will resist unless the hearer feels very strongly about the matter. (The effort will be exponentially greater, of course, if the hearer wishes to object to two items.)

Recognise the persuasive power of the way a complex noun phrase works to bring a number of different things into close association and have readers accept them as a set.

Complex noun phrases can be confusing. For example, does the phrase 'a new fabric detergent container' refer to a container of detergent for new fabric, or a container of new detergent for fabric, or a new container of fabric detergent, or even a new (made of fabric) container of detergent? Such phrases should be used with caution, and if confusion is possible some division of the elements should be made.

Recognise that complex noun phrases can be confusing.

Adjectives can be used to encode attitude and opinion to great persuasive effect (whether informally in describing an opinion as 'clever', 'too clever by half', 'intelligent', or 'bright'; or more formally in describing an idea as 'problematic', 'visionary', 'innovative' or 'newfangled'). The attitude may be clearly revealed, as in these examples, but it may also be less obvious, and hence more influential, as in 'We have a major problem on our hands', which contains the opinion that the problem is a 'major' one without specification, and 'That was a careless mistake', where the opinion is that the mistake arose from 'carelessness'.

Manipulate your use of adjectives to suit your evaluation of an event.

The use of pronominal adjectives can reveal attitude towards the matters being expressed, as in, for example, 'These plans are well done' compared with 'Those plans are well done'. The first shows the speaker to be less distanced from the plans (and possibly from their creator) than in the second. The same sense of distance is revealed in the choice of 'this plan' rather than 'that plan', or 'here's the plan' rather than 'there's the plan'. What the distance implies will depend on the particular circumstances, but such uses are worth observing.

Choose pronouns carefully, and observe others' use of them.

Choosing between noun and verb

When speaking of an event it can be realised by either a noun or a verb, with different effect. The use of the noun can allow the doers of the action to be omitted, and this will impact on the meaning. For example, there is a good deal of difference between these pairs of tokens – *absence/being absent*, *freedom/being free*, *protection/protecting* or *being protected*, and between these sentences:

> 'Experiments have shown it to be true.'
> 'People experimenting have shown it to be true.'

The first version gives a more absolute value to the experiment than the version where the doers are explicitly named, and readers can see clearly that 'showing it to be true' is the act of some people, not a universal law beyond the scope of people. In the second version, also, it is more easily seen as comparable to investigating, testing, hypothesising – all uncertain in their outcomes.

Consider the choice between naming a particular event by noun or verb.

Using verbs

Verbs as realisations of actions can be used effectively for naming purposes, for example categorising a particular act of speech as one which insults, offends, interferes or intervenes. This acts to persuade others to give that meaning to the speech. They might disagree with the interpretation but the naming could become the accepted view if they do not think to analyse it.

Always choose your verbs carefully.

Adverbs can add a judgmental meaning to the realisation of actions, for example, describing something as being done 'mistakenly', 'deliberately' or 'with malice'.

If you choose to use an adverb, remember you are expressing an attitude towards the verbally expressed action.

When representing an action, in many cases it is possible to choose between an active and a passive structure, for example between 'The secretary organised the meeting well' and 'The meeting was well organised by the secretary.' The difference is one of focus. In the first example the focus of attention is on the secretary, and in the second it is on the meeting. Taking the second option also allows for the possibility of deleting the doer of the action should this be useful – 'The meeting was well organised.'

Consider the different values in choosing between the active and the passive forms of the verb.

When the need is to represent an experience this can be done in such a way that the experiencer is either mentioned or omitted. So one can say 'I am worried' or 'This is worrying'; 'I am bored' or 'It is a boring meeting'; 'I am glad to see you' or 'It is good to see you.'

Choose whether to express or not express the experiencer.

The normal expression in English for many events is a transitive structure, that is, one in which an actor performs an action which has a definite result, for example: 'We organised the successful conference.' But it is also often possible to use a more intransitive structure, one in which the action is less controlled by the actor, or its results seem just to occur rather than to be the product of the actor's work, for example: 'We did the organising for the conference, and it was a success', which loosens the connection between the organising action and the success.

Some verbs in English remove the responsibility of the action from the actor to some external force, for example: 'it strikes me', or 'it is a known fact', or 'it is obvious', all of which are variants of 'I think', but disguise on whose authority 'it' is striking, is known, or is obvious.

Choose how you wish to represent (a) the actor – as in control or not, and (b) the result – as the outcome of the actor's work or not.

Syntagm choices

The two most important locations in a syntagm are first and last: putting a matter in first position indicates to readers that it is the major focus, and in last position it suggests that it is the matter which the speaker wishes the hearer to retain most in his or her memory.

Put the most important idea in a syntagm into the first position. Put one important idea into the last position.

Readers expect that the subject of a sentence will be at or near its start, and in statements that it will usually be an actor. This expectation can be used in order to attribute responsibility for an action to some source other than the real actor. So, instead of saying 'I can't get this thing to work', one could say 'This thing won't work', or one could say 'It escaped my mind' instead of I forgot', or 'It fell' instead of 'I dropped it.'

Consider how to attribute an action.

Within a sentence a speaker can coordinate events (ideas or actions), and in so doing imply that they are equivalent, though this may be a partial view. For example, '(There are three things to be done), I'll send out the publicity brochures, Peter will organise the conference, and Mary will publish the results.' Peter and Mary may feel this is an unfair distribution of work, since what is involved in each activity is not equal. Events may be coordinated more tightly through the use of 'and', or more loosely through the use of 'and as well', 'and also' or 'and moreover'.

Coordinate what suits you to be seen as equal, and analyse what others are implying to be equal.

The valuation of an action can be realised as positive or negative, as in the choice between 'It was good' and 'It wasn't bad', or between 'We must get together' and 'We must not leave it so long next time.' Changing from a positive to a negative focus of attention can significantly alter the realisation. Compare, for example, 'The letter is half done', with 'I'm only halfway through the letter', or 'I've nearly finished' with 'I haven't quite finished yet.'

Consider how best to use negation.

REALISING THE INTERPERSONAL

Speakers use language not only to realise events, but also to register their sense of the interpersonal nature of the communication encounter, and to influence the other participants to share that sense. They do this by negotiating the *bond*, *roles* and *tone* that will sustain the interaction.

Bonding

This can be registered in various ways.

1   Self-presentation   An absence of information given about the self argues a wish for a remote or looser kind of bond; where information is supplied, the kind and quantity suggest what sort of closer bond is wanted. For example, information about the speaker's achievements suggests a more remote bond, since these are matters of public record, and so treat the hearers simply as members of the public. Information about the speaker's problems suggests a closer bond, in allowing opportunity for the hearer to offer support (which would imply a bond between equals) or advice (which permits the hearer to adopt a superior role, that of one who knows better than the speaker). Information about the speaker's mistakes suggests a very close bond by making the hearer privy to matters not normally raised in public and in which the speaker reveals loss of face.

2   Personal vocabulary   The use of language tokens, such as personal names, nicknames and names that encode shared references, can create a bond. Decisions to use the hearer's first name, surname, full name or title imply different degrees of bonding. Referring to others in these ways can increase or diminish closeness, depending on whether the use is shared by the hearer. For example, the effect of the following exchange would be to stress difference rather than closeness: 'How's your Personnel Officer these days?' 'Bill? He's fine.'

3 Emotional language Whether it is expressing the speaker's emotions or making emotional matters the focus of attention, emotional language increases the closeness of the bond, since it expresses feeling, or permits an exchange of feeling, and this is perceived as rather more personal a matter than non-emotional matters, or non-emotional expressions. The closest bonding may be being sought if a speaker is jokingly insulting since this is one expression of intimacy in the close family bond. If the hearer misreads it, however, by failing to perceive the jocularity of tone, it can have the opposite effect from that intended, and make a breach in the bond.

4 Casualness in speaking Whether expressed as a deviation from the topic or carelessness in word use, or indeed as interruption and non-sequiturs, casualness in speaking can be perceived as closeness of bonding, if the speaker's aim appears to be to reveal himself or herself in a state of unpreparedness, to let others see behind the scenes of his or her normal public presence. (It would not be perceived in the same way if hearers feel that the speaker is *really* unprepared or careless, and has made no effort to present well.) Conversely, a speaker who speaks with logic, choosing words and topics with precision, and preferring to be silent rather than offer hesitant ideas or words, and who objects to others' lack of logic and precision, displays a wish for a remoteness of bond.

5 References to shared matters Referring only to shared experience or knowledge that is very public, and known to many others, produces a distanced bonding. Referring to less public or more private matters, particularly to shared secret knowledge, produces a closer bond. Referring to shared attitudes or opinions, because these can arise from deep feelings in people, can produce a very close bond.

There is a further means of producing bonding, using a shared language, which is called *restricted code* use. This is the kind of language which takes for granted a shared knowledge and experience, and works by minimal reference to the shared world, for example by the overuse of such inexplicit pronouns as *it*, *they*, *those* and *that*, and of such all-embracing terms as *thing* and *the other*, and of such vague verbs as *be*, *do* and *have*, in fact of all those words that require the hearer to have prior knowledge of their referents and do not provide clearly referential terms which could be understood by any hearer. An example of restricted code usage is 'Did you get it then? She said you would have', where *get*, *it* and *she* are unspecified and assumed to be known. The opposite of restricted code usage is called *elaborated code*, where all items are realised in such a way that anyone ignorant of the events dealt with could understand enough about them either to have a clear perception of them or to be able to ask reasonable questions to clarify them.

In each of these five cases, the hearers may not wish to reciprocate in kind or accept the degree of bonding the speaker wants, and part of the interaction will consist of negotiating what is ultimately to be the accepted degree and kind of bond for the duration of the negotiation.

6   Codeswitching   Every time someone speaks they can switch to the discourse of a different kind of interaction from the one in progress. So, for example, during a negotiation between colleagues over a work matter, one or the other or both can switch to the code of, say, melodrama, or comedy, or sermons, or journalism. All are codes with distinct speech routines (vocabulary, voice quality and so on), distinct kinds of bonds with hearers, and distinct kinds of role and social tone, which are (or are intended to be) instantly recognisable. One interactive value in code-switching lies in its capacity to provide a mechanism whereby an awkward speech act (such as ordering a peer to do a task or correcting a colleague's work) can be made less awkward by assuming a role in which ordering or correcting can be done in such a way that the speaker 'disguises' or distances himself or herself, because the role adopted is clearly not 'true' to the interaction, but has as one of its normal behaviours the awkward task to be performed. So, for example, a reprimand may be offered in the code of church minister, or a problematic question can be asked in the code of intrusive reporter. The choice of code to switch to could indicate whether the problem for the speaker arises from a sense of solidarity, a sense of distance, or a wish to conceal.

Hearers who understand the code switch not only hear what act is being performed (and so receive the order, correction or reprimand) but also work out from the very act of switching that the speaker feels awkward enough about the act to seek to disguise his or her role while doing it. They will read this complex behaviour in their own way, evaluating reasons, and assessing motives.

Role setting

A speaker can attempt to set roles for the participants in a negotiation before, during, and even after the event. In the preparatory stages of a 'chat' he or she can tell stories or anecdotes in which roles are declared for the speaker or for others. For example, tales can be told in which the speaker is the main actor and the others are observers, or in which one hearer is singled out for mention as an actor. The substance of the story may have little to do with the negotiation topic, but still role determinations can be set for those present. For example, a speaker may tell of an incident on the way to the meeting in which he or she successfully defeated an attempt to cheat him or her about an account. In so doing he or she comes across as a successful achiever in a world of cheats. There may be little connection intended between the cheating and the present encounter, but the success and the achievement declare how the speaker is currently seeing his or her role. Equally, an anecdote may involve one of the hearers in some capacity or another, and shows how the speaker is currently seeing that person's role. In both cases the hearers may either accept or attempt to renegotiate the roles being set.

Also in the preparatory stages, either in the chat or in the first part of the meeting proper, a speaker may overtly declare his or her role, perhaps by naming his or her position – 'I am the Personnel Officer' – or by stating where his or her power originates – 'I am acting as representative of the Department' – or by declaring the task he or she has been required to do in the interaction – 'I am empowered to seek answers to these questions.' He or she may also use the speech acts associated with some role, for example declaring, insisting, informing, requiring, questioning or organising, and may continue to establish the desired role during such major preparatory acts as setting the agenda and circulating drafts.

During the negotiation itself speakers manifest their roles by the quantity of speech they contribute, and how and when it occurs. Each speaker therefore produces a different profile of speech behaviour: some produce a good deal of speech; some say little except at crucial moments; some dominate by unexpected silence either throughout or at significant moments. Some only speak in response to others; some make marked interventions by striking initiations of speech; and some directly seek to change the speaking patterns of others by requiring strongly marked changes in behaviour, for example by indicating that enough questions have been asked and that the meeting ought to pass on to another topic. In addition, role can be indicated by the particular tokens used for each speech act: some speakers use strong terms like 'want', 'need' or 'require' to indicate their own role as one whose wishes will be attended to, others produce initiating speech acts like 'question', 'request' or 'ask for information', all of which require responses, and hence dictate the role they think another person should take. Speakers who speak positively and with few hesitations may do so in order to be taken for major actors; others who hedge and hesitate and offer tentative opinions, declare themselves to be of minor importance; neither may necessarily be accepted in these terms. The first may annoy by overconfidence, while the second may already be known to have social position and high rank, and the speech will be read as an attempt to disguise this.

After the negotiation, participants can still seek to take a particular role, for example by writing to the others with an interpretation of the value of the meeting (and hence seeking to impose themselves as major actors in the event). Other possibilities would be to raise a question about some matter left incomplete, or to ask if others have completed their tasks set at the negotiation, or to set up the next activity: each of these gives a role to the speaker, for example as interpreter of the actions of others, as one with the right to raise questions as to the achievements of the negotiation, as one who can check up on the task completion of others, or as one who has the right to set up the next event. Others may not accept that the speaker has a right to such a role, and may seek to adjust it.

Tone setting

A speaker can seek to set the tone of an interaction by talking of matters in the desired tone, for example by relating anecdotes of a serious or jocular kind, by describing actions in an argumentative or exploratory way, or by raising matters in a thoughtful or emotional tone. Tone can also be set by explicit declaration, as in 'We must be most cautious about this matter', 'This is no laughing matter', 'Circumspection is called for here', 'This is most urgent', and so on.

The tone can be set with respect to the matters to be dealt with, as illustrated above, or can be addressed to the behaviour of one of the participants, either the speaker or the hearers, as in 'We must all pull together on this one.' Tokens may be used which indicate that the speaker feels pleased to think of him or herself as, for example, creative and energetic, or thorough and careful; or which indicate he or she has a sense of the hearers as particular kinds of actor, as, for example, by showing admiration for them as clever, useful, and self-motivated, or by comforting them, so suggesting they are in need of support.

Tone can also be set for the negotiation, for example by producing acts which are seen as serious or less serious, by registering disapproval of the unserious acts of others, or by setting the pace at which matters are dealt with.

Part II

The management of spoken interaction

Chapter 3

Conversation: its nature, structure and 'rules'

GENRE

Genre is the name given to a set of communicative activities with shared characteristics to which particular instances of the activity can be understood to belong. So, there are genres within writing – poetry, letter-writing, report-writing, etc., and there are genres within speech – the conversation, the lecture, the interview, etc. People have a sense of the different genres, such that when they come across the signals of a particular genre they set their expectations of what will occur (and not occur). So participants can say 'That was a good meeting *as meetings go*' or 'We never considered the detail, you must do that *in a negotiation*.' And they narrow their focus, rather as a computer programmer could select a database from his or her memory store and begin to work only with that. He or she might not know what specifically would be used from the selected database, but would not expect to need data from elsewhere. The sense of generic expectations will affect the production, reception and understanding of the activities of the particular instance. (Part of many negotiations, and particularly cross-cultural ones, may be spent on establishing and agreeing these generic parameters before getting down to specifics.) The understanding of genre will also provide a means of comparing and evaluating the success or otherwise of any specific negotiation.

Genre is worth examining for several reasons:

(a) It enables the principles of the organisation of negotiation to be understood and used to effect.
(b) It enables comparisons to be made between negotiations, which can reveal the absence of important matters, the non-occurrence of particular acts, and so on, which may help in the assessment of a particular negotiation.
(c) It can be used to classify particular occurrences as types or instances of a negotiating activity, and so to understand something more about

them, for example recognising the acts performed on a particular
occasion as routine or peculiar, conventional or idiosyncratic.

(d) Negotiations can be summarised or paraphrased more easily if seen at a
generic level, for example: 'We didn't spend much time on preliminaries, but moved straight to the detail of the plan, then we got stuck on
the last clause of the contract and spent more time on that than we'd
expected.' Such a description is using generic perceptions of 'timing',
'detail', 'plan', 'got stuck', 'more time' and 'preliminaries'.

(e) We can put ourselves and others into the roles which we know from
experience are proper to the activity – presenting ideas, qualifying
them, objecting to the ideas of others, accepting them, expressing
attitudes, offering advice, providing procedural assistance, and so on.

(f) We learn how to measure comparative success and failure in reaching
the goal of the interaction.

(g) We learn to recognise stages in the progress of a negotiation, and so to
estimate the value of using a particular negotiating strategy, for
example, where best to place it for maximum effect.

(h) We can know who is the most difficult opponent present because we
can know what constitutes 'difficulty', and can read this in his or her
strategies.

(i) Finally, and very importantly, we can know what speech actions are
likely to occur, how to assess each one against the benchmark of
previously experienced ones of similar kind, and so both to hear
accurately what is being done by others and also to recognise what acts
we ourselves could perform, and how best to word them for our
desired outcome, and so on.

In other words, considering negotiation as a genre allows one to stand back
from the activity and know the framework within which it occurs, the
means by which it is achieved, and also enables one to assess and evaluate
the actions, procedures and outcome. All this is done by using comparison
and contrast with a 'model' negotiation derived from experiential knowledge of the genre.

NEGOTIATION AS CONVERSATION

To see negotiation generically it is necessary first to understand that it is a
sub-variety of conversation, partaking of many of the conventions or 'rules'
of conversation, but differing in having a narrower range of speech acts
available to it, having stricter rules of procedure, and a defined goal.

It also varies in having an extra two elements to the goal or purpose
behind the speech activity, in that:

(a) there is some degree of disagreement or opposition among its participants which is to be settled, and

(b) there is a need to produce some action or policy decision.

As a consequence, negotiation uses the conventions of conversation but also acquires its own set of conventions which will assist in their achievement. The conversational goals of bonding through sharing ideas and attitudes and of achieving ego satisfaction through being able to speak to others and have them hear one's views, remain true also of negotiation.

It is worth noting how often the end product of the negotiational goals, whether they are actions or policies, is linguistic. This means it may be misunderstood, because the words or phrases used will have different meanings to each participant. Negotiations can end in verbal agreements, written reports, memos, communiqués, etc., and these will need to be monitored carefully: particularly if one participant is put in charge of formulating the result. Make sure some provision is made for drafting and correcting before it is finalised.

The generic sense of a negotiation acts as a familiar framework for participants and so provides them with the comfort of a ritual, within which they can address the peculiar needs of any particular negotiating instance. Such comfort is necessary because a negotiation will require participants to change or adapt their views and may require them to lose an argument. This could be too threatening if there was no sense of routine about it all.

ACTS OF NEGOTIATION

The generic activities of negotiation will include:

1   the speaker performing such acts as:

(a) articulating a view on the matter under discussion;
(b) bringing into discussion – that is, into the hearing of others – his or her topics, opinions, needs, purposes, etc.;
(c) adjusting, adapting, altering, qualifying and omitting from these those elements which are unacceptable to the majority or, if it is a polarised negotiation, unacceptable to one side;
(d) prioritising the matters represented, ranking them and choosing from among them what can be put together to form an acceptable whole;
(e) formulating what will be the finished proposal;
(f) formulating the final communicative act, whether it is a plan, contract, verbal agreement or whatever.

2   the hearer reacting in the following ways:

(a) noting what others do as their major acts, for example proposing, suggesting, reporting, dismissing or arguing;
(b) analysing what criteria are being used by the participants to establish major and minor acts;

(c) noting what acts are not performed by others (which may be of significance);

(d) learning about the ideas of others;

(e) knowing when to provide support or refuse it.

PREPARATION

Before entering a negotiation a participant must consider the difficulties and consequences of these acts, as well as how best to perform them. Like all speech events, once a negotiation starts, it will affect those involved in many ways, and will act upon them so that from that time onward, for as long as the memory of the event lasts, their lives will be altered by it. For example, a negotiation will require a speaker to articulate views on a particular matter. In the process this will provide a firm outline to his or her thoughts on the matter, where previously he or she might have only vaguely registered it as something to consider one day. Once this is done the thoughts will acquire new value for the speaker, who may even fully comprehend them for the first time. Articulating them will also inform the other participants that this speaker thinks this thought, and considers it germane to the event, revealing to them his or her thoughts about two important things: the subject matter and the event.

Before entering a negotiation, a speaker should also consider the qualities that are important to the event and seek their achievement, for example:

equivalence of participants, seriousness, clarity, viability of subject matter, specificity.

He or she should note the kind of speech acts which are appropriate:

inform, tell, ask, discuss, advise, accept, etc.;

and the modulations of them that will be needed:

adapt, modify, qualify, reduce, recognise the contribution of, analyse, as well as *ignore, dismiss* and *reject.*

Before entering a negotiation, a speaker should consider what would be problematic in the event:

emotion, frivolity, vagueness, the mythical or unreal, too great a sense of urgency, behaviours or topics which are too unusual or innovative, or, worst of all, adopting the position of being anti-talk, as in 'I want some action round here' (which is the most unproductive position to take when 'talk' is the means by which negotiation must proceed).

SPOKEN INTERACTION – GENERAL

To reduce the complexity of negotiating speech to manageable proportions for its users, there exist structural and interpersonal conventions or 'rules' which act as controlling devices and operate both at the level of the whole interaction and at the micro-level of each exchange of speech. In each case, there are two kinds of agreed 'rules' of behaviour:

(a) regulative rules which can be broken with a variety of effects, some acceptable, some less so; and
(b) constitutive rules which cannot be broken without some marked consequence: from throwing undue emphasis on the speech act which caused the breach of rule to causing some serious damage to the interpersonal bond.

The rules may never be articulated by those who use them, but they are conventionally learned from experience. (In cross-cultural communication, where they may not be understood, they can be the cause of a range of problems.)

Examples

An example of breaking a regulative rule would be the interruption of another's speech. This acts against the rule that a speaker is allowed to finish saying what he or she intends to say. People do interrupt each other quite often, but it is never without some effect on the person interrupted, and on any observers who note it.

An example of constitutive rule-breaking would be the abrupt and unsignalled termination of an interaction, because the rule is that encounters must end by bilateral agreement. Abrupt endings do occur, of course, but they have the potentiality to cause serious social damage except in very particular circumstances which might excuse them.

Practice

Ask what you dislike most about the talking behaviour of your associates. You may be able to pinpoint what rule is at issue, and note its effects. In encounters where you can act as a bystander, note what acts of speech by one person adversely affect another. Is there a rule involved? There are many such rules; not only are they generally unwritten, but also no list of them appears ever to have been compiled. You can discover the ones crucial to your own negotiating activity by noting when damage occurs – expressed by displays of anger, signs of irritation, apologies, mistaken interpretations and the like. Set up a list of the rule-breaking acts you most dislike, and consider whether you need to adapt your behaviour in any way.

It is sometimes possible to pinpoint the difficulty by asking the one who is demonstrating that damage has occurred what they think the problem is, and then analysing their answers. The dialogue might proceed in this fashion:

John: 'Bill makes me wild, he's so arrogant.'
You: 'What does he do that's so arrogant?'
John: 'Well, I don't know, it's just . . . [Note that being asked to analyse a response may well cause hesitation.] Well, take the other day, he came into my office with several tasks that would take me all day to do, dumped them on my desk – shot off without even giving me the time of day.'

Such an account suggests several interpretations for Bill's behaviour and John's response. One is that Bill 'shot off without giving me the time of day', in other words broke the maxi-level convention that speech interactions should only be closed by mutual agreement. It is damaging to terminate an interaction unilaterally. This one act will, of course, be read in the context of his other acts, and John would interpret it in accordance with the goals and purposes he wishes for the interaction. It will still have some effect, however, even though the speech sounds quite trivial, and it takes place very quickly.

Other maxi-level conventions include the following.

(a) Speaking too slowly, or too formally, and offering only the polished product of thought is inappropriate in interactions where the sharing of ideas or a bonding relationship is a main concern, because no sharing of thought *processes* is offered.
(b) Producing only routine clichés and nothing more is boring and against the convention that we must provide some interest for hearers.
(c) But equally, using no clichés is also against the 'rules' because they serve at least one important use by slowing down the rate of information flow in a speech so that it is not too dense for the hearer to absorb. Clichés interspersed with new or complex information make for a more comprehensible speech action.

In order to discuss the structural elements of a negotiation, we will take as a model a single, informal discussion between colleagues during a normal working day, in which such activities as the following are likely to occur:

offering suggestions, asking advice, providing information, expressing feelings, disagreeing, showing acceptance, etc.

To analyse this further requires that we consider the structural aspects of the discussion.

INTERACTION STRUCTURE

At the maxi-level of speech interaction, a discussion has a structure which is conventionally accepted, and its phases serve conventional functions.

Initial phase

This begins with acts which have as their primary functions:

(a) the establishment or re-establishment, the exploration or declaration, of bonds of relationship;
(b) the declaring of the speaker's role – as adviser, organiser, objector, clarifier, etc, and the speaker's attempt to allocate roles to the hearer or hearers;
(c) the provision of information about the mood, attitude or personality of the speaker;
(d) the reception of this information by a hearer who will use its meaning for the interaction, and
(e) the making of decisions about the appropriate psychological tactics, speech acts and politeness strategies to be used from that time forward.

Any strangers present will use the time to become used to other speakers' speech patterns, voice qualities, mindset and personality traits. Whether they launch straight into business or spend a few minutes chatting while assembling, it still holds true that the opening moments provide the opportunity for interpretative work.

If all of them are friendly colleagues and meet every day, the need for such work is much diminished, and in some cases may be done on the first day of the week, or at the first meeting of the working day, and need only be hinted at thereafter, until the next major break.

Practice

Think what can be usefully learned of speaker B from the following possible responses offered as replies to this chatty comment by A:

A: 'How was the golf?'
(which seeks to bond with B by showing that A knows that B was to play golf at some time between the previous meeting and this one and that A is interested to know about it).
B: 'Don't ask!'
B: 'Went round in 85! [pause] How was the party?'
B: 'What? Oh right, not bad I suppose. About these plans . . .'
B: 'Well, we started off at about 6.30 a.m. then the car began making rattling noises and I had to stop by a garage to get it fixed. That took about an hour. It was the right brake drum . . .'

Jockeying for roles and status also takes place in this first phase. An instance of the kind of act used for this work would be:

'You look worried, is that contract causing problems?'

This could be read as friendly concern, but in it the speaker takes the role (and senior status) of one who (a) can assess the other's states of mind, (b) knows the other's tasks, (c) can make (tentative) judgments about the other's capacities for a task, and perhaps (d) knows enough to help solve the problems. It also puts the other's state of mind onto the topic agenda of the meeting while revealing nothing of the speaker's own.

Whether this act was intentional is not the point; what matters is how it could be read, what effect it produced. It could easily, for example, lead to the other person having to reveal to those present his or her difficulties with a problem, and so centre their attention on his or her lack of ability. It could also lead to such other consequences as that person being irritated by the assumption of inability or denying it or waiting for an occasion later to retaliate with an attack on the first speaker's inabilities.

Central phase

After the initial phase, there is a move to the central activity, the main reason for the interaction, which itself has a preliminary phase, a centre and a closing phase.

A phase transition is usually signalled by a boundary move, for example:

'Well now, we'd better get down to work on this . . .'

'OK then, everyone here? Well, let's start.'

'If we're all agreed on that, let's move to . . .'

'That's settled then, OK.'

'Next item for discussion is Agenda item 3.'

That is, it often names the next activity required, sets the agenda of behaviour for the next part of the speech interaction, or summarises or declares closed the previous part. It consists of two moves:

(a) a framing signal, such as 'Now then', 'OK then', 'Right' or words of this kind, given with strong emphasis – often with non-verbal signals – a bang on the table, a hand clap, etc.;
(b) a focus signal, which is a metastatement about some part of the negotiation; in the examples given above, the focus phrases are 'we'd better get down to work on this', 'let's start', 'all agreed', 'let's move to' and 'that's settled'.

Frame and focus usually occur together. They strongly indicate a change from one set of activities to another, or from discussing one topic to another.

It is very important to note who the members accept as being able to perform this phase-changing; it may be the chairperson of a formal meeting, or the boss of a set of co-workers, but if the meeting is of equals, then someone who seeks to change the group's activity from one kind to another is taking a leadership role. Where this is accepted (knowingly or not) by the others, they are in effect accepting that person as a leader.

Closing phase

The final phase, closure, also has conventions. The most usual has already been mentioned above, whereby a speech event cannot be ended unilaterally, that is, without a joint agreement to close. The existence of such a rule is the reason why occasionally one hesitates to leave a colleague's office, hanging on in the doorway for some little time (though there may be an excellent reason to hurry away) until the other agrees to end the interaction. The signal of agreement is often a very brief 'OK', or is given only non-verbally by a nod and turning away, but it has significance enough to cause trouble if it is not offered.

The less formal the interaction, the less signalling is needed. More formal interactions may require a whole series of signals. For example, the end of a committee meeting agenda has three stages of closure: a preliminary signal ('Any other business?'); a reference to the next meeting; and a terminating signal, such as 'I declare the meeting closed.' The first allows those present to offer an expression of disagreement about closure should they wish to; the second works to sustain the bond between members at its moment of greatest weakness (the moment of parting) by linking the present occasion with the next meeting, when it can be strengthened again; and the third makes use of formal signals easily recognised by all.

AT INDIVIDUAL ACT LEVEL

At the level of individual acts at every stage of the interaction, the focal point is the *speech pair*. This usually consists of two parts, that is, two utterances: an initial move and a response. The speech pair has power within the interaction because for each pair there is a requirement that the first part belongs to the class of acceptable initial moves, and that the second part relates to the first part in a socially acceptable way. The first part, therefore, restricts the options of the second speaker to the set of appropriate second parts. So, for example, every question as a first part requires an act from the set of answers for the second part.

The set of options available to the second speaker can be large or small. A broad question, for example 'What time is it?', could produce any of the following and more: '4.15', 'It's about 4', 'Why?', or 'That's the third time you've asked.' A more narrowly constructed first part, like 'Susan, did you get the report?', requires that one particular person responds (and no-one else should speak), and gives Susan roughly only three options: 'Yes', 'No' or 'Not exactly'.

Practice

Can you think of others that differ in essence from 'Yes', 'No' or 'Not exactly'? Can you think of the set of options that must follow a request like 'I'd like a copy of the report please', or an apology like 'I'm sorry I forgot the report.'? What differences are there in social significance between each option in the set?

It is, however, no difficult matter to discover a question not followed by an answer, and this raises a question about the status of the pair as a two-part unit. But it is noteworthy that the first part provides so specifically for the second that the absence of the second is usually conspicuous and has a strong social impact. People regularly complain in such terms as 'You didn't answer my question!', or 'Are you not going to accept my apology?', or 'Didn't you hear me? I'd like a copy of the report!'

Preferred responses

There is a further restriction on the second part: namely that the initiating move sets up both preferred and dispreferred options. The distinction between the two is crucial, and needs explaining. A preferred response is one which responds to the subject matter and form of the first part, and which recognises the aim of the speaker in making that speech act. So if a speaker says 'What time is it?', the hearer knows that it is a question, that the speaker wants to know the time, and that good answers would include information about the time, or a speedy admission that the hearer has no useful information, so the asker could ask elsewhere.

To provide the preferred response is easy: it is easy to decide on and to formulate, because something about the first part makes clear what the second part should say. However, to provide the dispreferred response requires more cognitive energy, because it involves adjusting your ideas from the preferred to the form you want to offer. It results in a less connected and usually more complex utterance. This happens partly because it may require politeness strategies to mitigate or excuse its not being the required or expected option; the very presence of such strategies indicates that there is something about the response that will need explaining or apologising for. (See Chapter 4, pp. 67–75 for an account of politeness strategies.) Favourite devices of respondents who know they should justify the dispreferred option are:

(a) the use of pause or hesitation, as a signal that something inappropriate is about to be said;

(b) providing explanations for doing the dispreferred act;

(c) offering apologies;

(d) offering thanks or other appreciative recognition of any initial act which offers itself as doing something good for the hearer, like offering advice or giving an invitation, while producing something which does not fit well with it;

and also, since the dispreferred form will jolt the first speaker's mind by being unexpected,

(e) using tokens which signal the disjunction between what is wanted and what is to be delivered, and which could be pauses or vocalised hesitations: '. . .', or 'OK, but', or (drawled) 'Well . . .'.

Preference is a very powerful concept and can be used to explain the occurrence of quite a number of other speech behaviours as speakers try to avoid having to perform dispreferred second parts. For example, it is thought better that the speaker correct his or her own mistakes rather than have others correct them:

A: 'But I think these resorts are not very well presented.'
B: 'What?'
A: 'These resorts, they are —'
B: 'Resorts?'
A: 'Oh sorry, I mean reports.'

Speakers use pre-invitations and pre-requests, which are ways of inviting and requesting which seek to avoid loss of face for the initiator if a dispreferred response is likely and would result in the offer or request being refused. For example, if you wish to request that someone do something for you, a typical pre-request would be:

A: 'Are you busy at the moment?'

(hoping for the response 'No', so that you can then say 'Could you do X for me?') The pre-request would be recognised, and the hearer would decide whether to allow the request or not. If not, then the following exchange might occur:

B: 'Yes, why?' (dispreferred)
A: 'Oh, nothing, I just wanted a word but it's not urgent.' (Avoids making the request and so saves face.)

The most frequently used speech pairs are question and answer, request and response, and statement and response, but there are also such other pairs as accuse and deny or compliment and acceptance, and so on. (See Chapter 7 on speech acts for an analysis of a set of important first parts.) Each kind of first part – question, request, statement – exerts a different kind of power over the hearer, but it inevitably encourages him or her to take the path of least resistance and to respond with the preferred second part.

Questions

Take the following first part as an example (this one happens to be a question, but every kind of first part creates a set of ranked responses):

Fred: 'Have you seen that report anywhere?'

A sample set of possible responses to this are (listed from most to least preferred):

1 'Here it is.'

This answer is most preferred because the speaker here has recognised that the question is really a double act – a hidden preliminary question (pre-request): 'Where is the report?', and a request: 'Can I have it?' – and has moved straight to the request and fulfilled it.

2 'There's a copy in that red file.'

This also answers the hidden pre-request in such a way that Fred can achieve his goal, but it does require him to take steps to do so.

3 'Mary has it.'

This answers the preliminary question in a preferred, positive way and enables Fred to make the request to the appropriate person, Mary.

4 'Bill was supposed to have it today.'

This is not a helpful response and must be called dispreferred because (a) it only responds to the pre-request question and does so somewhat vaguely and (b) it sets up for Fred a whole series of actions: having to ask a second question and make a second request to Bill, and with no guarantee that they will be productive.

5 'No. Were you wanting it urgently?'

This is a negative response, but has two parts to it. The first part of the response, 'No', is efficiently speedy; so while it is not wanted by the speaker, it is nonetheless a perfect response to the question's content and form, and so it is a preferred form. It may be inconvenient, but it is not dispreferred. (Note that if Fred gets such responses to his questions more than about 30 per cent of the time, he is inefficient in his assessment of who has what information.) The second part of the response is more problematic. In one sense it is gratuitous, neither helping nor hindering Fred with his goal of getting the report, and so could be read as dispreferred. On the other hand, it expresses concern about Fred's situation and offers him the chance to express it. Fred may find these interpersonal qualities in the response pleasing.

6 'Yes, I saw it yesterday somewhere.'

Although this example answers the question positively with 'Yes', the vagueness of the response, and therefore its uselessness in helping out with the underlying request, makes it dispreferred. It could be more annoying than a straight 'No', because it appears to provide information while not actually doing so, and because it shows no recognition of Fred's real purpose. Unless the speaker goes on to clarify the location or assist the search in some way, it is worse than useless.

7 '. . . . .'

Silence is the worst response in some senses. Provided it is certain that the question was heard, it shows no sense of social duty or awareness of the nature of interaction. It is baldness itself, the antithesis of politeness, and will result in some damage to the interpersonal bond. It will never be understood as meaning nothing at all. What will be understood is that the speaker has offered the most dispreferred response, and that will be read as having meaning within the interpersonal part of the interaction, for example refusal to cooperate with Fred. It will also be interpreted with respect to the context of the question; Fred would consider what '. . . . . .' means in connection with the terms 'see', 'that report' and 'anywhere'. Is the 'seeing' a problem? Perhaps the speaker is too low in hierarchy for access to reports and is insulted by the implications of the question. Is 'that report' a problem? Perhaps the speaker wanted to write it and someone else got the task, and so is angry at the question. Is 'anywhere' a problem? Perhaps the speaker has lost the report, or has seen it somewhere without permission. Or is it that the whole act by Fred is so problematic that silence is the one polite or even possible response? Perhaps the speaker cannot find the report because he knows he is not meant to see it, for example it contains the news that his position is to be terminated. If this were so, then silence could be a sensible refuge, though it may be misunderstood by Fred.

This last aspect of the first part's power is worth further consideration. Not only does a first part restrict the hearer to a set of options for the second part, but the initiating move also raises a topic, addresses some issue, brings some matter into the talk and requires the hearer to speak about it. It may be the very last thing the hearer wishes to hear, or speak about, but he or she will have to say something in response. Whatever is produced by the second speaker, his or her unwillingness or reluctance to address the topic may be hard to conceal. Any avoidance strategies tried might only act to focus the first speaker's attention on them, and give rise to speculation about their use. The following are examples of questions that are likely to elicit a reluctance to respond.

1 The 'difficult' question which asks for an opinion:

'What do you think of the boss's new proposal?'

which the respondent would not like to speak about at all, or at least not with the particular person asking the question.

2 The awkward subject:

'How are things going at work?'

where the hearer has just become unemployed.

3 The complex first part, which contains several assumptions the hearer cannot accept, and cannot easily argue about:

'You are interested in the new project, aren't you? Well, we've managed to get rid of that incompetent architect, without any fuss; we won't hear from him any more, and you'll be glad to know we've appointed John Smith to do the work. You thought highly of his work on the last project, didn't you?'

If the hearer is not interested, thought the original architect competent, knows there will be a court case about getting rid of him, is not glad about John Smith's appointment and thinks badly of his work, he will be faced with a difficult or even no-win situation. Yet the question has been posed, and he must respond in some way.

Commands

Commands are also powerful acts. To the kinds of influence mentioned above for questions must be added two extra factors:

(a) the act required by the command may be a major imposition on the hearer; or
(b) the authority and senior status of the speaker may be such that the command cannot easily be refused.

Should the hearer wish to resist, a good deal of mollification using politeness strategies, will be needed.

Statements

Statements may appear superficially to be quite minimal in the demands they make on a hearer, but they do, nonetheless, require some interactional work. They must always receive some response, and the preferred response is agreement. In many cases it is enough to supply what are called 'support noises', verbal signs that the hearer is paying attention. Most people have one that it is their habit to use, such as 'mhm', 'aha', 'right', 'yeah' or 'yup'. Non-verbal signs are also used, including nods, smiles or a fixed gaze at the speaker. It is crucial that some version of these responses be produced if hearers wish to present themselves as listeners. Being a listener is an active role and signals must be given to this effect, or else speakers will respond badly and question whether they are being attended to – 'Are you listening?', 'Do you know what I mean?', and so on – or they will repeat, reiterate or expand their utterance because they think its substance is producing disagreement, which they will try to overcome.

Whatever the kind of speech act, every kind of initial move influences the interaction, not just by the constraints it sets on the second move, but well beyond that. Every utterance represents ideas, opinions or attitudes, and does so in a particular way. Specifically,

(a) it mentions some matters and excludes others; and
(b) it emphasises some things and subordinates others.

Inclusion and exclusion by one speaker, particularly when he or she initiates a speech pair, can strongly influence what will be spoken about by others, and what they will reject, forget or ignore. It is always hard for hearers to ask themselves what is not being said about any given matter. Yet it may be of vital concern to a successful outcome that this be done.

The placement of words in sentences can put a strong emphasis on some ideas, reduce others to insignificance and can make particular associations between matters (by juxtaposing them, coordinating them and so on) – in short it can affect how hearers assimilate the ideas, and so perhaps can influence them either to accept or reject them. As an instance of how placement can affect the presentation of material, consider the following:

'After our decision on this matter last week, what we need to do now is to consider its implementation.'

'We need now to consider the implementation of the decision we took last week.'

In the first version the decision appears to be still available for discussion because it is in the focal position – that is, where the main point of the sentence is put – while the second version puts 'implementation' in that position. The same change of emphasis is present in the next two examples.

'If the new parking centre isn't built the city's congested streets will come to a standstill.'

'The city's congested streets will come to a standstill unless the new parking centre is built.'

'We can achieve our target if we can increase production.'

'If we can increase production we can achieve our target.'

TURNTAKING

One of the most general conventions of spoken interaction is that one and not more than one speaker talks at a time. It is a regulative rule only, and is frequently broken by overlapping speech, but it nonetheless has power, as can be seen from the way one or other of the simultaneous speakers will soon fall silent. Overlaps are usually very short.

Another general convention is that silence is noticeable, and may be problematic in some circumstances. Silence can have a variety of meanings.

(a) In a close relationship it can signal complete accord as people relax quietly in each other's company.
(b) In a frozen encounter it can signal the opposite – a breach of some sort – for example, disapproval or distance.
(c) At the start of an encounter it can suggest discomfort, and can appear rude or antagonistic because of what is not being done – no bonding is taking place, no exchange of ritual gestures of acquaintanceship.
(d) It can be menacing or disconcerting, according to its circumstances, particularly if it is unexpected.

So silence on the whole is viewed somewhat negatively in spoken interaction, and even a pause, which is a short silence, is often taken as negative behaviour in some circumstances, of which the following are examples.

(a) Pausing before a response suggests hesitation and may even signal disagreement.
(b) Within a speech move, whether an initiation or a response, pausing can indicate an extra effort in producing the utterance and so reveal a problem point for the speaker.
(c) Pauses within speech can be irritating to a quick listener who anticipates what is coming next and yet has to wait for its production in speech before replying (because of the convention against interruption).

The main feature of turntaking, however, is the way in which it orders utterances so that the roles of speaker and hearer can be exchanged frequently and easily. The practical aspects of taking turns rest on yet more conventions.

(a) Holding the floor as speaker is perceived as a socially important act.
(b) All present are entitled to a turn at holding the floor, though they may choose not to take it.
(c) It follows, therefore, that no one speaker should hold the floor too long, because this denies opportunities to others.
(d) An exception to this is if all present agree that one person can dominate the talk. For example, this is acceptable practice if the speaker has important information to give, has a highly ranked position in the group

of talkers (one of the privileges of high rank is talking at length), has a good story to tell (much will be forgiven a good storyteller), and so on.

Practically speaking, there are four possibilities of behaviour involving the speaking turn, two as current speaker – yielding a turn and holding onto a turn – and two as current hearer – claiming a turn and listening.

YIELDING A TURN

A speaker has a variety of strategies by which to signal willingness to yield the floor to others, and hearers can recognise these as the approach of an opportunity to speak.

1 The grammatical construction of the speaker's language can indicate that a possible 'termination point' is approaching, and this can be taken advantage of by the hearer to begin speaking. For example, in 'The orders that you were worried about came yesterday', a unit of thought has been expressed, and the sentence could be seen as complete. However, it is possible that the speaker could intend to continue with 'and they were all as per the invoices'. If the hearer began a speaking turn after 'yesterday', it should not be perceived as impolitely interrupting the speech because the speech sounds as if it is finished. (Though the first speaker may take the first pause that follows as an opportunity to finish it off.) If, however, the second speaker began to speak after 'the orders that you', it would be grossly interruptive because the sentence is clearly incomplete at this point.

2 The voice quality of the speaker may indicate an approaching termination point, for example a slowing down in pace, an increase in drawling, or a drop in voice pitch to one lower than usual.

3 Certain phrases can signal the approaching end of the turn, for example 'and so on', 'and things' or 'so, anyway', where these sound as if the speaker has run out of things to say. Each speaker will have a routine set of phrases which are readily spotted by a keen listener.

4 Several non-verbal signs can accompany the other strategies: an increase in directness of gaze (where the gazer has been varying his or her gaze to and away from the hearer during the turn), or a glance away (where the gazer has been staring for most of the turn), and physical 'retreat' from the floor, by literally moving the body back to some degree, settling the arms to a resting position, or relaxing any signs of physical tension.

In signalling an intention to terminate the turn, the speaker may well produce a complex set of signs by using several of the above possibilities together.

There is one act which the speaker can produce which always yields the floor, and that is when he or she asks a question, either addressed generally or to someone nominated by the speaker as in 'Mary, what do you think?'

HOLDING THE FLOOR

A speaker may not wish to yield the floor, and can resist attempts at dislodgment from that prominent position. This can be done by one of the following methods.

1 A long turn can be set up by announcing that it has several parts, for example 'I wish to make three points', thus indicating that the turn is not terminated until the end of the third point, so anyone who jumps in before then is interrupting.

2 When someone looks like interrupting, rejection phrases can be produced, such as 'Just a minute', 'Let me finish', 'Hang on' or 'Just wait.'

3 Terminating signals can be withheld, for example by speaking in 'periodic' sentence forms where the completion of the sense is held up until near the end of the sentence, as in:

> 'Because our new office equipment is not yet fully operational, and therefore the report is delayed (though I hope it will not be much longer than next Monday), we must not offer to take on any new, or indeed revise any old, projects *till we have cleared the decks.*'

This last phrase is the first possible termination point. Compare it to the following, which could be terminated at any of the italicised points:

> 'With our plans now established, we could proceed with the *project*, though we should make sure the agents understand the *deadline*, and the sales staff are equipped to deal *with it. That's my opinion*, but I'd be interested to hear what you *think, Bill.*'

4 A turn can be held by not pausing for breath, and by speaking loudly or quickly.

5 The speaker can avoid looking at the person who is indicating a wish to take a turn. This acts to make it difficult for the person to speak because there is a convention which requires that eye contact occurs between speaker and hearer at the moment of turn exchange. (The convention is captured in the familiar phrase 'trying to catch someone's eye'.)

6 Assertive non-verbal signals can be used, such as leaning forward and increasing the quantity and intensity of gestures, i.e. holding the floor by sheer physical dominance of it.

CLAIMING A TURN

The hearer who wishes to claim a turn has several possibilities for action, which are listed in increasing order of acceptability.

1 Notice a possible termination point and then begin to speak quickly.

2 Overlap in speech with the speaker.

3 Interrupt in a pause by the speaker, either where the sentence is incomplete, or where the whole turn is incomplete.
4 Begin to speak hesitantly; stutter the first few words and then stop. It may have to be repeated later if it does not cause the speaker to come to a speedy termination.
5 Offer supportive noises, in agreement with the speaker. These may encourage the speaker to stop, because agreement appears to have been reached. You can then begin to speak – either in agreement or not, as appropriate. The noises could increase in volume as an indication of a turn-claim. Since they are supportive of the speaker, he or she may be more willing to relinquish the floor in response to them than to such adverse noises as 'but what about . . .' or 'yes well, but . . .'
6 If invited to respond to a question as an initiating move, go beyond the response to initiate a move of your own, as in:

A: 'So, what do you think, Bill?'
B: 'Oh, I agree entirely. But I would also want to say that . . .'

7 Use non-verbal language to show a wish to claim a turn, for example lean forward, increase gestures in intensity or number, raise a finger, or tap the table.
8 Try to catch the speaker's eye.

It is worth noting one particularly strong strategy for claiming the floor, for what it shows of the games people play to avoid an appearance of dominance in floor holding. In interaction, one of the strongest initiating moves is to call out someone's name: it is almost impossible not to respond to this call. The result of this move is to get the attention of the one called; and, frequently, he or she produces the response 'Yes?' or 'What?' or 'What do you want?', which are questions, and so yield the floor. If then, as an example, Bill wanted to get the floor, but wanted it to appear as if the floor was given to him rather than just taken by him, the following speech could be used:

Bill: 'Mary!'
Mary: 'Yes, what?'
Bill: 'I must tell you about the new project . . .'

Bill then has the floor, and Mary has given it to him.

LISTENING

Oh – I listen a lot and talk less. You can't learn anything when you're talking.

(Bing Crosby)

A good listener is not someone who has nothing to say. A good listener is a good talker with a sore throat.

(Katharine Whitehorn)

A particular member of a group discussion may be content in the role of listener, either temporarily or for the duration of the encounter. This attitude can be indicated in two ways:

(a) by offering support noises, from the most minimal indications of willingness to listen such as 'mhm' or 'aha' to the fully supportive 'Yes', 'That's great', 'Exactly', or 'I agree entirely';
(b) by offering positive encouragement to the turn-holder to continue, as in 'Go on', 'What happened next?' or 'Tell them about the X'.

The importance of listening as a conversational act is clear from the quantity of time spent on it (it is estimated that between 50 and 60 per cent of speech interaction is spent listening), and also on the work it does in contributing to the success of the event. This is measured by the way it does two things, which together could be called 'making sense' of what others say.

The first part of listening involves hearing what is said, while the second involves incorporating what is said into one's mind, adding it to the store of ideas already there, adjusting some ideas to take account of the new one, as well as reorganising categories of ideas already accepted.

Good listening requires that the listener decide its purpose, and then find the appropriate method for doing it. Typical purposes are to attend to the speech of others just enough to get some information or to get the gist of a matter, or to acquire a detailed understanding, or simply to give the appearance of listening (if, for example, an important speaker is being boringly repetitious).

LISTENING FOR MEANING

The most important part of the process of listening requires that the person not only hears the sounds made by another but also recognises them as systems of meaning. To do this it is necessary to filter out any extraneous noise, whether physical discomfort, or literal noise like the hum of air-conditioning, or psychological noise, such as fear and anxiety, which can prevent the hearer from knowing clearly what has been uttered. Attitudes too, if strongly enough held, can prevent hearers listening, and can cause them to attend only to what their own needs and attitudes suggest they should hear. So, some listeners perceive every speech as an attack, or, because they dislike some participant, treat every speech by that person as in some way bad. Listeners can also easily resist paying attention to speech which is vague, carelessly structured, or cognitively complex because of the amount of mental energy it demands to decipher it.

MAKING MEANINGS YOUR OWN

Cognitive energy is always to some degree required because of listening's second part: the incorporation of the matters heard into the listener's repertoire of ideas. The problems of doing this are compounded in negotiation when the speaker has to make extra judgments, deciding what incorporations and adjustments will suit the particular event, and help it to a successful conclusion, and which new ideas must be resisted either at all or with respect to the particular negotiation.

It is obviously necessary, therefore, that time within the encounter be provided for such work to proceed. Speakers who supply a heavy information flow of ideas, without any respite, reduce the chances of their ideas being listened to and accepted. Success will attend those who reduce the information flow to a rate more suited to the listening task. What rate is suitable can be gathered from observing the rate used by others (the bonding parts of the encounter should be used for this purpose), or from noticing the reactions to other speakers' information flow levels during the negotiation proper.

There are two listening pitfalls to avoid:

1 selective listening, which hears only an occasional word the other person says and invents the rest from the imagination; and
2 adaptive listening, which is more difficult to spot, in which an idea presented by another is assimilated into the memory store so successfully that later it is impossible to remember where it came from, and it may be thought of as one's own original idea.

Both can seriously distort the other's idea; the first by ignoring much of it, the second by interpreting it in the light of remembered acts of a somewhat similar kind, and adding their qualities to it or assuming it does not vary from them.

To ensure that more than surface listening occurs, listening skills can be improved by the following methods.

(a) Translate into 'telegraphese' the key ideas and terms used in others' speech.
(b) Reduce others' utterances to their basic propositions.
(c) Note emotive language when it occurs, then try to erase it from the words being spoken and seek the underlying rationality (if any).
(d) Use your judgment about the rhetorical tactics used in speaking in order to note which are the main points being made, and which therefore require most consideration.
(e) Make generic judgments. Does a speech act that you hear fit well into the negotiation genre? Into what category of negotiation should it go? What variants are possible, that is, how else might it be put (use a

paradigm and syntagm analysis) – what, therefore, is the meaning of this particular example?

(f) Use your generic sense to notice what acts are missing, or what propositions or topics are being excluded or avoided.

Listening is not only for the purpose of adjusting to the ideas of others, but also in order to note the intensity with which they hold those ideas; to sense the feelings involved in the encounter. Without some awareness of this it would be impossible to gauge how best to achieve your ends. It matters to know that Bill cares deeply about some item on the agenda, while no-one cares very much about another. It also provides information which can function to sustain the bond between participants. The information can be found by listening for occurrences of emphasis in speech, or emotive vocabulary, in particular those signs of emotion which are very minimal but which do give away indications of attitude, particularly when they are often repeated, as might occur with some such phrases as 'I feel . . .', 'I am concerned that . . .' or 'We must . . .'. The first is a verb of (mild) feeling, used instead of something like 'I think . . .' or 'I know . . .' (which say something different about the speaker); the second expresses (mild) concern; and the third expresses a (mild) sense of compulsion (and adds to it an indication that the speaker sees him or herself as a member of a group).

Where it is very important to get the listening right, check your results by seeking clarification. This should not be done by asking 'Did you mean . . . ?' or 'Did you say . . . ?', which rarely proves successful because it relies on speakers being able to recapitulate what they have just said. It is better to articulate the results of your listening and ask if you have got it right. Your paraphrase could be signalled by 'Let me check it', or 'Are you saying . . . ?'

Never produce a response act until you are absolutely sure you have heard the initiating act correctly.

TOPIC

The last aspect of negotiation management that needs attention is topic. Both its general use, and the movement and manipulation of topic throughout an interaction need to be considered. In one sense there is no need to define 'topic of negotiation'; it is obviously the subject matter, varying with each event, so it could be, for example, a new wordprocessor which has been delivered to the office, a sales campaign, a repair on a production line, or whatever. But there is a real need to define what a topic *does* within an interaction.

For a start, the subject matter must be put into propositional form; it is not possible to negotiate 'a word-processor', but what can be negotiated are propositions about 'who will use it', 'who will pay for it' or 'what its uses will be', for example. In a negotiation without an agenda, that is, without a set of formal or informal propositions (or motions) notified in advance, the first part of the encounter will be spent trying to decide on an appropriate proposition to debate. If this happens, it should not be treated lightly, as merely a preamble to the proper business, since once a proposition is agreed on as the agenda it will dictate the terms of the meeting, and be used to accept matters raised as relevant and germane, or to reject matters as off the point.

Once a proposition is settled on, it acts as a macro-topical structuring, or map, for the ensuing discussion. From then on, the speech acts produced will affect it in various ways to suit the participants. They will reinforce it, explain its terms, repeat it, seek to vary some term in it, select part of it for attention, argue that part of it should be deleted, seek to weaken its force by adding qualifications, generalise from it to show its strength and validity, exemplify it (either to strengthen or weaken it by the selection of the particular example), narrow its applicability, distract others from its weakness, and so on.

The end result of these acts should be, if the negotiation has been successful, some modulation of the basic proposition which all present can now support. With any subordinate proposition that arises, the same processes apply. Not every act produced will relate to the central macro-proposition. Irrelevancies may be introduced, perhaps inadvertently as some word brings other possibilities to a speaker's mind, or perhaps intentionally as a distraction to prevent some thorny issue in the proposition from being noticed.

Many negotiations have more than one macro-proposition, and where this occurs participants will want the transition from one to another to be done in a way satisfactory to all. So it is important to mark any such transition by an appropriate framing and/or focusing signal. There is a set of standard ones, each with different implications. The following examples are worth considering, either when others use them or you do so yourself.

1 'OK then' implies agreement with the previous activity (vaguely), and signals termination of the propositional discussion.
2 'Right then, that's settled, let's move onto . . .' resembles 'OK then' but with the addition of a good deal of authority assumed by the speaker, as one able to lead the discussion from one point to the next, and who will seek to set the terms of the next macro-structure.
3 'That reminds me' states a link, albeit a personal one, relevant to 'me' and not necessarily clear or acceptable as a link for others.
4 'Oh by the way' declares that the new topic being introduced is irrelevant, quite 'out of the way' of the previous one, but for some unspecified reason worth mentioning at this point. Such apparent irrelevancies should be examined closely to see whether there is some hidden link which might be of interest, and to understand why the speaker feels it

possible and necessary not only to raise irrelevancies but to label them as such. He or she may be signalling something negative about his or her attitude to the previous topic and may be revealing how he or she ranks the topic raised as 'by the way'. It is certainly worth considering why the speaker deliberately reduces the linkage between the two topics and yet still *does* bring in the 'by the way' topic.

5 'Incidentally' also declares that the next information is not of major importance. A hearer should consider whether this is an accurate description of what the speaker says next.

6 'Oh I forgot to tell you' may be quite literally meant, memory failed and is now working again, but one could ask what has jogged the memory, what link between the previous topic and the new one did the trick. One could also ask how it was that the person concerned had time to be jogged into remembrance, and whether he or she had been paying attention to the discussion.

7 'Talking of which' suggests that there is no break in topic, but in fact it often heralds a new one, and may be used because the speaker wants to sneak in a new topic without it being noticed. A variant of this is 'While we're on the subject'.

Because the conventions concerning suitability of topic are regulative rather than constitutive, speakers may raise a subject matter or a proposition which is then found unsuitable by some or all of the hearers. When this occurs they can perceive the speaker to be inefficient or not alert to the current topical work being done by the others; as ignorant of the customary behaviour of such interactions; or as arrogantly seeking to adapt the meeting to some personal goal. In most cases this will be met with disapproval.

Practice

It should be possible for an observant member of a series of negotiations to list those topics which get a poor reception, and are judged inappropriate or awkward to deal with. They may be verbally rejected 'That's not relevant' or 'That's a matter to be dealt with by others, our job is to . . .' or just be received in stony silence. The list would have two uses: it would enable you (a) to check your own rejections of particular topics and consider why you respond so strongly to these and not to others, and (b) to avoid introducing them and meeting with rejection.

Once a topical proposition is selected and agreed on, then the process of discussing it will begin. In Western culture this usually means a focusing on one or other of such things as:

(a) its definition;
(b) its contrasts and comparisons with other subjects;

(c) its qualities (good or bad, better or worse, short or long, more or less attractive, etc.); and

(d) its causes and effects;

The proposition used to present a topic should be judged for any contradictions inherent in it, or between it and others to be dealt with, and for any circumstantial factors which influence its validity.

Its truth value, that is, what authority supports or rejects it, what laws justify or forbid it, what statistics confirm or deny it, should also be considered. (See also coverage of topic in Chapter 7, pp. 121–4.)

Practice

While preparing for a particular negotiation it is worth noting the topics dealt with at previous events of a similar kind, and the propositions preferred by each participant (individuals have their own routines, so one speaker will frequently raise, say, the consequences of a matter, while another always asks for statistical evidence). Remembering their propositional behaviour in this way could enable you to make well-planned contributions, to anticipate topical difficulties, and decide how best to make your own topical interventions.

If as the negotiation proceeds, it deals only with a rather restricted set of topics, or has a narrow agenda, then this should be taken into account when preparing material for it. If you select a topic which fits the agenda it should receive fair treatment from the others; if, however, you wish to venture beyond the limits of the agenda by introducing a new topic it may meet resistance because it is unexpected, on the other hand it may move the negotiation in a useful direction and prove a very valuable contribution. Much will depend on the way the new topic is phrased. If, for example, this is done by linking it somehow to the established agenda topics, or if its value is declared overtly, or if its newness is disguised, it may be more favourably received than a bluntly expressed violation of the tried and true topic conventions of the meeting.

It has just been pointed out that some propositions tend to be routinely chosen. So, the amount of new information they provide may be minimal; in such cases notice the opportunity they offer for work towards relationship maintenance and ego satisfaction.

Example

At a regular office meeting, the topic of work allocation is a standard item on the agenda: 'Who will do what next week?' Its parameters are well known to the habitués of the meeting – the rank of staff members, their previous experience of the type of work, their general ability, matters outstanding since the previous allocation, etc. Such matters have been raised before, in much the same words, and with much the same results. So what role does the topic actually play in any particular meeting? First, it provides the security associated with routine, because it does not require new thoughts to be activated about a new matter. Since most people are cognitive misers, refusing to expend more mental energy than is absolutely necessary, this will be a welcome relief. Second, it sets up the discursive routines by which participants understand their social role in the world of work, so one person gradually learns that their role is to query the fairness of work allocation, while another learns that their role is to point out the consequences of a particular allocation.

Topic use and development in the negotiation can reveal much about the interrelationships of the negotiators, which may be of assistance in working out strategies to use in the encounter. If, for example, the bond is strong between two members, they may combine to support a proposition and block any alteration of it. If there is strong antagonism this may produce objection and resistance to the proposition, even if unwarranted by any defect in the proposition. Observable tokens of bonding may be references to shared experience in negotiation or other aspects of life. While it can be generally assumed that sharing personal experiences creates a close bond, this is not always so; it may create enmity or social awkwardness. Shared rank creates close bonds too, and so does sharing a workplace. And so, of course, do shared attitudes or emotions.

To understand what degree of bonding exists, it will be necessary to analyse the initial part of negotiation where the small talk may be very revealing. Notice there the use of, for example, unspecified references – to 'it', 'him' and 'that' – and that some people understand these without explanation while others do not. In addition, note the use of 'our' or 'we'; keep an ear open for similarities in phrasing between people; be sensitive to the ability of one person to instantly find examples, references or figures to support another; note the use of nicknames; and, finally, notice how people react to jokes, for instance whether they reveal that they have heard a particular joke before or not.

With all these factors involved in the presentation and use of topic, it is no wonder that its movement throughout an encounter appears quite random. It certainly does move a good deal in many cases, yet it is not fair to assume that it is random, except perhaps in extremely loose and unstructured meetings. The links are there when you subject the event to close analysis. What is true is that no speaker who introduces a topic can expect to retain absolute control of it. As soon as the initiating move is finished in which a topical proposition is put forward, the other speakers, though influenced by the standard constraints or responses on speech pairs to retain it as their topic, may move immediately away to another proposition of their own preference. The pattern of topic development in the initial stage of a dyadic encounter might well take the following pattern:

A: initiates move, begins topic 1
B: responds then initiates with topic 2
A: responds, then seeks to restore topic 1
B: responds, then seeks to restore topic 2

This kind of topic patterning may continue and become a serious concern where there is no set topic agenda, since the conflict then threatens to influence the course of the whole negotiation.

CONTROL OF TOPIC

The following strategies represent what can reasonably be done in such circumstances to make your topic dominant.

As first speaker:

(a) ensure that your initiating move restricts the respondent's options as far as possible (see speech pairs for suggestions);
(b) criticise others' moves away onto other topics as poor responses – call them irrelevant, trivial, unproductive or out of place.

As respondent:

(a) provide a linking phrase between your response and the initiating move, for example, 'Yes, indeed!', 'Exactly!' or 'I know what you mean', and then add 'but', and move to your own topic choice;
(b) declare that there is a similarity in meaning between your topic and the initiator's topic, or go further and declare that they are the same (even when this is not strictly true): 'It was the same in a case of mine' (not really the same); 'Or in other words . . .' (not the same proposition); 'I'd rather call it X, it's more accurate' (where you are in fact changing the central term of the proposition), and so on;
(c) subsume the other's topic under a more general heading and then deal with your own topic within that heading, for example:

A: 'We must consider the effect of this plan on our sales people.'
B: 'I agree, but I'd suggest what's really needed is a consideration of the effect of this plan on our whole operation [and then moving away to your own topic], and particularly on our production target for next year.'

(d) argue that your topic has priority, for example because it must be discussed first in order to make sense of someone else's topic;
(e) argue for the prime importance of your topic over another, or over all the others.

(These last two strategies will depend on your ability to argue, and also on the keenness with which the others adhere to their topic preferences. Even if you fail to win topic priority, it could be useful to know how others defend their topics, and to be aware of the degree of personal involvement invested in them.)

Exercise

Consider the following transcripts of two parts of a natural conversation. Note the speech pairs, the turntaking, the evidence of listening, and the movement of topic:

Dialogue 1

A: 'Well, eh – well, well, er, um – anyway, as far as, eh, getting something – getting some action on this thing, you know, if they've got this stuff in the States they could be able to fly it out within, you know, a couple of days. Um, I'll give him a ring on Monday.'

B: 'You'll have to indent it – er, it's the paper work that takes the time rather than getting it through the air.'

A: 'Oh yes, I – I – I appreciate this but if – if its – if they, you know, rush the damn thing along, um, surely it shouldn't take any more than a week.'

B: 'Well he – he told me it would be better to buy a locally made one in case of replacement requirements and that Smiths were prepared to supply it but its not very clear what's going on.'

A: 'And uh – uh – they're sure that it is suitable for this machine?'

B: 'Oh well, I guess it would be suitable for this machine.'

A: 'Yeah, okay.'

B: 'The machine is not, you know, terribly easy to operate.'

A: 'Yeah, yeah, fair enough.'

Dialogue 2

A: 'Well in fact I'll – I'll clear it up today.'

B: 'No no wait! No no no, don't bother to, you know, even, um . . .'

A: 'I'm not bothering'

B: '. . . even to take a chance of offending him because, um, he's – he's bloody good and ah, you know, I – I can get in with him and learn something about it. You know this doesn't worry me in the least bit.'

A: 'All right, well it worries me only to the extent that the filter might be, em, exposed to light and this kind of thing. These . . .'

B: 'Oh.'

A: '. . . are the important things which you and I'd . . .'

B: 'Yes that's right.'

Chapter 4

Particular problems

INTRODUCTION

Within negotiation there are two major problem areas that this chapter will discuss: first the need to maintain good social relationships during the kind of encounter which, by its very nature, must put them at risk; and second dealing with members of other cultures.

Negotiation is only necessary when there are differences among people, whether of opinion, interest, priority, purpose, or all of these. Moreover, the differences must become the focal point of the interaction, must be addressed, dealt with, and somehow incorporated in the final outcome. Some participants might have to make serious adjustments to their goals, and to accept compromises in accommodating themselves to an agreed settlement. All of this can be accomplished more easily if the cooperative relationship between them is sustained. In addition, if further encounters are necessary, and further dealings have to take place, it would be helpful if the good relationship could be sustained into the future.

Also, if the negotiations are likely to attract public notice, it is important that they demonstrate to anyone who might wish in the future to engage in negotiation with the people concerned that they would find it a well-conducted and amicable affair.

If the other participants belong to other cultures, then added to the inevitable difficulties of negotiation will be the possibility of fundamental misunderstandings and serious social damage.

This chapter will suggest ways of dealing with the likely problems in both cases.

STRATEGIES FOR GOOD RELATIONSHIPS

In every human interaction, whether it is a discussion, a formal debate or a negotiation, there will be present first a strongly developed personal need for face-saving, and second a strong social preference for agreement or, at worst, manageable disagreement. The two are intertwined, and between them affect the formulation of a very high proportion of the speech behaviours produced in interaction.

'FACE' WORK

By 'face' is meant the universal desire to have one's ego recognised and taken account of, to have one's views heard, and to some extent accepted by others, or at least to have others accept one's right to hold them. It is a basic human need and is called *positive face*. At the same time, there is another aspect to human ego needs. We all feel the need to be granted some degree of freedom of action, within the established constraints of social laws and conventions. This requirement that our actions are not impeded is called *negative face*. As a corollary to these needs, we must recognise that others have the same needs, and therefore, where possible, provide ego-support for others (on the do-as-you-would-be-done-by principle).

In each culture the kinds of face needs can be different, and so can the means by which face recognition is formalised in words and actions.

AGREEMENT

By 'agreement' is meant the presence of a cooperative spirit in social encounters, which recognises what the other person's purposes are, and does not seek to impede them more than is necessary to sustain one's own purpose. It does not mean saying 'Yes' when wishing to say 'No', but it means concealing the force of a disagreement, perhaps disguising it in oblique or indirect forms of speech, or perhaps making the disagreement clear to the other without being confrontational. As an example of such obliqueness, note the response in this speech pair:

Ann: 'Did you see the excellent adjustments we've made to the plan?'
Bill: 'Er yes, you've done well, but I'm not sure why you've done . . .'

Ann clearly wants approval of the 'excellent' adjustments, and just as clearly Bill cannot give it. But his response begins with a compliment before he raises a question about them. The hesitation 'er' and the reduction in praise from 'excellent' to 'well' would make it obvious to Ann that Bill is in some disagreement with her view, but equally they reveal that he wishes to disguise his view somewhat, and so take account of her 'face'. He also separates his resistance to the 'adjustments' from his recognition of her work, which he praises ('you've done well'), further supporting her face.

Ann would be in no doubt, from the moment Bill hesitated, that he did not agree, but by the end of his response she would equally be in no doubt that Bill wishes to remain in an amicable relationship with her. She, of course, made it particularly difficult for Bill to avoid damaging her face, by leading with her chin in saying so clearly that she approved of her own work. Had she merely asked whether he had seen the adjustments she could have saved her face from potential trouble. Any request that another person approve what one has done is a face-threatening act (FTA) since it allows the other person opportunity to offer not only approval but also, of course, criticism or disapproval.

Agreement also means, as this speech pair suggests, that where possible the respondent gives the preferred response to the initial move. This is a face concern too. Speakers set up their speech acts in such a way that one particular response is the easiest, simplest and least troublesome to produce. It suits their face needs to have this response. Where they make a statement, the preferred response will be to agree with it; where they ask a question, the preferred response will be to answer it; where they make a request, the preferred response will be to fulfil it, and so on (see pp. 48–52 for a fuller account).

Example

Ann: 'You do approve the plan don't you?'

sets up as the preferred response the answer 'Yes', and if the respondent wishes to disagree, but also to address Ann's face needs, then he or she will need to produce some indirection to disguise the disagreement to an appropriate degree. This will require judging how much face-saving is necessary, taking into account such factors as:

(a) the speaker's sense of self as displayed so far;
(b) the degree of speaker commitment to the speech move he or she made;
(c) the degree of disagreement the respondent needs to make;
(d) whether the speaker and respondent have been disagreeing earlier or whether this is the first time;
(e) the strength of the social bond between them, and so on.

As well as considering such factors, there are other ways of achieving agreement, and avoiding face trouble. Some suggestions follow.

PREPARATION FOR THE EVENT

(a) Study the people who will be present to discover how they phrase their questions, statements, requests, etc., and consider how best to phrase responses to them.
(b) Study how the others tend to respond to questions, statements, and requests, etc., and note what degree and kind of face work you might expect from them.

(c) Do some face work in advance, incorporating it when circulating any of your opinions or questions in advance, whether in printed or spoken form, to test them out.

Practice

Study your own practices as initiator or respondent, from audiotapes of your interactions where possible, and see where adjustments may need to be made.

Do some preparatory work by considering the speech acts you will want to make at a meeting, and articulating them in advance to those who might be able to advise you about their prospects of success.

DURING THE EVENT

Consider how to produce your speech with due concern for face and agreement factors.

Some acts can be performed quite bluntly, with no regard for face concerns, though in fact they may seriously constrain the hearers' freedom of action – their negative face. This bluntness is acceptable if the hearers agree that the act must be performed bluntly for efficiency's sake, as when a convener calls a meeting to order by saying:

'Now then everyone, take your seats, I want to start the meeting.'

There appears to be a strong face-threat involved in the bluntness (there is not even the 'please' of a polite request), and in the egotism expressed in the reason given, which sounds as if everyone must move just because one member 'wants' to do something. Yet, no objections should occur, because the convener is acting not for ego-fulfilment, but because it significantly adds to the efficiency of the meeting for everybody. But think how much less acceptable it would be if the following words were spoken by a member of the group to the others in mid-meeting:

'Now then, Bill, sit down, I want to talk about my report.'

This could be quite face-threatening, and cause trouble.

Some acts can be performed bluntly because they are very obviously to the respondent's advantage, and hence support rather than threaten his or her face, as when a doctor tells a patient to 'Say aaaah' in the process of helping him or her to health.

Some acts by their very nature are more likely to be perceived as non-face-threatening, for example *inform*, *discuss*, *report* or *tell*; whereas the following ones are riskier for face: *argue*, *assert*, *direct*, *offer* or *promise*.

But it is not possible to negotiate without using some FTAs, so you should seek to become skilled in learning how best to produce them with least risk to face, including your own. The list that follows gives first the main FTA possibilities, and then some strategies to reduce the face-threatening aspects.

Positive face threats

A speaker threatens the hearer's positive face by appearing to pay little heed to the hearer's right to self-esteem, as in

(a) acts like *accuse, criticise, disapprove, insult* or *reprimand*;
(b) acts like *challenge, disagree* or *reject*;
(c) interruption of a turn, and not giving signs of active listening;
(d) forgetting the hearer's name, opinions, and so on;
(e) raising subjects, or speaking in a manner, that would embarrass or annoy the hearer;
(f) raising subjects, or speaking in a manner, that would divide the others from the hearer, perhaps even isolating him or her from the rest;
(g) creating an unfriendly, uncooperative atmosphere while the hearer is speaking, or while the hearer is responsible for some part of the event.

Supporting positive face

If any of these acts are thought necessary given your goals for the negotiation, then they can be performed in a way which lessens their face-threatening qualities. This can be by using a friendly manner, or making reference to some bond that is shared. In particular, you could (1) claim and stress some common ground, or (2) show that you and the other person are basically good cooperators.

Common ground can be claimed by:

(a) showing you share the hearer's goals; so, for example, a criticism can be mollified in this way:

> 'I agree we should be producing a forward estimate, but you haven't gone the right way about it – this plan is no good.'

(b) showing sympathy with the hearer's situation, or recognising a similarity between his or her needs and those of your own, as in this example of a *challenge* act:

> 'I know your department, like mine, is overworked at the moment, but these figures just won't do.'

(c) using in-group language to show a bond with the hearer, for example in mollifying an act of disagreement:

> 'Oh come on, mate, I can't accept that, it certainly won't fit the PFT plan will it?'

(d) using token agreement, as in the example of Ann and her 'excellent adjustments' above, or in:

> A: 'Is it a big company?'
> B: 'Yes, quite big, well biggish, certainly it's not small.'

(Note that even a question like this one, which might seem to be an inquiry with no set expectations about the size of the company, nevertheless prompts the respondent to accept the terms of the question, in this case the large size of the company.)

Common ground may be established in other ways: for example in the small talk, which acts as a bonding agent from its first occurrence in the initial phase to the end of the interaction. Any speaker who knows that he or she will be opposing a particular person later on, and so be face-threatening to them, can seek to store up good-will to offset this future activity. So shared jokes and friendly inquiries about personal matters (attending to the hearer's face wants) can be a good investment for the future of the negotiation proper.

Showing cooperation with the hearer can be achieved in the following ways.

(a) Cooperation can be taken for granted, for example by assuming the hearer will willingly help the speaker:

> 'You'll lend me that report won't you? I know you have three copies.'

and, as in this case, suggesting that the speaker knows enough about the hearer (which is ego-bolstering) to know that he or she has three copies.

(b) Respect can be shown for the hearer at the same time as doing an FTA, as in the following criticism:

> 'You are the expert on this I know, so I can't understand how you came to make this mistake.'

The example also leaves room for the hearer to respond easily: 'But I didn't, it was X's mistake.'

(c) Respect can also be shown by providing explanations for the act while performing an FTA, which suggests that the hearer deserves to know the reason for the act and that there are reasons for the act – that is, it is not a gratuitous insult. For example:

> 'I can't approve of that, it's a very poor piece of work; if we built our plan upon figures like that we'd lose out to our competitors within six months.'

Negative face threats

The hearer's *negative* face is threatened when the speaker intrudes upon his or her freedom of action, restricting it in some way, and thus treating it with disrespect. Negative face-threatening acts include:

(a) acts like *request* (probably the most face-threatening in its various forms, which can be as severe as *command* or *order*), and *require*, which put pressure on the hearer to do something he or she may not want to do;
(b) acts like *advise* or *suggest*, which are less strong than *request*, but which nonetheless put pressure on the hearer to take the advice or follow the suggestion;
(c) acts like *remind*, when they imply that the hearer has forgotten something and is therefore at some degree of (mild) fault, and when they are meant as an indication that the hearer should do something;
(d) acts like *warn* which, in one sense, imply that the speaker will take action in the future to inhibit the hearer's freedom, as in 'I'm warning you, don't seek to claim damages.'

Supporting negative face

Two negative face work strategies, which minimise the restriction placed upon the hearer's freedom, are outlined below.

First, if you must be direct, then make the act as brief as you can. Use conventional forms so as to minimise the force of the FTA by making it less conspicuous – a routine event rather than an outstanding one. It will still impose upon the hearer, and it may even constitute a serious imposition, but at least the manner of issuing the *advice* or *request* or whatever will not in itself have been face-threatening.

Second, judge carefully the degree of indirectness to be used. There are some well-established conventions for performing indirect speech acts, and the following examples should all be quite familiar in form. The value of these conventions is that there can be no doubt about what is being performed, so the hearer will realise that you are simultaneously imposing on him or her *and* trying to save his or her face. (Only in cross-cultural communications could there be problems of misunderstanding here.)

'I'd like you to do this report.'
'I'll get you to do this report, if I may.'
'Can you do this report, please?'
'Could you possibly do this report?'
'Let's get this report done, shall we?' (where the speaker will not do the report at all)
'You're doing this report, aren't you, Bill?'

Memories of previous uses of such routine tokens of indirection will provide the clue to understanding them. It is these same memories that enable people to read what degree of face-threat reduction is being used. We then respond to its appropriateness, or lack of it, and feel more or less threatened.

Indirect acts

The two main principles to be followed in choosing the tokens of indirection are outlined below.

First, do not presume or assume too much of the other person. Hedge your acts of questioning or requesting to reduce the imposition they form. This can be done by using appropriate phrases.

(a) Phrases to reduce the *power* of the act would include: 'it seems to me', 'there is some evidence that', 'as far as I remember' and 'if you'll allow me'. As in:

> '*As I recall*, we asked you to do the report, Bill. Is it done?'
> '*As you know*, we've arranged for your office to deliver these. Is that OK?'

(b) Phrases to reduce the *importance* of the thing requested would include: 'roughly', 'more or less' and 'to some extent'. As in:

> 'Could you tell us the *approximate* figures, Bill?'
> 'Could you *just* tell us the figures?'

Second, do not coerce the other person. Allow the hearer to avoid the imposition if he or she wishes. So use the following sorts of strategies.

(a) Express doubt that the hearer could do it, using phrases such as 'Would it be possible' or 'I wonder if you could'. As in:

> 'Could you possibly see about this report?'

(b) Acknowledge the hearer's status or position by showing deference, for example, by using titles such as 'sir', or 'Dr . . .', or by a form such as:

> 'This query should perhaps be addressed to your assistant, but I wondered if you yourself could just . . .'

and so on.

(c) Apologise, that is admit that the act will cause the hearer trouble, indicate your reluctance to cause this trouble and give reasons to justify the imposition; or ask forgiveness.

(d) Impersonalise the act, or omit yourself from it, as in 'It would be appreciated if . . .', or 'I have been delegated to ask', and so on. Here the act appears to just be 'there', or to come from outside or from some anonymous group 'we', as if the speaker were not exerting any *personal* authority over the hearer.

CROSS-CULTURAL COMMUNICATION

After all, when you come right down to it, how many people speak the same language even when they speak the same language?

(Russell Hoban)

(Although the examples of foreign cultures provided here are gathered from a variety of sources, they provide only a sampling of the possibilities of difference in discursive usages. Examples of English discourse are given here also, because a greater awareness of the home culture's practices can help a negotiator (a) to recognise any differences in others' practices and so pinpoint problems of understanding; and (b) to know how the others will read English discourse, and the problems they are likely to have in so doing. Throughout this section we assume a correlation between language and culture: the reasons for this should be clear from Chapter 1.)

Members of the same culture share an understanding of the nature and functioning of discourse. They agree on:

(a) the means by which discourse realises happenings (and they share many of the ideas, opinions and attitudes it manifests);
(b) the means by which discourse functions as a social event, with appropriate roles and actions, and possible goals.

They share perceptions of all the factors of discourse, from the macro-level of speaking itself, to the micro-level of the meanings of their words and grammatical forms, and the value of the length of a pause between utterances.

These understandings are built up from the many thousands of discourses experienced by the members of a community, each of which plays its part in establishing that community's cultural and social knowledge. A cultural community categorises the world into roughly the same set of events, and makes roughly the same kind of inferences about the intentions of speakers and the value to be attributed to discourse behaviours. Moreover, it assumes that its system of discourse use is self-evidently appropriate. A native speaker can, therefore, know what is happening in a new discourse occasion because the language practices are similar to others previously experienced, and the situation, roles or goals of the present action resemble others. It is the absence of this build-up of shared, familiar, and usually unexamined, knowledge and its importance in providing a frame by which to measure new discursive actions that can cause problems of cross-cultural communication. To prevent or rectify such problems it will be necessary either to find some means of acquiring practice in the other culture, or else to acquire an extra sensitivity to the procedures of the home culture as well as to those of the foreign culture.

Practice

Gaining access to as much discourse as possible in the other culture can be achieved by visits, by talking with visitors, by reading the novels of the other culture, or by viewing their television programmes and films, provided that in each case attention is focused on discursive practices which might be relevant for a negotiator's purposes.

This data should be subjected to analysis, for example examining the repertoire of discourse events that occur and the way each is socially perceived; and listening to the dialogue and noting what is said and what is not sayable, the priorities raised, the concerns declared or implied, the agendas that are set and the speech forms preferred.

Speakers can decide either to use the behaviours that are customary within their own culture, or to accommodate their actions to the other's cultural expectations. Before making a choice between these options, a negotiator needs to estimate the ability and willingness of the others to make discursive allowances.

If a decision is made not to accommodate to the requirements of the other culture, it will be necessary to make it clear (perhaps by constant references) that the occasion is being treated as containing two distinct sets of cultural practices, and hope that this will produce toleration for 'inappropriate' discourse. This may simplify matters, since each party may then make straightforward allowances for the other's 'difference'. However, the other participants may not be capable of making adjustments to another culture's discursive practices, or may be unwilling to do so, and this would put the speaker at a disadvantage throughout the encounter.

Adaptation to the other's cultural expectations, while avoiding these problems, may cause others, since the other participants will not be sure how to read particular acts, which may be either attempts to do things in the other culture's way, or examples of the speaker's own cultural frame of reference. The best solution may be to make it clear which practices are being used when any moments of misunderstanding occur. On the whole, however, avoidance of problems in cross-cultural communication can be best achieved by increased awareness of the general differences in language and discourse use between cultures, and by knowledge of likely sites of difficulty.

The points raised in this section are intended to provide awareness of those elements of discourse which most need to be considered in cross-cultural negotiations. They are presented as a checklist of those aspects of communication where problems are likely to arise, with illustrations where this assists understanding of the point, and strategies for the prevention and repair of discourse damage. (Efficient use of this section will be enhanced if reference is made to other sections of the book where fuller accounts of specific discursive factors are given.)

GENERAL

The first thing to determine is whether an interaction is one which contains cross-cultural factors: language and ethnicity are the main causes of difference, as indicated earlier, but within a culture differences can also be caused by region, class, age and gender. The obvious example is US–British interactions, which can founder on the false assumption that because the English language is shared (together with many cultural assumptions), there will be no differences in discursive usage between the two regions.

Difficulties in cross-cultural communication can arise through ignorance of the language, or through ignorance of the discursive practices of another culture. Language mistakes, that is vocabulary or grammar errors, can result in particular misunderstandings and ambiguities, or they can reveal the speaker as generally ignorant of the language, or bad at languages in general, and so result in a social loss of face. Any of these can be detrimental to the good outcome of the negotiation, but much more important are the mistakes that arise from ignorance of the cultural framework within which the other party is operating. This can affect the setting of negotiation agendas and roles, can hinder the smooth running of procedures, can exclude matters, foreclose possibilities, and produce inappropriate conclusions.

Practice

It is crucial to discover early on how someone who makes linguistic or discursive mistakes, a non-understander, is viewed in the other culture. Some cultures tolerate non-understanding and take it as an opportunity to assist; others see it as a sign of powerlessness and hence something to be taken advantage of. Listen to how they refer to non-understanding, and note which strategies for seeking clarification they use among themselves and so might find acceptable from a foreigner.

Sites of difficulty in cross-cultural interaction can be found in each of the following aspects of negotiation:

- discourse
- genre
- the management of spoken interaction
- speech acts

DISCOURSE

(See Chapter 2 for a full account.)

The cultural value given to discourse

Cultures can vary in the value they place on discourse, and there are two important areas that can be used here as examples. First, Westerners see talk as valuable, using it for social purposes as well as task performance, and see silence as indicating a lack of interest, shyness or hostility. Asians, however, value silence and discourage the social expression of ideas. (The Taoist view is that one who speaks doesn't know, one who knows doesn't speak.)

Practice

Note how talk and silence are perceived in the culture in which you are interested.

Second, in Western cultures it is usually acceptable to declare explicitly at certain points what the negotiation is about, that is, to use 'metalanguage', declaring in words what is happening in words, for example, saying 'May I just ask a question?', or 'Have we discussed this enough?'. However, this would be seen as unacceptably domineering in those Middle Eastern and Oriental cultures where participants have strongly ritualised social behaviours, and therefore expect that the ongoing activity will be understood by all without being described in words. They could therefore perceive a metalingual comment, such as 'So, as I see it, what we are now doing is agreeing the terms', as an inappropriately authoritarian attempt to influence the direction of the negotiation.

Practice

Note how the other culture views metalanguage.

The nature of the negotiation experience

Cultural differences can be perceived in the very nature of the negotiation, and three such differences can be examined. First, Westerners accept that many negotiations can have casual elements, for example either beginning with the friendly exchange of information and opinions on unrelated topics before launching into the first part of the business, or throughout the encounter moving from business to chat and back again. In some other cultures even the chat requires a greater formalisation, either in procedure or in seriousness of tone.

Examples

A more ritualised first stage with specified topics (not including politics) is used in the Middle East, so that a (Western) casual statement of a political opinion might not be taken as part of the ritual, and could be judged as a comment of significance for the business interaction, and so play a more active part in the negotiation than the speaker intended.

As another example, while Indian culture does not insist on formality of structure or tone, it does require a very long introductory element, and uses it for a good deal of social exploration. This enables the Indian participants to investigate the exact roles of the others and to establish their own as, for example, arranger, petitioner, serious or less serious potential buyer, adviser, principal or agent, client, or consultant, in order to determine what speech acts will be suitable for the main part of the business. If the introduction is cut short, confusion of roles could result, and the behaviours that follow may be incorrectly understood.

Other cultures can be characterised by a discursive preference for formal distancing of behaviour, or by suspicion of strangers, or by a sense of self-importance; each will react differently to the presence of informal chat.

Second, preferences concerning the structure of the negotiation will vary. One culture may require that there be clear recognition of each stage of the negotiation (to assist in the interpretation of behaviours), and that this involve both the naming and clear marking of each stage and its boundaries, in some cases with ritualised behaviours, actions or words. Another may not feel comfortable with that degree of specificity, preferring to see the action as more flexible. There may also be differences in the kind of marking signals preferred, for example it may be enough to use an inexplicit signal, 'OK then, that's that. Now then . . .', or it may be necessary to be more specific, as in 'OK, that's settled the terms. Now then, let us proceed to working out the delivery dates.'

Third, modes of closing interactions may differ; for example, one culture may expect informal chat while another expects a summarising statement. This may lead to confusion, with the summary seen by one as a method of friendly closure but by the other as another stage in the substantive business of the meeting. In some cultures, the right to close an encounter belongs to the one who called it into existence, though he or she will check that the other party accepts closure at that point. In New Guinea the one who stays behind after a meeting to tidy matters up is the one with the right to close it off.

Practice

How does the other culture structure negotiation, and how does it set the tone of the interaction? What kind of social distancing, degree of formality, etc., does it prefer? How are these manifested? In the other culture, who closes interactions, and what rituals are involved?

Speaking and hearing roles

Cultures have different senses of what it is to be a speaker in any discursive interaction. For example, when a Japanese acts as *speaker* and refers to himself or herself as 'I', it does not have the same meaning as in European languages: it means not a personally responsible self, but an agent within an action set by the system in which the 'I' operates, and in which the 'I' performs a set role. So, for example, a Japanese executive who said 'I accept your offer' is not declaring a company decision, but rather is stating that he or she will perform their assigned task with regard to accepting offers, and this may be only to pass on the matter to those in whose hands such decisions rest. (It is this reduced sense of 'self' that makes a Japanese find self-disclosure or the exchange of personal information inappropriate; and so possibly misread the significance of a Westerner's offering of personal comments alongside business talk.)

Western culture allows for speakers to underplay their individuality where the setting is very formal. So Western business negotiators may not think it appropriate for an interest to be taken in their personal lives and may see themselves as just role-players, for example announcing themselves just by their positions: 'I represent X' or 'As the marketing director, I . . .', without offering a name or giving an indication of personal attitude or interest. For Indians any negotiation must include the exchange of names and other personal indicators, and they may spend much time on such personal matters, seeing fellow negotiators as individuals first and role-players second. For them the absence of the full and personal introduction is incapacitating, and may be interpreted as deceitful, distant or impolite. It can be made worse by the Western preference for understating one's position, saying, 'I'm John Smith in charge of X', rather than 'I'm Sir John Smith, Vice President in charge of X.'

Practice

How do the members of the other culture introduce themselves, refer to them-selves, or see themselves, when they act as speakers or hearers?

The *hearing* role may vary from culture to culture, reflecting different views of the responsibilities of recall, of consequent action and of the passing on of information to those who need it. Differences here can lead to confusion about responsibility for future stages in the negotiation. How to act in the listening role also varies; for some it involves silent attention, while for others it requires attentive comments and vocal encouragement (see the sections on support noises, pp. 52 and 58).

Practice

How do participants from the other culture see their role beyond the face-to-face part of the negotiation? Check what is expected to happen, and who will take responsibility for what. State clearly what responsibility you will take.

Relative weighting of speech and writing

In some Western cultures a businessman's (spoken) word is his bond, and the (non-verbal) act of shaking hands on a deal can be understood as the finale to a business deal. A written version is only a useful confirmation, which could be delayed without consequence because the parties know that the business has been concluded and matters can proceed on that assumption. A member of another culture, however, may wait for the written form before proceeding, perceiving this to be the proper con- clusion to the business, and so cause unanticipated delays.

Practice

How does the other culture value speech as against writing? Take the appropriate action.

Strategy

For each aspect of discourse mentioned above, analyse whatever data from the other culture you can get access to. Observe how each element of discourse is dealt with. The topics may be irrelevant to your interests, but focus your attention on the way the discourse proceeds, and on how the speech event is realised by those involved in it, and the differences between this realisation and the nearest equivalent in English.

GENRE

(See pp. 39–40 for full account.)

There are historical and social factors which govern the way the generic activity of 'business negotiation' is perceived and these may differ between cultures.

There is the way *business* itself is regarded within the culture. Its historical development will influence (a) what social value is given to business compared, for example, with the professions or government; (b) the value of the particular kinds of business, for example commercial or manufacturing, within business in general, and (c) the social prestige granted to a particular firm or institution.

There is the way *negotiation* itself is perceived in each culture, for example how highly it is regarded within the business community (compared, for instance, with research and development, production or marketing); or there is the question of who performs negotiation within the business enterprise, and how they are socially valued – that is, what is the social awareness of the roles of senior negotiator, advertising executive, deputy administrator, and so on.

There is the way negotiation *procedures* are set socially, with a common understanding of what stages should occur, in what order, and what amount of time should be spent on each, and so on. Which goals can be achieved through speech and which are appropriate to the written elements of the negotiation is also a social decision.

There is the way the culture institutionalises the pattern of *discursive behaviours* for negotiators, and shares a sense of whether these can be flexibly worked out on each occasion, or must follow an unvarying formula. This pattern includes the manifestation of status differentials, and what behaviours to use, for example, when the speaker or hearer is a consulter or an arranger, a petitioner, an arguer or a counsellor, and so on. It also involves sensing whether a particular kind of act, such as *summarising*, is acceptable at all; who is permitted by convention to do it and at what points in the proceedings; and what value it will assume for the interaction.

There is the way a culture develops a sense of the appropriate styles for *speech acts*, for example how to do the acts of 'consulting' and 'arranging', of 'managing' and 'deciding', and of talking to one's own team or to the members of the other, and so on. Cultural parameters also dictate how attitude and tone should be realised, and although some attitudes are signalled in the same way across cultures (a smile is a universally recognised sign of friendliness), many of the more complex attitudes are less easy to read.

In certain cultures there is an added complexity, because two language variants are possible: a formal, complex variety used for serious matters and for recording them for history, and a 'low' variety used for informal interactions. In Greece, for example, there is both the classic language and the demotic; in the Arab world there is classical Arabic and a multiplicity of informal, regional languages. This has two points of significance for cross-cultural communication: the first is that the classical form can be acquired by foreigners, complete with the canon of historical examples which have supplied its meanings, so that someone who speaks it can be relatively sure of being understood in the right way. The second point is that in such cultures switching to the colloquial from the formal (classical) language during a negotiation has more consequence than a similar move would have in English, since it will not be perceived as a move from formal to friendly, but a move from serious to trivial and unimportant. Matters raised in the demotic form will not be treated as important, so an English speaker who speaks with Greeks or Arabs and uses casual colloquial English (which they could see as demotic) in order to make friendly overtures, may be perceived as acting very inappropriately, wasting time by talking trivia in a low style, using an avoidance strategy, or, at the least, doing something very odd to be viewed with suspicion.

Any new instance of negotiation in business will be assessed and interpreted in the light of this background of social expectations; all previous such encounters will act as a framework within which to evaluate the new one, and to understand it. Within a culture, conformity to the framework will make the negotiation easily understood, while variation from it will usually be perceived as individuality or eccentricity, or as marked behaviour of some other kind and be judged accordingly. But across cultures this knowledge is missing, so neither conformity nor variation from the framework will be recognised: the words and grammar may be clear, but the value of the speech act may not. Awareness of the social values of negotiation activity in the other culture is essential for good understanding.

Examples

The different valuations placed on the social status of participants would have implications for the 'etiquette' of a negotiation between a businessman of a culture which gives high respect to lawyers, and a solicitor from a culture which gives social precedence to commerce.

Also, when a person from one culture which has a rigidly formulaic sense of procedure enters negotiation with someone from another who thinks it can be formulated on the run, there can be confusion. The first thinks they are just having uncommitted discussion before the formal routine begins, while the second thinks the negotiation has begun and they are jointly formulating substantive proposals, with resultant misconceptions.

Sometimes the negotiation activity of a group from one culture is split, according to standard practice, into tasks performed by two different people, with, say, one agreeing the major points while the other deals with consequent detail, but if the group from the other culture has no such division of roles, there could be difficulties in assessing the value of the speakers' contributions. It would help, of course, if the roles were clearly stipulated, but this may not happen because both groups take it for granted that their own interpretation of roles is standard, natural, or universally accepted.

The social distance set for negotiators can vary between cultures and this may give rise to serious misreadings. For example, in a culture where a reference to the personal is not expected, a friendly enquiry about the other's bad health could be read as a (formal) attempt to put him or her at a disadvantage, while an anecdote about losing credit cards and suffering financial strain could be read as a (formal) plea for better financial terms in the business deal.

Strategy

Consider your own behaviours and your expectations of others' behaviours with respect to the generic factors of negotiation, and see what will need adjusting in a cross-cultural encounter.

Find out from whatever sources of information are available (including memories of previous cross-cultural encounters) how the generic factors that are appropriate to your particular negotiation actually work. Aim to have a clear idea of what to expect in terms of procedure, roles, goals, personal versus business behaviours, and so on.

Establish clearly in your own mind how you are reading a particular instance of the genre, and anticipate (and perhaps prevent) difficulties by sharing this with the members of the other culture. If it is thought advisable, then it could be declared overtly, as in, for example,

'We understand today's meeting is only preliminary. When we have discussed the matter a little, we will report back to our board, then put our thinking on paper and let you have a copy. We would then like to hear a response from you. We will then present to you for your ratification or emendation a final version which can form the basis for our next meeting. Is this procedure acceptable?'

Or it could be dealt with covertly, perhaps by questioning the others as to their understanding of the ongoing event.

Accept that negotiations which are cross-cultural have an extra dimension of difficulty. At each stage in the procedure it may be necessary to establish that understanding has been achieved before proceeding to the next stage. This cannot be done by general questions such as 'Is that understood?' or 'Am I making sense?' You need to be more specific, for example by requiring paraphrases from others to check that they have understood your meaning, or else paraphrasing their acts for them to check that your own understanding is accurate. (But judge carefully the social value that will be placed upon this strategy by the other culture: it may be found oppressive or too precise or too authoritarian, and have a deleterious effect.)

THE MANAGEMENT OF SPOKEN INTERACTION

Speech pairs

(See pp. 47–53 for a full account.)
The problems with speech pairs in a cross-cultural negotiation are all micro-level ones.

First, you must be able to recognise the kind of initiating move that is offered. The grammatical form used will not always indicate the kind of act that is being used; for example, in English, question forms can be used to make requests as in 'Could you tell me the time?'; statement forms can be used to ask questions as in 'I'm borrowing your pen, OK?'; and command forms can be used to make offers as in 'Have dinner with us tonight.' Such instances may be very familiar to members of a community but are liable to misreading by foreigners. In some languages the grammatical forms may perform different work; for example, in Russian, the interrogative particle *razve* predicts a negative response, so that a positive response would be difficult for the questioner to interpret.

Second, each culture may have a different sense of the proper person to offer certain kinds of initiating moves. For example, only seniors can ask juniors (or some professionals can ask their clients) certain intrusive or personal questions, make certain requests and offer certain kinds of statements. Equally, it may only be proper for certain rankings of people to respond in certain ways: a very junior person should not answer a question about the company's policy by explaining matters which are the proper business of senior members of staff. How the initiating and response moves are allocated will depend on how each culture sees the weighting of each kind of rank or role, and of each act – statements may be seen as more or less influential, questions as more or less intrusive, and requests as more or less commanding.

Third, foreigners might not make the appropriate responses, particularly in the ritual kind of speech pair (the equivalent of the English: 'How are you' – 'Fine thanks'), but also in less ritualised speech; for example, they may not realise when an acknowledgement should be supplied after a statement, or where a comment is needed after a request. A foreigner might also have difficulty in recognising that a speech pair makes sense, as in the following:

A: 'What time is it?'
B: 'The boss has just gone.'
A: 'Oh, right.'

Here the cultural framework for the exchange is contributing much: A and B know that the boss goes regularly at 4 pm, and it is only this that enables A to make sense of B's response. If A were a foreigner he or she could be thoroughly confused by B's words.

Practice

While watching interactions in the other culture, note any differences in the speech exchange modes from those in English. In your own cross-cultural negotiations observe those occasions where speech pair activity causes problems and seek guidance from those of the other culture as to the site of difficulty and a suitable solution.

Turntaking

(See pp. 54–7 for a full account.)
   Several aspects of turntaking can cause difficulties.

Acting as hearer

In some cultures listening is a silent occupation, requiring only an interested facial expression. In others (including English) it requires vocal noises as an accompaniment to the speaker's words.

   Some require a listener to offer many noises as support, others only a few. These 'support noises' include 'mhm', 'mm', 'right', 'yeah', 'good', 'fine', and aphorisms like 'That's always the way', 'Things always work out', etc. Problems may arise because of the tokens used in another culture, for example, Urdu speakers use 'very nice', as support, and this can be misread ('My name is Bill Smith.' – 'Very nice.') Many of them depend on the tone of voice in which they are uttered rather than on the words used, so there can be problems with tonally based language users. Japanese, Indian and other Far Eastern cultures may misread an English tone as disagreement or impatience rather than the support that was intended. An English speaker can dismiss Tamil listeners' support as exaggerated and false, since they use extremes of tonal variation.

   Where the noises are placed also matters; each culture develops a synchrony in smooth-running speech, and as part of this, support should be offered at moments of maximum information. The emphasis the speaker gives to the information is echoed by the hearer's murmur of agreement. If the noises are offered at points of little information it will seem that the listener is not paying attention (so children can understand when a parent makes suitable noises but is only half listening), and this produces an awkwardness or discomfort which is a sign of communication failure.

   Support can be offered by echoing the last words of each sentence of the speaker. This may be seen by some cultures as eagerness to share in the interaction and a willingness to join in; others may see it as a form of overlap and a rude cutting short of a speaker's turn, while yet others see it as paying too much attention to the surface value of the words (and too little to the in-depth meaning).

Some people provide support noise in the form of questions ('Is that right?', 'Did you really say that?'), which show that the listener is alert to the way the speaker's mind is working. They may be seen as signs of an excellent listener by speakers with similar habits, and they will note, but not respond to, the questions. Other speakers accept them quite readily as supportive listening but also answer them, contentedly enough, when it suits their own purposes; this often results in a disjointed conversation that a third party might find confusing. But in some other cultures such questions will be read not as support but as interruptions, each of which has to be answered, thus disturbing the flow of the speech and irritating the speaker. This can be particularly evident when the questions are fast, overlapping, pointedly personal, or abruptly delivered. When the speaker answers the supportive questions it can also confuse or irritate the listener, who needed and expected no answer, and may not even be aware of the form of words he or she used in the questions, since they are habitual clichés and not thoughtfully intended. With both parties confused and irritated, good cooperative negotiation is unlikely.

Turns

Cultures differ as to the pause that is permissible when there is a change of speaker. For some, any pause is seen as unfriendly and to be filled instantly; for others, pausing is quite acceptable up to a certain length. Some cultures, including Spanish, may even prefer a measure of overlap in voices to pauses, taking it as a sign of attentive friendliness.

Turn-yielding

When an English speaker relinquishes the floor to others, either by asking a question or requiring information of some named individual ('What do you think, Bill?'), he or she would expect there to be no pause before the hearer begins to speak. If there is a pause it will be assumed that the hearer is rude, has nothing to say, is taking evasive action, is hiding something, is not clever enough to answer quickly, etc. If the hearer is Indian or South American there could be many long pauses because in those cultures a pause before responding is a sign that care is being taken to produce a good answer.

Turn-denial

When a speaker refuses to allow another to speak it can be done with more or less face work. English phrases used range from the polite 'Just one more point, if I may', through 'Let me finish' to 'Don't interrupt'. The degree of face work may be mistaken and cause offence.

Turn-claiming

When a listener wishes to claim a speaking turn several strategies may be adopted, depending on the cultural norms of the listener. Indians increase the volume of their support noises; Britons repeat their support words and increase their pace. In each culture there are set phrases which are recognised as turn-claiming. In English such phrases as 'but', 'but what about' or 'no no no' (said with strong emphasis) are common, but their value as turn-claimers may not be recognised by one of another culture. There are also many non-verbal signs; in English these include a physical moving forward, an intensity of gaze, and other appropriate gestures. For other cultures any one of these could be problematic, for example the gaze could be read as objection to the speaker's opinion or attitude (particularly if accompanied, as it often is, with a frown of some sort), and could have entirely the wrong effect, causing the speaker to continue in defence of the point.

There are two further general points to be made about turntaking. First, in many cultures it is antisocial to dominate the floor for too long, though in some hierarchical communities those of senior rank may speak at very great length; this may cause problems in societies with either a different sense of social ranking or a different sense of the correct length of turn. Second, long turns may be intrinsically justifiable for many cultures, because the matter being spoken of is of great interest to the hearers. How interest is measured may, however, differ between cultures.

Practice

Observe how turntaking proceeds in the other culture, with special attention to (a) how speakers refuse to yield the floor, (b) how speakers relinquish the floor, (c) how hearers make support noises, and (d) how hearers try to gain the floor.

SPEECH ACTS

Every time someone speaks, three events take place: an utterance is made (a locution); a speech act of discursive power and intended influence over others occurs (with illocutionary force); and an effect on the listener is generated (a perlocutionary effect).

Locution

Every culture uses rhythm, intonation, pace and volume to give meaning to their utterances, and takes for granted their role in speech. When, therefore, the overall rhythm and intonation pattern of speech differs between cultures, this causes a basic discomfort because it signals that there will be little predictability about the speech, and more cognitive energy will be called for to understand what is being said. A very strongly marked rhythm can make the words difficult to hear; it can also make it hard to distinguish some speech acts in cultures where they are usually marked by intonation. For example, in English it is only intonation that indicates whether the sentence 'John is at home' is a question or a statement. English uses a rising tune to indicate questions; Pakistanis use falling intonation. Such differences indicate that the participants are 'on different wavelengths' and this can create such uncertainty that it may even cause a listener to feel that the foreigner's language is unprocessable. However, the difference need not give rise to negative effects; it does give a warning that misinterpretation is possible, and so can make people listen more carefully.

Prosodic features, such as tone, pitch, loudness, pacing and pauses, can distinguish important ideas from less important ones and can show the speaker's personality or attitude to what he or she is saying, for instance serious or joking, and also whether he or she likes or dislikes the hearer. Rhythm in some cultures indicates what social value is placed on the interaction; for example, Indians use a slow, ponderous, highly contoured rhythm and a low pitch to indicate seriousness of purpose. For them, the things said slowly and in low tones are the things that matter. Unfortunately both of these characteristics are likely to cause non-Indians to interrupt, with unfortunate results.

The Japanese use a high degree of palatalisation (where the blade of the tongue touches the palate, as in the English sound *dz* at the start and end of *judge*) to indicate that an intimate topic is being raised. English speakers speak quickly when dealing with such topics. Tamil speakers use a creaky tone to indicate that they are offering a complaint. Such differences may not easily be registered or dealt with correctly across cultures.

Illocutionary force

Neither the denotative value of the words used nor the grammatical forms employed clearly indicate what is intended by way of illocutionary force; it is rather the combination of such factors with the circumstances of the act, the roles and status of the speaker and hearer and the prosodic features that show what force the act has. Therefore this aspect of cross-cultural communication is particularly prone to misunderstanding. Since we negotiate on the basis of the illocutionary force we perceive others to be using, it is important to spend time examining the factors involved.

Direct speech acts, or baldness of speech, would be a simple matter for other cultures to translate, and would avoid many of the difficulties that more indirectly realised speech actions present. But most cultures and most people in each culture show an aversion to bluntness because of its negative effect on social interactions. They prefer to use strategies which not only perform an act, for example a request, but simultaneously work for the establishment, maintenance or adjustment of social relationships. This is done by couching the act in an indirect form which both gives due recognition to the other's status and role and realises the speaker's sense of his or her own position, as well as persuading listeners to accept the act. Only if urgency or efficiency demands it should speech acts be offered and accepted in bald form ('Watch out!', 'Fire!', 'Come in', 'I'm on the phone. Be with you soon'). Poles and Black Americans are exceptions as cultural groups in declaring a preference for bluntness, and while some English speakers throughout Western culture will loudly declare that they 'like people to be straightforward and not to beat about the bush', the same people are equally concerned to maintain good social relations, insisting that you have got to get along with other people, and this may require face work.

Face work

Baldness is avoided by the use of face work or politeness strategies, but the expectations of face work and the choice of strategies depend on a reading of the discourse factors involved, and this is difficult across cultures. A sample of strategies is given here to show some of the possibilities of misunderstanding.

(a) Use the correct form of address, which recognises the other's status and the degree of relationship. This varies cross-culturally. For instance, an Indian speaker may use 'brother' to signal a moderate friendliness; an English speaker will associate this with trade unionism or communism, and mistake its intention.

(b) Use 'please' and 'thank you' in offers, requests and questions. Japanese speakers might use 'sorry' instead while offering a gift, as in 'Accept this gift, sorry', since in Japanese and Korean cultures receiving a gift entails some obligation to reciprocate. The apology is for imposing the nuisance of gratitude.

(c) Pay attention to the speaker by support noises or the like. Indians of superior status in an interaction recognise no obligation to signal attention to those of lesser status.

(d) Use the deictic distinction between 'here' and 'there' (see p. 193 for a full account). Speakers use 'here' to indicate their own location, or their main point of interest, while locating the hearer 'there'. In some cultures this is reversed, so polite Japanese speakers will locate a hearer 'here' and themselves 'there'.

(e) Use small talk. A sufficient quantity of this, provided it is on the right subjects, with the right tone, and at the right place in the interaction sets a framework of face work in which blunter forms can be accepted. Trouble may arise because the other may not recognise the signs of small talk. English indicates small talk by using certain topics which have little referential value ('Isn't it lovely weather?' is not seriously offered as a meteorological statement) where other cultures would use very different topics; Mexican speakers indicate chat by sprinkling their talk with instances of the particle '*ala*' ('a little'). Trouble may also arise if one culture thinks the other is using too much or too little to suit their sense of the social parameters.

Reminder

Beyond basic face work there are two particular face work types addressed to saving face: positive, which seeks to express solidarity and shows that the speaker values the hearers' self-esteem, treats them as a friend and respects their wishes; and negative, which seeks to maintain the hearers' freedom of action, position, or territorial rights, and to avoid troubling them. (See pp. 68–75 for a full account.)

Positive face work can take some of the following forms.

1   Speakers indicate that the matters being spoken of are of interest or value to the hearer, or are intrinsically interesting, and so worth the hearer's attention. Cross-culturally, this requires a knowledge of what interests the hearer, where this may differ from what could be expected in the home culture.

2   Speakers acknowledge shared experience and claim common values or opinions, for example by using 'we' or 'our' (rather than 'I' or 'my') as in 'our plans', to suggest that both speaker and hearer want what the speaker does. While a common strategy in English, it may cause cross-cultural problems, either because it is not recognised as intending to include the other but read as referring to the group to which the speaker belongs, or because if the 'plan' is *not* in fact shared, the person from the other culture may find it confusing, and could also find it difficult to say so without causing social damage.

Sharing common ground can also take the form of stressing agreement and avoiding disagreement. In English it is polite to show disagreement only after agreeing as far as possible. For example, if asked 'Wasn't Bill's presentation good?', you could reply 'Yes [agreement], well, I thought the first part was good, but his conclusions were rather weak.' The question here, of course, expects agreement, and it is polite to fulfil a speaker's expectations if at all possible. Some cultures would find it even harder to express disagreement and would use more oblique ways of doing so; some would find it impossible if the speaker were of high rank. For them the initial agreement may therefore be mistaken for the truth, and the other points seem just mild reservations.

Probably the clearest way of indicating positive face work cross-culturally through acknowledging common ground is by using the real shared experience that builds up during the negotiation, and referring to it.

3   Speakers assume that they and the hearers are cooperating in a joint exercise and have the same goals in the interaction, for example by optimistically presuming the hearer will accept what they are asking for. Therefore such forms as these are used: 'You won't mind if we move this agenda item, will you?' or 'We'll go and have a look at the merchandise now, OK?' Cross-culturally this may be too much of a presumption and cause problems.

Negative face work can take some of the following forms.

1   Speakers use titles or other honorifics and explicitly or implicitly acknowledge the hearer's status as high, while downgrading their own. This is an important strategy for Japanese, Korean and Indian speakers, all of whom have a strong sense of hierarchy, and who need honorifics to set and maintain the status of all parties to the interaction. It is uncommon in English, and may be difficult to handle well in a cross-cultural situation. Yet, even if an English speaker does not use honorifics, the others will assess his or her rank and judge behaviours accordingly.

2   Speakers hedge or speak hesitatingly in order to indicate that the act being performed is not intended to impose on the hearer or to restrict his or her freedom, for example by using a phrase like 'more or less' as in 'It's more or less settled then, isn't it?' This allows the hearer plenty of room for objection. Or they use a form like 'This matter must be settled soon' when it is the hearer who must settle it. The form distances the speaker from the act involved, as compared with 'I think the matter should be settled soon', and distances the hearer too, compared with 'You must settle the matter soon.' It is as if the 'settling' is requested by no-one in particular, and must be done by no-one in particular. One problem cross-culturally is that such hedging tokens may not be recognised by the other culture. Equally the foreign tokens may not be read correctly; in Japanese and German, hedging is performed by particles attached to certain words or phrases, and these may be wrongly translated by the speaker when using English. Another problem is that different cultures expect different quantities of hedges to be used as indicators of deference, and may use too many or too few to please a foreigner.

3   Speakers use polite signs that indicate they are not imposing a serious burden on the hearer in wanting him or her to do something. So modifiers are used to belittle what is required, as in 'We need just a brief account from you. There's no hurry', where 'just', 'brief' and 'There's no hurry' reduce the

nature of the 'account' that is required. These tokens may be taken quite literally by another culture, and produce an unfortunate result.

4   Speakers use polite signs that indicate they are pessimistic about the outcome of what is being requested, as in 'You are very busy I know, but it would be good if we could have another meeting soon.' A foreigner might attend to the first part and see the second as of less importance, and so the speech that follows could take a wrong direction.

Indirection is a third and important variety of polite face work.

Many speech actions, whether they are statements, questions or (particularly) requests, are realised through indirection in order to avoid loss of face for speaker and hearer. For example, invitations (requests for the hearer to attend some event) may be offered obliquely to allow for refusal without social damage. A speaker may say, as a face-saving pre-request 'Are you doing anything tomorrow?' In English this is recognised as preliminary to some intrusion on the hearer's time, but it may be taken by a foreigner as the main speech act and dealt with accordingly.

There are many other general cross-cultural problems which can arise from such uses of indirection.

1   Assessing when indirection might be an appropriate strategy is difficult across cultures, requiring knowledge of the others' self-esteem and social ranking, as well as the imposition that is at issue when the speaker performs a particular act.

2   The purpose for which the indirection is used may be unclear – it can act to save the speaker's face, minimise the force of the act being performed, minimise the task being required of the hearer, save the hearer's face, or some combination of these, and any of these may be mistakenly interpreted.

3   The ways in which indirection is signalled are extremely dependent on cultural experience and knowledge. For example, saying 'There's just one more small matter I would like to raise' is an indirect means by which an English speaker might indicate that he or she has some hesitation about raising the matter; it need not mean that the matter is 'small' – that is, insignificant – yet a member of another culture could read it thus, since this is its literal meaning. English speakers use such mollification devices as standard practice for indirection. For example, many English speakers use 'OK' to mean a mollified 'no' as in 'OK, . . . but it won't really work.' This can, of course, be misread as 'yes' by others. Other such tokens include 'What about', as in 'What about doing X?', which could be read as a question rather than a polite indication that the speaker wants the hearer to do X; and 'I don't think so' or 'not really' meant as a polite 'no', which could also be taken the wrong way.

Strategy

Examine how the other culture indicates its version of indirection, when it uses it, and what social relationships seem to call for it.

The more indirect the act the worse the problem. While a relatively direct form like 'I wonder if you would care to consider . . .' may be fairly clearly understood to be a request that the other consider something (though the exact social value of the expressions 'I wonder' and 'if you would care' may not be fully appreciated), a very indirect form like 'Have you anything scheduled for next Friday?' (meant as a face-saving pre-sequence for a request) could be read as an intrusive inquiry about the details of the other's business practices; while 'Are you ready to move on to the next item of business?' (meant as a polite way of discovering whether the other has matters still to raise concerning the present item) could be read as a criticism of the other's lack of preparedness to deal with the next item, and provoke an angry or irritated response, such as 'I am as ready as you are' or 'I have been ready for some time.'

Some cultures prefer one strong marker of mollification, others prefer many weaker ones. The preference among most English speakers is for a series of weak markers, as in 'Oh well, I just thought if it's convenient we might have a brief look at the matter of X', where there are six mollifiers: 'Oh well', 'I just thought', 'just', 'if it's convenient', 'might' and 'brief'.

Mollification in English can take the form of surrounding a difficult or forceful speech with small talk using the friendliness it engenders to lessen the force of the act in its midst. These bonding tokens, with their extreme looseness of meaning, are often very difficult for foreigners to understand. Even the familiar 'How are you?', used as a ritual greeting and expecting a response like 'Fine thanks, and yourself?', has been taken as a true question by those of other cultures, and has produced a response with full details of health and/or emotional state. Luckily modern language teaching methods include awareness of such tokens and their values, so the problem is likely to be found now only with older members of another culture.

In any culture the effort involved in producing indirect speech acts is part of what is taken as a token of concern not to offend the hearer. It will not work unless that effort is obvious to the hearer, and this may be lost across cultures.

Perlocutionary effect

The perlocutionary effect can obviously vary more between cultures than within one. Unintended effects can result easily where the cultural presuppositions of speaker and hearer differ, and these may be hard to predict. For example, if an English speaker says 'Would you like a drink?', it may be a simple invitation to take some liquid refreshment from the drinks available in the room or nearby, but it may also be said as a means of extending the current interaction by some time spent in social intercourse. The speaker may be suggesting that people adjourn to another venue, perhaps a hotel, club or restaurant, where drinks are on offer, but where socialising, not quenching thirst, is the purpose. A member of a culture without this perception could assume that only liquid refreshment is being offered, be puzzled by its apparent absence, or, taking it literally, might reject the offer because not thirsty, and so miss an important part of the negotiating exercise.

Luckily, in most cross-cultural encounters, the extra caution that is used to read the other's speech should ensure that such difficulties are rapidly solved by enquiry. So, in fact, the alertness of participants could result in more appropriate perlocutionary effects than in intracultural encounters.

Speech act occurrence

The very occurrence of some speech acts may differ in acceptability between cultures.

(a) It may not be permissible to *ask* some questions of some people in any form. For example, in Tamil it is impolite to ask where someone is going, because of local beliefs in destiny's control over such things (it is rather like asking an English person 'How do you think God has planned your future?')

(b) In Western culture, formal business dealings are expected to exclude the act of *beseeching*, though it is quite acceptable in some Eastern cultures.

(c) In some Middle Eastern and Far Eastern cultures, *joking* may never be a suitable act in serious negotiation and both its presence and the words and matter used in it may be misunderstood.

(d) *Blaming* others is seen as socially unacceptable in South American Spanish culture where the person blamed is of senior rank, so instead they use a passive construction with no agent mentioned as in 'The matter was left undone' rather than 'He forgot to do it.'

Of those acts which are acceptable in both cultures, some will differ in values.

(a) North Americans expect more *praise* and *acknowledgement* than Europeans do.

(b) In Japan the act of *specifying precisely*, which is valued by Europeans, is seen as a poor tactic, even when planned to improve matters, since for the Japanese what is *not* said has greater importance than what is said; so dwelling at length on an awkward point may be seen as impolite and is hence to be avoided, since for them face work takes precedence over detailed clarification. A better strategy would be to avoid the matter and find other matters to deal with in which extra face work can be used, to balance the lack of it in the previous act.

(c) *Declaring* one's wishes may be unacceptable in some cultures, because it could be taken as a more purposeful act than was intended: some would see it as agenda setting, or a declaration of the only acceptable goal.

(d) In oriental cultures, while it is possible to express one's wishes or feelings, it is not possible to report the wishes or feelings of others, that is, one cannot say 'he wants' or 'she feels', but must say 'he shows signs of wanting' or 'she gives the appearance of feeling'.

Cultures may also have different expectations about the acceptability or timing of specific acts within a negotiation. They may, as a consequence, find certain versions of the three major speech acts – *statement*, *question* and *request* – more of a social imposition if they occur early in an encounter and less of one if they occur later; or they may misread a declaration of goals as too authoritarian because it occurs too soon for them and is not negotiated by both parties.

Cultures may differ in their understanding of the role in negotiation allocated to certain speech acts, for example *recapitulation*, which may be taken by one culture to mean 'offering an opinion as to what happened, for correction by others', and by another to mean 'establishing the basis on which the next stage will proceed', and by yet another to mean 'reiterating those aspects which strengthen one's argument'. So also *to summarise*, which may be taken as meaning 'helping to keep the discussion tidy' or as 'dictating the agenda'.

Feeling that certain acts are proper to certain stages in the interaction applies not only to the business in hand but also to the relationship being formed by the negotiators. Some cultures, like German and French, formally mark the stages of relationship: for example, intimacy is marked by the move from *sie* to *du* and from *vous* to *tu*. German culture also marks the appropriate time for this move in ritualistic ways; French does not. English speakers have no formal marking, nor is there a sense of the proper time for a move to greater intimacy.

Strategy

For more information about communication with members of a particular culture you should consult a specialist text which deals with communication in that culture.

Create your own checklist of problem areas which you have noticed, or which others suggest might occur. Keep such information accessible, and read through it as a preparation before your next cross-cultural encounter.

Take every opportunity to watch people from different cultures interacting among themselves, and note what you can of their discursive practices.

Remember that the others will also be trying to make adjustments to intercultural communication, so that their behaviours may not be understandable as, say, standard Japanese acts, because they are those of a Japanese person trying to imitate English practices.

Final note

Non-verbal language, as it involves proximity, touch, gestures, gaze, territory, turntaking, support noises, and so on, can vary much from one culture to another. Be careful to note how people from different cultures interact non-verbally, and try to come some way towards accommodating or imitating their different practices.

Chapter 5

Media interviews

PREPARATION

The first thing potential interviewees should consider is their reasons for engaging in the interview, and hence the goals they hope to achieve. What do you want to say, and what specific elements of the vast audience who might receive your words do you want to address? (The interviewer should not be your prime audience, though this will be difficult to manage, given the difference from ordinary conversation, where your interlocutor is usually the proper audience.) Interviewees should constantly remind themselves of their goals throughout the distractions that engaging in the interviewing process will bring.

It is fairly obvious why the media themselves like to use interviews: they are a cheap form of programming, and they provide audiences with the feeling that they are sharing in the ever-evolving nature of current affairs. They are attractive also because they link people (interviewees) and ideas, and so support the social understanding that more can be known about ideas if the person holding them can be seen discussing them, and that an apparently sincere person 'proves' the value of the ideas he or she presents. Also, interviews can give the appearance of spontaneity, and for viewers this can provide the exciting possibility that something could go wrong while they are actually watching. Like watching someone on a circus tightrope, it is particularly gripping if there is no safety net: similarly the media is more exciting to watch if it is live to air.

The genre of interviews also needs to be considered. There are various types of interviewing including the press conference and the crush of reporters outside an important event. The model interview, however, differs from both of these. It is a cross between a conversation and a legal cross-examination; it is expected to show signs of a relationship between interviewer and interviewee; it is required to have a theme or story, to form a coherent unity, to be more than the sum of the questions asked and the answers given; it should give the impression that it is an in-depth interaction

– investigative, probing, and personal. It is both planned and unplanned: that is, it may present errors of information, idea and speech, though it has been radically edited, revised and checked.

The media will seek to obtain interviews when an event occurs which is seen as suitable material, and will consider several criteria in assessing its suitability: whether the event influences a majority of its audience, whether it can be clearly understood, whether it is unexpected (within certain limits), whether it can be seen in personal terms, or whether it is negative ('bad news') in some way. An event is also likely to be considered fit material if it has already been dealt with in other media; this enables an interviewer to build upon and use the previous knowledge that readers will have acquired (though in this circumstance an interviewer would look for a different angle to take in order to create a complementary sense of newness).

Understanding how the media work

Although the media differ in what they emphasise most in an interview – radio is very sensitive to nuances of mood and attitude, as well as hesitation; television gives priority to visual images rather than words; and print can influence through its ability to use the rhetorical devices of composition – they all have certain features in common. By examining these it is possible for interviewees to understand how best to package their views for media consumption.

All media distinguish between interviews for news or current affairs and features purposes. The perfect *news* interview is a very brief one: press reporters may want the interview to deal only with what is newsworthy, and why, how, when and where it occurred; and radio and television *news* reporters may want only enough newsworthy comment by the interviewee from which to take a thirty-second segment, which might amount to no more than fifty words. The perfect *current affairs* interview on radio or television can be slightly longer, perhaps a two- or three-minute segment, and is preferably one which does not need editing; it might consist of only two or three questions and amount to approximately 300 words by the interviewee, though in the press it could be given much more space. Since most of these are short, a potential interviewee should be prepared to compress and select the most important aspects of the matter to be dealt with. It is worth practising some suitable comments and trying them out on colleagues. These should be shorter than a sentence in length to be sure of inclusion.

Interviews of such brevity are made understandable to their audiences, because the media utilise society's general stereotypical perceptions of the interviewee and of the interview's form and content as a framework. This has important consequences for the interviewee.

The interviewee

The stereotype of the interviewee is based on standardised views of such factors as age, gender, social role, occupation, and kind of involvement in the event in question. The media use it when deciding how to manage the interview; they know what they want and choose an interviewee who can be guaranteed to perform in a certain way. They expect the interviewee to say certain things, and when these have been said they bring the interview to a close. They thus predict both the content and meaning of the interview and set up their questions accordingly. They are unlikely, therefore, to endorse any variation from their plan, and could ignore it as problematic.

In more general terms, they are also unlikely to give social endorsement to any variation from the stereotypical, so that an interviewee who knows that his or her words might appear as a variation from this stereotype must reckon with resistance in the interviewer and the audience. Since the mass media repeatedly work in this way, their output reinforces the stereotypes, and maintains a widely understood sense of the established social order.

Example

An interviewer might ask such a question as 'Won't that badly affect ordinary families?', expecting everyone to understand that there is something called a family which is everywhere much the same, without questioning the assumption by asking, for example, 'How exactly do you understand the term "family?" ', or 'Do you mean the single parent family or the dual parent family?' An interviewee who asked such questions, or who answered the original question with 'It depends what kind of family you mean', would not only confuse the interviewer but could also face problems with audience understanding, until such time as society generally accepts the fact that the 'family' no longer has a single meaning.

Expectations also exist in the audience's minds as to what content the interview will have, what topics will be raised, and what views will be expressed, and any deviations may be resisted as troublesome. For example, people have a standard view of a banker, and every banker is expected to look and sound the part. When confronted by a banker who differs in some way, they could miss much of what is being said while making adjustments to their mental stereotype. Such stereotyping can occur with respect to every element of the interview's content: the matters mentioned, the actions taken, the attitudes expressed, and so on.

Example

If the interview is about a physical event, then the assumption is usually that there are only three roles to take – actor, victim or bystander/commentator/

expert. If it is about political or business information, it is assumed that the interviewee's role is one of representative or spokesperson with no power to affect the issues, or of 'objective' expert outside the issue, or of official actor with some (named) responsibility for the outcome. There is also a general assumption that in all matters every person involved can be put into one of two groups, those affected by the matter at issue or those affecting it, thus ignoring the possibility of gradations of responsibility or effect. If the interviewee's role in the matter is of a complex kind, it will need to be declared and explained if it is to be generally understood.

Potential interviewees should consider the influence these factors may have on the speech behaviours the interviewer will use, and hence on their own contributions. They should acknowledge the form their own stereotype takes, and if they wish to do something unexpected, for example vary their role or make a maverick comment, they should be aware that this may cause a basic problem of understanding. One tactic to overcome this would be to make some overt acknowledgement of the intended deviation and so enable the audience to place the comment in relation to their stereotypical expectation: for example, 'I may be unusual in this but . . .' or 'Although in the past bankers might have done X, nowadays we do Y.'

Interviewees should be aware that any departure from the expected might be highlighted by virtue of its difference, and this could result in its having a more powerful impact than intended. In a case where the audience has a vested interest in retaining the stereotype (for example where it serves as a scapegoat for a social problem), any departure from the expected may be received wholly negatively. Equally, it is worth noting that if you do not wish to be remembered, then fitting yourself perfectly to a stereotype could act to make your words less distinguishable from others in the same category, and so perhaps in time make them less personally attributable.

The interview form

The form of the interview is also stereotyped in order to assist interviewers to handle efficiently the many different people they must question, and its patterning also helps to ensure that the audience can cope with the brevity and compression of the event.

This routinisation of form can be used by interviewees to anticipate the style of their own interview by close scrutiny of the patterns that are followed, both generally in the output of news and current affairs interviews, and specifically by the particular programme and interviewer seeking to interview them. The interviewee can be made a prisoner of its power unless the form of an interview is understood in advance. Interviewees should notice, for example, the kind of audience the organisation caters for;

whether the interviewers are chosen for abrasiveness or subtlety; whether they sharply control the exchange of ideas, or leave room for the interviewee to adapt the topic; whether they build on a single topic or spray topics around; and whether they adopt a fast or slow pace of questioning. They should particularly notice the interviewer's most used or favourite topics, attitudes, and questions.

Where a company has several employees likely to be involved in media interviews, it may be worth getting a professional to do a thorough analysis of the relevant media programmes, the interviewers' methods, and so on, but it is vital that potential interviewees acquire their own personal sense of what to expect.

Not only should the internal form of the interview be considered, but also the formal media context in which it will be produced. An interview will occur as only one item amidst the many others in the news – car accidents, royal babies, world crises – and its memorability will be affected by this. Meanings are therefore less likely to be established once and for all during or immediately after the interview; they may be changed by what else happens both in and out of the media in the ensuing days and weeks.

A media interview is often heard or seen with divided attention by the audience, who may be simultaneously talking, standing on a bus, eating and drinking, waiting for the quiz show that immediately follows the news, or still laughing at the comedy show that precedes it. In short, they may be giving it very little close attention. Unless the matters presented in the interview are seen to have personal relevance or interest, the audience may even completely disregard it. It is a myth promulgated by the media themselves that they are a powerful force because they are attended to by all, and thus provide potential interviewers with access to the attention of millions. Certainly those with an urgent interest in the matters raised will attend carefully, but it should not be forgotten that the media can also be treated with scant respect; the newspaper is skimmed and the radio or the TV set and its output given as much attention as any other piece of furniture.

It has been estimated that some 40 per cent of television viewers pay little attention; that, irrespective of content, the attention of some 20 per cent is strongly influenced by their antagonism to, or approval of, the interviewer or interviewee; that 10 per cent misconstrue what occurs; and that 10 per cent have mixed views by the end (the remaining 20 per cent are either children or the elderly, whose response is likely to carry little social weight). Potential interviewees should realise how little control they have over the audience's interpretation.

They cannot control the way the audience adapts and accommodates media material, both content and mode of presentation, to its own concerns, hearing and seeing what it wishes to hear and see. The meanings that are created through the media interview are not necessarily those carefully designed by the media practitioners themselves, let alone those planned by the interviewee. Audiences can base their interpretations quite loosely on the material supplied in the particular interview, and may even conflate it with material from other sources, and from their own opinions, with the result that they make mistakes about what occurred, what exactly was said, or even who was interviewed. If members of the public cannot remember names or faces they will be unable to make accurate attributions, and instead could produce vague categorisations of an interviewee's performance such as 'just another expert trying to blind us with statistics'.

Accurate retention appears to be more strongly influenced by the presentation of personality and the speech acts performed during the interview than by the subject matter. Retention is also likely where the reader perceives there to be some content of personal relevance in the interview, or where the interviewee has a (stereotypically) recognisable role in the community's affairs (for example, the role of a manager or owner of a manufacturing company will be better understood, and his or her words better remembered, than that of a finance expert from a consultancy firm).

Apart from the general audience, however, there is another group to consider: those with specialist knowledge of, and interest and a part to play in, the affairs raised. Interviews are also seen by colleagues, business rivals, members of the same profession, and within the media themselves, where specialist feature writers and journalists are looking for copy: these too should be kept in mind. Though their perception of what occurred will probably be more accurate and detailed than that of the general public, it will still be true that their own interests and goals and also their ability to accommodate the interview's contribution to their world view will have a strong effect on how they interpret and remember what is said.

The interview content

The content of the interview is also stereotyped. Interviewers ask questions to which they already know the answers, for the sake of their own control of the encounter, and they keep the talk focused on their own perception of the topic. Among other things this means that stereotypical answers will best please the interviewer, and be accepted with little comment or query, while maverick comments will not be taken up unless they provide an opportunity for one of the favoured tactics of interviewers – creating a conflict. Setting up a conflict makes good entertainment and interests the audience, whether it is between one person and another, one group and another, or between people and nature, people and fate (as in interviews about accidents, fire, famine and flood), or even the interviewee against an earlier self. Interviewees should decide what entertainment they will provide, for example what conflicts they are prepared to introduce themselves or accept when raised. This may prevent the interviewer from bringing up others which would be less acceptable.

Specific preparation

First, make sure that you record all that you and the interviewer say together if there is any chance at all that the interview is being recorded or filmed. Second, make sure that you take a copy or recording of the published or broadcast interview. In the case of discrepancies between what you were given to understand about the nature of the interview and what actually occurred, your hand will be strengthened if you have recorded the evidence.

Immediately before an interview consider those factors involved in media production which could affect you psychologically and so impact upon your performance. Significant factors include the medium in which the interview is conducted, and how intrusive its production needs are; the participants of the interview, whether it will be a dialogue or a group interaction; and the topics that will be raised.

The medium

A press reporter may use the phone as the channel of communication, it is therefore important to be circumspect on the phone with anyone who might be attached to a media organisation. Do not make any off-the-cuff comments, and do not move straight into an interview there and then, but ask that it take place later. Ask for details of the interview's format, its goals, topics, length, the other interviewees, in what programme it will be broadcast, and so on, and then consult with colleagues and think about the problems. A reporter may appear in person accompanied only by a notebook or recorder; the small amount of disturbance he or she will cause should not be taken to indicate that talking to the press is an inconsequential event: words in print may last longer than an electronic image.

Radio and television interviewers require more obtrusive equipment for their work, and the upheaval they cause makes it very clear that the occasion is significant. The upheaval can, however, distract the interviewee by claiming his or her attention, to the consequent neglect of the words being used and elicited. It may be particularly hard to concentrate on what is important when an interview takes place live in a studio after a good deal of technical preparation involving make-up, lights, and camera positioning. Interviewees who wish not to be distracted would do well to consider their likely reactions to being so little in control of events. Before the time of the interview itself, a useful technique is to practise what might occur once the interview proper takes place, using a mirror to note facial expressions, gestures and posture and using a sound-recorder to monitor speech, but realise that things might not go according to the rehearsed plan; like conversations, interviews are negotiating interactions and can therefore have wayward and unplanned outcomes.

It can also be a useful technique to rehearse mentally the studio activity which will be involved so that the actuality creates as little psychic disturbance as possible.

Participants

Establish who the interviewer will be, and whether anyone else will be present during the interview, or whether interviews with others are being sought. Analysis of the programme's habits could help to show this, but also ask directly about it before agreeing to be interviewed.

Topics

Establish what topics will be raised, and declare any topics which you will refuse to discuss. Be prepared, however, for the interviewer to mention the forbidden topics, and have a suitable response ready, for instance 'You agreed that that topic would not be raised.' This lays the blame firmly on the interviewer for any awkwardness which ensues, whereas a form like 'I said I would not discuss that' sounds as if the blame is yours, and also opens the way more easily for the interviewer to ask why you are refusing discussion.

On the day itself, interviewees should allow enough time to recover from the journey to the studio; ask for a quiet place to compose themselves before the interview begins; ask to see the interview location as soon as they arrive at the organisation's offices; try the chair provided, and get used to the distance from the interviewer, and to the lights, heat and bustle; and ask for any (reasonable) alterations that would produce more comfort.

THE INTERVIEW

To understand the actions that take place during an interview, consider the goals and the strategies adopted by media interviewers and reporters.

The standard goal of a good interview, as described by both journalism textbooks and experienced practitioners, is a combination of information and entertainment. Journalists would find it complimentary if the following words were used of their work: clear, well-informed, crisp, entertaining, provocative, revelatory, unusual (though this last would be restricted to the stereotypically unusual). They seek to produce these qualities by setting up certain situations or prompting certain responses from the interviewee. These are listed in descending order of priority.

1 A conflict can be set up by, for example, creating an opposition between the interviewee's opinion and the standard opinion held by the professional group to which the interviewee belongs, or between views of the interviewee and those of someone of equal standing, or between the interviewee's currently stated views and those he or she has stated at an

earlier time. The interviewer will also always be on the look-out for any apparent contradictions in the interviewee's words which would create another kind of conflict. If no obvious conflict presents itself the interviewer may resort to such generalities as 'Most people would say . . . yet you seem to disagree.'

2 A revelation of ideas or facts, particularly one which the interviewee seems unwilling to make, can be sought through a question such as 'Is it true that your company is currently seeking a merger?'

3 A revelation of personal feelings behind the presentation of facts can be prompted by questions like 'But won't this be a disaster for your employees?'

4 A clear structure to the interview could be achieved in a narrative account – who did what to whom and with what climax – but also in an account of facts and figures through such devices as 'There are three main points to note . . . The most important point is . . .'

5 A significant statement from the interviewee would be something along the lines of 'There will be no increase in the cost of . . . this year.'

6 A pithy, quotable, and memorable phrase, such as 'Our competitors have missed the bus', 'People won't stand for it', 'People want the best deal', which appeals to standard cultural views in everyday words.

This last response can be particularly entertaining if it is a good encapsulation of some complex matter of public interest, or if it offers something new or of particular public interest. (If in the process it shakes the expectations of the interviewer, it may allow the interviewee to have more control over the interaction from that point.) If in addition it is presented at speed, with no hesitation or qualification, it may well be picked up for a thirty-second 'grab' on the news.

An interviewee should always provide more than the basics of the matter, since if he or she does not the interviewer certainly will. He or she should decide which is the highest priority goal he or she is prepared to meet, and supply that early in the interaction. The chances are that this may satisfy the interviewer's needs and shorten the interview, leaving more troublesome matters untouched. Its virtue is that it keeps control of the event at least partly in the hands of the interviewee. If the interviewee does not play an active part in the achievement of any of the media's goals, the interviewer will aim first for conflict, the situation with the highest priority in the list, and this, clearly, could put the interviewee at a disadvantage.

If interviewers achieve any of these goals, this will certainly attract audience interest, and that feature of the interview may be remembered and even taken up by other media. So, unless interviewees want the event to be remembered, they should prepare to satisfy none of the interviewer's goals. It may be managed in some instances by appearing dull, bland or ordinary. In that case the interview may not be used at all, or if used it will be easily forgotten, and all that will remain is the faint memory of an undistinguished person. Colleagues and competitors will not take it amiss, will understand, while general public opinion may have little significance for the interviewee apart from providing him or her with a bruised ego for a few days.

Strategies and counter-strategies

Remember that everything that the interviewer does – smile, frown, be silent, or speak – is intended to produce a particular response in the interviewee. Both in the warm-up session and in the interview itself interviewers begin gently: they will often use silence to get the interviewee to talk, or use their own anecdotes to draw others from the interviewee, watching for verbal or non-verbal signals of discomfort, so that they can home in on what is generating that discomfort as a subject likely to rouse strong passions. As counters to these an interviewee could practise: being silent rather than saying something trivial or inappropriate; listening to anecdotes without volunteering anything of their own; controlling their expression, gestures, and posture to support the verbal message and to give away as little else as possible, while all the time resisting appeals to the ego (which are primarily intended, after all, to bruise the ego later). Interviewees will also watch for signs of the interviewer's self-perception and manifestations of his or her ego, in order to make tactical use of this knowledge in the interview. Hard though it may be to achieve it, potential interviewees should try to gain enough self-knowledge to be able to resist such tactics.

Once the interview itself begins, interviewers employ standard strategies as provocative as the following.

1 They could play devil's advocate, by saying something like 'Some would say that what you have done is bad.'
2 They could presume they speak for particular social groups, for example 'ordinary people' who, it is claimed, do not understand or accept the interviewee's views or actions, by making statements such as 'Most people would say you were foolish to do that.' This needs a careful response so as not to imply that the interviewee despises the views of ordinary folk (who are watching the programme).
3 They could make assumptions or take for granted things which the interviewee should question. For example, they could say: 'With manufacturing industry in such bad shape, should your firm be expanding in this way?' The assumption about the shape of manufacturing industry should not be allowed to pass without comment. If it goes unnoticed or is not dealt with, then it can be said later that the interviewee has agreed with the assumption. This could be confusing and could distract from the interviewee's preferred topics, throwing him or her onto the defensive, and perhaps making it difficult to retain authority.

4 They could quote an unattributed statement which seems to conflict with the interviewee's present views, which may later be declared to belong to the interviewee or to someone with whom the interviewee would not like to disagree.
5 They could change the topic with no warning. This can make the interviewee slow to follow the change, and hence to respond, which in turn can be misread as hesitation about the issue itself rather than adjustment to the new topic.

Most patterns of behaviour adopted by interviewers are centred on the questions they use. On the matters to be raised, standard strategies include asking:

1 (using their standard order of questions) what it is, to and by whom it was done, and how, why, when and where it occurred;
2 what its social significance is in general, for 'ordinary' people, for the country as a whole, and for a special interest group with particular links to the matter;
3 what its causes and consequences are, particularly as these relate to the interviewee's role and responsibility;
4 whether the interviewee as an individual has behaved responsibly within his or her role (and they may attempt to suggest a clash between the person and the role – another version of conflict).

The forms used may be a simple question which is too sweeping to answer easily, or a complex question which is either difficult to follow, forcing the interviewee to have to ask for a repeat (thus sounding as if he or she cannot understand things said), or cannot all be answered, forcing the interviewee to select one topic to deal with first (thus sounding as if some of its elements are deliberately being ignored).

Journalists know that, all things being equal, a short question will draw a short answer and a long question will draw a long answer; they are aware that a kind of rhythm of turns is built up in interactions, with each seeking to equal the turn of the other. Since interviewees cannot use one of the ordinary conversational ways of equalising their turns – such as asking questions of the interviewer – they may instead use a lengthening of their answer (and perhaps say more than they should). Interviewees should beware of this 'Matarazzo Effect' (Jucker 1986: 32).

To counter these strategies, interviewees should have answers rehearsed. They should be clear in their own mind what they want to say, and what to conceal. They should think of the questions that would be hard to answer and expect these, think of the question they would least like to be asked and prepare an answer. They should have with them detailed information on every aspect of the matter likely to be raised – its background, any useful comparisons and contrasts, any results, and so on. (Any quantification that may be asked for should be supplied in very basic terms – simple percentages, vulgar fractions or ratios only – if it is to be understood by the general viewer.) Interviewers like to balance facts with attitudes, so if it is a matter of figures, interviewees should try to combine a personal response to them; if it is a matter of personal attitude, then they should supply facts to help put it into context.

To decide what might be raised and in what terms, it is worth considering what has been raised in the media on the topic in the recent past, or in any previous media contact you or your organisation or competitors has had. If it seems that you will frequently be required to give interviews, you could prepare a media file on the matters you are likely to have to deal with, using newspaper cuttings and notes on television and radio interviews in order to remember the kinds of questions asked, the comments raised and any other ancillary matters that were introduced. Also make a note of those who have previously spoken or written on the matter and what their views were, so that before each encounter with the media you can get into the appropriate mode of thinking and be prepared. It is also worth consulting a colleague or a friend who is good at estimating what the general public is likely to want to know about the matter, and being prepared to have that focus used, and those terms.

The interviewer's language

During the interview itself, problematic words or phrases likely to crop up are those involved in the confrontational speech acts: 'confront' itself, 'demand', 'contradict', 'challenge' and 'oppose'. Have alternative phrases ready, introduced with, for example, 'I'd prefer to put it another way.' If the word 'confront' is used, seek to have it changed to 'argue from strongly held views'; change 'demand' to 'consult with', or 'state a strong negotiating position', or 'make a reasonable request in our own terms'; change 'contradict' to 'take a different view'; change 'challenge' to 'state a strongly held view'; and change 'oppose' to 'offer a healthy expression of differing views'.

Certain other phrases used by the interviewer signal trouble, for example 'You said last year . . .', '[The opposition] thinks . . .' or '[Someone of importance] has declared . . .', and could be the prelude to conflict of some kind. (Beware! It is not always the obvious conflict. For example, if the interviewer says 'You said that the price of your products would go up by only 1 per cent this month', the standard strategy might be to prove you wrong, but more subtly the focus may be put on the word 'only' and produce 'Have you any idea of the weekly food bill for an ordinary family, and the effect on it of "only" a 1 per cent rise?', producing a conflict between you and ordinary people.)

Note who are the subjects of the sentences that the interviewer is using – the danger terms are 'people', 'you', 'your boss', 'your rival', 'another expert', etc., and the rest of the sentence could either crucially oversimplify your view or contradict your known position in some way.

Be prepared to resist the attribution of some bad action to yourself or your firm, and have a better term ready to use, if one of the following verbs is used by the interviewer – 'cover up', 'make a mistake', 'make an error', 'change one's mind', 'hurt', 'give respectability to', 'disagree', 'delay', 'move too fast', 'act', or 'do not act'.

Be prepared to argue, as appropriate, that the following 'good' groups are not affected adversely by your actions: people (particularly the poor, the elderly, the young, the sick, or the otherwise disadvantaged) and your country; or that the following 'bad' groups are not being assisted by your actions: the bureaucracy, the criminal classes, an alien group of foreigners, or the rich and powerful.

An interviewer should not be allowed to dictate the terms of an interview without question. If an interviewee accepts the words, and just answers yes or no to the *substance* of the comment or question, then this could be reported later as the interviewee's agreement with the terms used. Be prepared, therefore, to rephrase the interviewer's words, for example, replying to 'You say you don't know what goes on in other companies. Isn't that an admission of defeat?' with 'That's not what I said. I said I'm not privy to the details of how other companies work'; and to 'Are you saying you've never forced a resignation?' with 'No I didn't say that, I said . . .'

Recognise that you do not have to answer directly any question put to you, though it will be tempting to do so, because this is how we would behave in ordinary conversation. The options are: you can take up a word used and expound on that; you can resist a word and seek to change it; you can begin your answer at a point so far in advance of the direct answer that you will never get to the point; if given a complex question you can answer that part of it which suits; and if the interviewer objects that the question is not being answered, you can reply 'I am answering the first part of your question about . . ., and I'll come to the other part in a moment'.

Monitor your own speech

As self-defence

Some of the greatest harm to an interviewee's spoken contribution can be done by media editing, which can ignore the clarifications you make and broadcast a misleading simplification of your views. Therefore, seek to produce language which is compact and cannot be easily split up. There are several strategies which might prevent this.

(a) Remember that the question may be missing from any edited extract published or broadcast, so ensure the inclusion of crucial matters by actually naming them within your answer.

(b) If you wish to make a qualified statement, place the qualification in the middle of the sentence. If it is at the beginning or the end it can be edited out very easily. For example, it is less good to say 'Provided exports increase, a small fall in interest rates is possible by the end of the year' or 'A small fall in interest rates is possible, but only if exports increase' (which could both be edited to read 'A small fall in interest rates is possible') than it is to say 'Interest rates are linked with exports, and if these increase then rates will fall' (which cannot easily be edited).

(c) Practise producing the right form of words for any crucial statements that are to be made. During the interview repeat it as it seems suitable rather than trying for elegant variations of phrasing, which might lead you to make a mistake, and have it focused on for debate.

(d) Consider the value to be gained from using the powers of grammar to help put your point. Use large noun phrases that cannot easily be split up to put those matters together that you do not wish to have separated, for example 'Our company, which was one of the first to take environmental issues into account, is not changing its policy', rather than 'Our company was one of the first to take environmental issues into account, and we are not changing our policy.' (From the second version, the last clause could be used alone.)

(e) Use anaphora, which does not permit easy editing, as in 'They [sc. interest rates] won't fall till the end of the year.' (Though it should be noted that this usage would not prevent someone quite properly reporting that you 'said' that interest rates would not fall till the end of the year.)

(f) Take advantage of the passive form and so avoid naming the agent of some questionable act, as in 'Mistakes were made' (rather than 'X made a mistake'), or 'It was suggested that there might be discrepancies' (which does not name the suggester, and also does not attribute the discrepancies to anyone).

Since the media and its audience disapprove of such things as changing one's mind and being ignorant, it is important to have ready phrases to account for apparent changes of mind, such as 'Circumstances have changed and therefore our policy has had to change also', or 'More research has been done since then, so this is no longer appropriate.' Ignorance can be avoided by preparation of figures and facts in advance of anticipated questions. (Remember that it is best if these can be given without apparent recourse to notes, but if this is not possible then use them; it is better to be accurate than not.)

If in doubt about what to say, take your time to speak. Since you do not want to be asked another question while you are pausing, nor do you want the pause to appear to be the result of ignorance or embarrassment, it is best to control the pause yourself. This is done by beginning to speak and then pausing, as in 'Well . . . in my view . . . it is . . .' If the interviewer begins to speak in one of the pauses it will be seen as an interruption, and can be dealt with as such.

As attack

Attacking strategies must be carefully planned and executed if they are not to rebound to the interviewee's disadvantage.

(a) Never be rude or criticise the interviewer directly, as in 'That's not true', or 'That's the wrong way to put it.' Audiences see this negatively and usually spring to the defence of the interviewer, who, of course, is a more familiar figure to them than you are. Criticism should be more oblique, as in 'People are more interested in . . . than in the answer to that question', or 'Most people want to know . . . [and not what the interviewer has just asked]', or 'Our experiences have shown that a more important question is . . .' or 'The word I'd rather use [than the one used in the question] is . . .'

(b) When asked a question (and therefore when given the floor), take the opportunity to initiate whatever speech you wish to make before answering it. Say, for example, 'Look, it would be helpful if I could just clarify a few points before answering that . . .', or 'Look, I think people would first of all be interested to know . . .', or 'I'd prefer to put it this way . . .', or 'That isn't how I would put it. If I might just rephrase it . . .', or 'That's interesting, but I think the more important matter is . . .' Such interpolations may be hard to make given the conventions which rule conversational behaviour, so they should be practised.

(c) Be prepared with a strategy to deal with interruptions, for example the use of such forms as 'I am answering it', 'I'm nearly finished' or 'That's a complex question and needs a complex answer.'

(d) Prepare sentences to cover those moments when you do not wish to speak at all about something, for example 'I cannot comment on that', but note that without some explanation of the refusal the interviewer may well ask for reasons. It could be better to use some such form as 'I can't be expected to reveal things like that to our competitors' (note that it is phrased so as not to blame the interviewer as it would have been if it were phrased 'You can't expect me . . .'), or 'It would be improper for me to answer that' (to which could be added 'at this particular moment' or 'until I inform my colleagues. . .', and so on, as appropriate).

Chapter 6

Using the phone

INTRODUCTION

People in business appear to spend on average about 10 to 15 per cent of their time using the phone. The majority of calls are short, around 2 to 8 minutes in duration, and they are perceived as useful ways of directly contacting people for a whole range of purposes. The most obvious of these are finding and giving information, giving and receiving orders and arranging face-to-face contacts. Internal phone calls generally act as substitutes for memoranda within an organisation, while outside calls initiate and receive business, or make and receive inquiries. Not only does using the phone achieve a good deal, but it also generates a lot of ancillary work, and so every call must be carefully used to ensure this can be done efficiently.

In order to learn to achieve success in the use of the phone, first ask yourself the following questions about your phone practices.

(a) How many different people do you contact? Is there a small set whom you repeatedly telephone as individuals, or is there a large set, where the people concerned only act in certain capacities, for example as buyer, seller, client or supplier?

(b) Do you have working relationships which use both face-to-face and phone contact, or only the latter? This will make a difference, since the two kinds of interaction can be used to support each other, whereas a relationship which depends on phone contact alone will need to supply a good deal of social bonding to maintain it in good condition through the one medium.

(c) Do you concentrate on the calls you make and receive, or do you treat them lightly, taking the opportunity to read or make notes while on the phone? If the latter is true, you could be neglecting opportunities for greater efficiency, or useful knowledge.

(d) For what purposes do you make calls? Is it for a range of primary activities to do with your work, or is it to arrange face-to-face contacts where such primary work will then be done?

Then check your strategies in each case.

THE PHONE CALL

Public opinion can provide useful information about the nature and value of the phone as a form of human interaction, and human business contact. Much of this useful information has arisen in response to the advent of the answering machine, which suits business very well, but is meeting strong resistance from members of the general public. They perceive it as an unsatisfactory means of communication, even though they can give information to it, receive information from it, or use it to set up a person-to-person call. The reasons given are (a) that it shifts control of the interaction to the person who is called and away from the caller and (b) that it is lacking in personal interactive communication, as well as being too brief and too task-centred.

These observations draw attention to two of the most important factors in telephone calls which can affect their success.

(a) the caller expects to be in control, that is, to initiate the call, to draw the other into interaction, to name the purpose for which the call is made and have that accepted as the prime focus, and to be in charge of closure;

(b) the caller wants some personal interactivity.

It would be a good idea to try to meet these expectations as far as possible.

Strategies

First, if you wish to vary from the caller's plan, for example by taking the opportunity of the call to raise a topic of your own, then acknowledge that it is a variation and ask permission to raise it using some such phrase as 'Oh, while you're there, could I raise the problem of the . . .?' Contrast the attitude expressed there with this alternative: 'Oh, while I've got you there, I must raise the problem . . .' In the latter version, the speaker suggests that he or she has actively caught the caller's attention. A caller may, subconsciously, resent this as denying his or her authority, particularly since it takes a dominant position in saying, without mollification or apology, 'I must'.

The caller in many cases (though this seems to vary with age and with region) believes that he or she has the right to initiate closure of the call. This involves a complicated series of pre-closure steps, starting with perhaps a signal that the topic is nearly done, 'One last thing . . .', or is absolutely finished, 'That's all I rang you for.' Alternatively, indication can be given that closure is approaching, 'Well I must be going now' or (more humbly) 'Well I mustn't keep you any longer', or there can be a bilateral agreement to close, perhaps 'OK?', 'OK', followed by the appropriate farewells. The ideal phone call ends with both handsets being returned to their rests simultaneously. (People record their disapproval when this does not happen in such phrases as 'She hung up on me.')

Second, treat the lack of a satisfactory interpersonal element as serious. Judge how best to substitute for it. Note, in particular, that phone calls may lack one of three important interpersonal elements.

Feedback

It is important to provide the speaker with feedback or responsiveness. On the phone such reactive behaviour will require a different means of expression from that used in face-to-face interactions. It can be provided by substituting for non-verbal signs an increase in articulated signs, for example 'fine', 'good', 'I see.' More extreme modulations of tone of voice than those found in face-to-face meetings can also be used, for example excessive drawling for hesitation, extra stress for approving noises, and, perhaps, exaggeratedly long 'nooo's for rejection. Pauses can be used on the phone, but must be carefully placed in case the hearer thinks there is a problem with the machine. They can be used for effect with the same meaning as in face-to-face interaction provided that they are exaggerated, and occur within utterances, and not after possible completion points.

Calls for reassurance by either speaker may well be more frequent: 'Do you know what I mean?', 'Are you with me on this?', 'Do you have a copy there?', 'Are you familiar with the problem?', and so on.

Signs of attitude

We need cues to each other's attitudes to sustain us as we interact; we use them to measure the success or failure of a speech act, or to judge the degree of politeness required. Ideally we use the presence of our whole personality to create complexity in our acts by particular combinations of physical signs and uses of language; so, for example, in a face-to-face encounter we might perform a complex act which is at once partial agreement and mild hesitation by producing a wry look in response to a particular word used and coupling this with producing the spoken response 'OK.' Unfortunately this is rather harder to do on the phone, but can be achieved by a combination of words which produce complexity, as in 'yes, I see – but then – well I suppose – do you think so?' as well as an exaggeration of voice qualities such as ironic laughter, harshness of vowel sound, or variation in tempo.

Without some degree of bonding work, the phone call can become too oppressive for personal comfort in its task-centredness. It can also be a bad means for conducting negotiation since it can become too uncompromisingly focused on the task and not allow the other elements of negotiation to have their place – for example, the expression of different shades of opinion, the declared recognition of others' attitudes, the provision of opportunity for all to speak, even if not all will be happy with the eventual outcome, and so on. A phone call is more likely to produce a polarised debate than a negotiation. This is true even of group calls unless care is taken.

Structure

A successful phone call should show signs of structural organisation. To achieve an orderly progression through an interaction to its goals, there is a need for markers of topic change as well as movement from major to subsidiary concerns. Many of the same verbal markers can be used on the phone as in face-to-face interactions. The main difference is that more of them may need to be used to substitute for the non-verbal ones, and to ensure efficient progress. The frame marker and, especially, the focus markers (see Chapter 3 for a full account) will be of particular use. For example, a focus marker like 'Have we finished with that?' can substitute for glances around the table, and one with the frame and focus combined, like 'OK then, let's go on to the . . .', can substitute for the shuffling of documents. Markers like 'Pardon' or 'I didn't quite catch that' are more frequent on the phone, substituting as they do for a querying look. Callers who wish to speak may have to bid for speech more overtly and orally than when face-to-face ('Can I say something?' or 'Can I come in here?'), and may actually have to nominate another person to speak more than would be usual in face-to-face interaction if the phone call links up more than two people ('Mary, what do you think?' or 'Bill, can we hear from you on this?').

The representation of the business matter in phone calls also differs from that used in face-to-face interactions, and requires special care with the language used.

First, since there is no single shared context, deictic references (such as the pronouns *this* or *that*) must be avoided or clarified: it makes no sense to say 'It's in this report' if your hearer cannot see the report you are indicating. A better strategy is to over-specify rather than under-specify; use titles, names and full descriptions wherever you have doubts that the matter will be understood.

Second, the act of listening must be more vocalised and more exaggerated; there may be an increased loudness in the 'mhm' or 'aha' sounds, or an increase in positiveness in any support noises used, for example 'Exactly' instead of 'Right', 'Yes' instead of 'Uhuh'.

Because of the narrowly task-focused nature of business phone calls, the speech acts in them are likely to belong to a smaller set than that used in other kinds of interaction, and will mainly be questions and answers, or requests and responses. You should consider the parameters of these acts in particular and judge how best to perform them in the light of the above comments.

Self-monitoring

To check on your phone-call speech behaviours, it would be worthwhile to record yourself (be careful, however, of the legal implications of this) to see what the major kinds of speech acts are that you engage in, and what your speech routines are within them. Ask a colleague or friend how they respond to your routines. Note what routines they use, and what is done by people you feel have a good phone technique. Compare them with your own, and consider whether to make any adjustments. Test any new routines on friends before using them in important work.

Part III

The management of written communication

Chapter 7

Written communication

INTRODUCTION

Since negotiation is above all an interaction with goals and aims, those taking part in it who have to make written presentations will need to consider what strategies will assist them in the achievement of their goals. The best way to examine the strategic use of written communication is by way of classical rhetoric, which is the body of thought, rules and instructions which has stood the test of 2,000 years' experience in assisting writers to use the best means of achieving their goals. This chapter will therefore provide a classical rhetoric account of the ways and means of producing successful writing. It will also add some suggestions for presentation and distribution after the writing is completed.

CONTENT

For the purposes of this account it will be assumed that the subject matter is already known, is already set as part of the task in hand; it is a 'given' of the writing situation. You may have to write on a new product or a matter of law, you may have to communicate about a meeting or a staff grievance, and so on. Whatever the subject, the procedure for writing has much the same stages.

1 Make sure all important aspects of the matter are covered.
2 Set up your main proposition.
3 Prepare any data needed.

COVERAGE

To ensure that you achieve topic coverage, the following questions should be asked of the matter in hand. Consider them as a checklist. Go through the whole list. Doing this can sometimes act to jog the memory about an important aspect of the subject which might otherwise be forgotten.

Ask yourself the following questions and then select appropriate sections from the groups of questions that follow.

Is the matter:

(a) an entity which is current (for example, a machine tool, a contract, or a staff member)?
(b) a group of entities?
(c) an event (for example, a meeting, an exhibition display, or a factory opening)?
(d) a group of events?
(e) a concept (for example, competition between suppliers, contractual obligations)?
(f) a proposition (for example, that new office space should be acquired)?
(g) a question (for example, 'Why did the sales figures fall below expectations?')?

(a) Where the subject matter is a currently existing entity

What are its precise characteristics (*shape, size, dimensions, composition, regulations, membership*)?
To what degree and in what ways could it be changed and still be identifiable as the matter in hand?
How does it differ from things that resemble it?
From what points of view can it be examined?
What sort of structure does it have?
How do its parts work together?
How are its parts put together?
How are its parts proportioned in relation to each other?
To what class or sequence of items does it belong?
Who or what produced it in this form? Why?
Who needs it? Why?
Who uses it? For what?
What purposes might it serve?
How can it be evaluated for these purposes?
Would it be useful to compare or contrast it with something the reader is likely to know? (*This may cause problems if the compared item is not in fact known, or if the comparison raises irrelevant matters.*)

(b) Where the subject matter is a group of entities

(*Add the following to the questions given above for single entities.*)
What makes them a group?
What implications follow from grouping them?
What do the entities have in common? How do they differ?
How are they related to each other if they have no common characteristics?

How could the group be divided? On what basis? To what effect?
Is the group a member of a larger set or class?

(c) Where the subject matter is a current event

What is happening?
Who is doing it to whom or what?
How is it proceeding? At what stage is it?
When and where did it begin, and when and where will it end?
Why is it happening, why did it begin, why will it end?
What caused it? What will be its consequences?
What were the circumstances in which it began and what are the circum-
   stances now?
How does it affect its context? How has its context affected it?
To what other events is it linked, if any?
What, if anything, does it show of some general condition?
To what class of event, or kind of structure, might it be assigned?
Is it good or bad? By what criteria? How were the criteria arrived at?
How do we know about it? How might the reader know about it?
What is the authority for our information? How is that authority to be
   judged?
How might it be altered, repaired or improved?

(d) Where the subject matter is a group of events

(Add the following to the questions given for single events.)
What makes them a group?
What implications follow from grouping them?
What do the events have in common? How do they differ?
How are they related to each other if not by chronology?
How may the group be divided? On what basis? To what effect?
Is the group a member of a larger set or class?

(e) Where the subject matter is an abstract concept

To what practicalities and specificities does the concept relate?
What characteristics must an entity or event have before you would apply
   the concept to it?
How do you distinguish this concept from those closely related to it?
Do others use the term in the same way? How can you accommodate any
   differences to ensure there is no misunderstanding?
Is there a point about the concept that does not fit the present occasion of
   use? Are there several such points?
Has the concept persuasive value for you? In whole or in part? Would your
   reader share this view?

(f) Where the subject matter is a proposition

What prior propositions does it assume?

What implications follow from it?

What must be established for your readers before they will understand and accept (or reject) it?

What are the meanings of the key words in it?

Into what sub-propositions, if any, can it be broken down?

To what class of propositions does it belong?

Can it be compared and contrasted with similar propositions? What distinguishes this particular proposition from the others?

What does it include and exclude?

Should it be anchored to its causes, and should its effects be predicted?

Should any details of the context in which it has arisen be supplied?

How best can the proposition be argued?

How can its truth or falsity be argued – by observation, authority, deduction, or statistics?

What might your reader argue in opposition to it?

(g) Where the subject matter is a question

Why does the question arise?

What does the question assume?

What are the meanings of the key words in it?

How does the question differ from others like it?

What is in doubt? How can it be tested or evaluated?

What answers can you predict?

In what data might answers be sought?

To what would the answers give rise? (*Also refer to the sections on* ask *and* answer *in Chapter 7.*)

This material has been adapted from Richard L. Larson 'Discovery through questioning', *College English* XXX (1968), 126–34.

CHOOSE which questions in the sections above best address the issues and make these the main topics of your particular subject matter.

ESTIMATE from the available evidence which questions your respondent is likeliest to want answered, and which you can handle best, and choose those.

The special case of problem-solving

When setting out to communicate a problematic matter which requires a solution to be contributed either by yourself or another, the following strategies should be helpful.

Where the communication requires a definition of the problem, use the preceding questions to clarify it.

Where the *process* of problem-solving is at issue, ask the following questions:

Who is to solve it?
Does the solver already know the solution?
Does the solver already know the rules for obtaining the solution?
Will the solver learn the correct responses during the task?
Has the solver to select and evaluate operations for obtaining a solution?
Has the solver to reformulate the problem and/or produce some unusual method of solution?
Has the solver to realise that a problem exists at all?
(*Also refer to sections on* advise, direct, *and* inform *in Chapter 7.*)

PROPOSITION

In order to keep focused on the purpose of the communication, it is important to make a careful selection from what should be an oversupply of ideas from those suggested in the section on *Coverage*. Take the ones with most relevance and rank them in order of value, given the purposes of the communication.

If they are not already propositions, put the most important into propositional form. A true proposition is a thesis or theme which can be argued and discussed and developed at length. It can have evidence brought to bear in support or refutation of it. It can form the backbone of the composition. It is the residual element that would be left if the whole text were reduced to one brief summary sentence. It should be the answer to the question 'What do I want to say in this text?' If you cannot reduce it to a single sentence, then you haven't really focused it enough.

The following are all acceptable propositions, in that they assert or deny something and could all be the focal point of a text.

(a) 'Our company needs a formalised grievance procedure.'
(b) 'This machine tool will not do the job efficiently.'
(c) 'These suppliers will not be able to fulfil the order in time.'
(d) 'The Personnel Department has not behaved unprofessionally in this case.'

Practice

Re-examine your old written communications and see if you can formulate their theses. If there is no clear proposition, consider what improvements you could make. It helps to say the proposition out loud; the change to utterance can make the proposition more obvious.

Sometimes, it may help to begin writing the document before the prop-osition has been determined; as the process continues, the proposition may be gradually discovered. But, if this happens, the document will then have to be extensively rewritten to suit the proposition.

Decide whether any subsidiary propositions are necessary. If they are, keep them quite separate from the main one, and make the distinction in importance clear to your reader, if necessary by overt markers or signals.

The next stage is to decide how best to develop the proposition so that your reader will accept it. There are three possible ways of doing this.

1 Use rational arguments. Most negotiators use this as their main strategy, assuming that their readers will accept a good argument. But it may be as well to utilise the other two possibilities to support your reasons.
2 Exert your authority. Use your expertise, your qualifications to write on this matter, your reputation and your experience to defend your pos-ition. Represent these things in your text as seems appropriate, but with due regard to modesty since this will be better received than arrogance.
3 Appeal to your reader's emotions. If the subject matter of the text might produce an emotion such as anger, fear, anxiety or surprise, which could prevent your proposition from being accepted, then write to reduce the emotion: calming the anger, reducing the fear and anxiety, or explaining away the surprise.

If you can take advantage of an emotional response to win your point, then rouse or play upon your reader's emotions. If, as is usually the case, the text is primarily a reasoned account, then consider what methods of reasoning could be best used from among the following:

1 Build the reasoning around the definition of any terms in the proposition which require explanation. We will take as illustration an example given above: 'The Personnel Department has not behaved unprofessionally in this case.' You might define what (or who) you mean when you write 'Personnel Department', and you would certainly need to define 'unpro-fessionally' and 'this case'.
2 Compare and contrast the terms in your proposition with others of relevance, for example the behaviour of other departments with respect to similar cases, or the behaviour of personnel staff in other companies or institutions. The comparison can be made with an idealised Personnel Department, or with the procedural rules with which yours was first set up, or whatever.
3 Consider the causes and effects of the propositional matter, for example the causes of the involvement of the Department, the causes of the case, the effects of the Department's involvement, the effects of the case, or the causes and effects of the accusation stated in the proposition.

4 Investigate the question of what is possible or impossible about the matters in the proposition, for example what might possibly have been done to earn the accusation of 'unprofessional', and what could not possibly have been done. Is it possible that some other department was at fault, or is it possible that the accusation was faulty – perhaps as a political move in an inter-departmental struggle?

5 Consider the past as it affects the matters in the proposition – what did happen, how did it happen, when, where and even why did it happen? If you have little evidence on the matter, ask whether it is probable that it could have happened, why it is thought to have happened, and so on.

Practice

Take some examples of old communications of yours and examine them thoroughly in the light of these possibilities. Are there any particular ways of developing a proposition which you favour? Do you regularly omit any? Among the communications you have received from others, which development strategies do you find most persuasive?

SUPPORTING DATA

Consider carefully, using the topic coverage list, what support your proposition will require. This may be documentation, dates, figures, or references to supporting sources. To ensure this is both relevant and comprehensive, keep the proposition firmly in mind as the focus of the text, and reject figures or tables which though perhaps ready to hand would contribute little to propositional support.

The supporting evidence may also include more general backing for the ideas in the proposition, for example, any testimonials in support of you, your ideas, or this particular proposition. Are there any laws, conventions or precedents useful for your proposition, and so on?

It would be helpful to develop a cross-indexed filing system for such material in order to improve your access to it. The main requirements of such a system are (a) that it has useful markers for the content of the materials, for example by means of keywords and (b) that full details are kept of the information necessary to retrieve the material. Seek advice from those experienced in your field; notice the sources of others' information and add that to your own.

DESIGNING THE TEXT

This involves setting up the text; considering your reader and yourself and determining what style to use; attending to its physical presentation; and ensuring its proper distribution.

The special quality of written communication is that it is a planned exercise within the control of the writer, and it is thus in sharp contrast to spoken interaction. It is important, therefore, to take full advantage of this and produce a well-designed text.

The reading of the text will be performed in quite a different way from that of a hearer listening to another's speech. A reader can stop and start to suit his or her reading needs, and this means that (a) more information can be packed into each sentence (where a hearer could not cope with a dense information flow) and (b) the text's sections must be well signalled, and its propositional material coherently organised, because the reader's attention will move backwards and forwards to suit his or her needs and the ideas will become disordered unless there are markers in the text to prevent this. For example, at sentence level there are such items as *first*, *second*, *however*, *therefore*, *and*, *but* or *finally*, while at paragraph level there could be such signals as 'The most important point is . . .', or 'As an example we could take . . .', and so on. It can be particularly helpful for the reader if there is a thesis sentence early in each paragraph which guides the reader's thinking through a stretch of text.

ARRANGEMENT

As a structural principle to govern the planning of the text design, the following classic five-part composition has much to recommend it.

Introduction

Use some means to ease your reader into the text. In a letter, for example, the first line acknowledging receipt of 'yours of the 1st' can serve this purpose, but it is better to use something of your propositional content. Possible methods include the following.

(a) Explain your purpose briefly.
(b) Indicate the value of your subject matter.
(c) Show how the text came about, for example by request, by command, or generated by your own interest.
(d) Make it of interest to your reader.
(e) Show that the matter has not been treated at all before, or has been badly misrepresented or unfairly dealt with, and indicate that you intend to rectify this situation.
(f) Use a case study or illustration to give your proposition vitality and to rouse emotion in your reader, or choose some aspect of the matter which addresses the particular concerns of your reader. (So, in the proposition about the Personnel Department, details of the case about which the accusation is being made could be provided at the start of the text.)

(g) If you consider that your proposition and the textual means you will use to support it are likely to meet with rejection, then use the introduction to reduce the chances of this happening by apologising, anticipating or answering the rejecter's arguments, and so on.

Statement of proposition

The most important instructions here are to be brief and be precise. Brevity is relative of course, but what it means here is saying just as much as is necessary for a reader to be able to understand the proposition. It should be no more at this stage, with no examples, no qualifications and no irrelevance. Equally, it should not be too brief to be clear; it should not be a shorthand version of your meaning, with too much between the lines rather than in them. Nor should it be so brief as to be too obscure for a reader to grasp without several re-readings. Try to produce the kind of sentence that would be suitable for 'marking' by a reader's pen to highlight it within the text.

Precision is necessary because the proposition will form the backbone of the textual development, and vagueness at this crucial point would render the rest of the text much harder to follow and very much harder to see as an argument or exposition of the proposition's meaning. So, if you consider it useful, briefly define or clarify any terms in the proposition, especially any that your readership could misconstrue because of their lack of specialised knowledge or because they might apply different meanings to the terms.

If your readers are familiar with the kind of proposition you wish to produce, for example if the text is one of a series, or a regular occurrence, and the subject matter is of a well-known kind, the need for brevity is even greater, since you are merely reminding your readers of your proposition and your subject matter, fixing their attention on it in the midst of a host of other texts and propositions that are sitting on their desks. If it is a very provocative proposition it will need to be more fully developed to counter any likely resistance. If it is a very new, unusual or original proposition it will need fuller and more careful expression because it will not be able to rely on the readers' memories of similar ideas but will contain all its own ideas. With such new propositions it is essential that they be well organised and fully explained.

The aim of the statement-of-proposition section of the text is to show off the proposition to the readership, and, like a shop's wares displayed in a window, it should be an honest statement of what will be 'for sale' in the rest of the text. It should present itself as of concern to readers, and should appeal to their interests.

Confirmation of proposition

This section of the text contains the arguments for the proposition. These will be both logical statements in support of it, and also proofs from outside sources, such as statistics, research conclusions, and authoritative support from experts.

The first important decision concerns the order in which the arguments and proofs are offered; one way to decide this is to use the order of elements in the proposition.

To use the Personnel example again ('The Personnel Department has not behaved in an unprofessional manner'), the order of arguments might deal first with the Department, then its behaviour, and then unprofessionalism. If the proposition were that 'we should employ more secretarial staff', then the argument might deal with the topics of 'we', employment, 'more', secretarial staff and staff.

Another order is that of chronology, provided that there is a natural sequence to the events behind the proposition.

Most rhetoricians suggest that the weakest arguments should be put first and the stronger ones at the end, so that the text moves towards strength and not away from it.

If the proposition is likely to attract opposition, then the order of arguments may be crucial; go over the arguments and see if a useful order suggests itself. There may be some obvious precedence among the arguments collected, but, if not, one useful strategy is to begin with those with which the readers are most familiar and would support, and then to move on to the more complex ones with the readers already feeling some support for your argument.

As to what arguments should be used in support of a proposition, this must depend on the particular circumstances of each text's production, but the following suggestions may be helpful.

(a) Build on what you and your readers can agree on.
(b) Move from simple ideas to complex ones.
(c) Be ruthless in cutting out irrelevances which will distract your readers from your point.
(d) Make it very clear which arguments relate to your major points and which to subsidiary ones, so that readers can know what importance to give each one.
(e) If possible, link the arguments to one another so as to make it easier for readers to move from one to another in a smoothly flowing reading process.

Refutation of opposing views

It is not always necessary to do this where, for example, you expect little resistance to your proposition. It may indeed be unwise to do this unless your arguments in refutation are really strong; it would be a pity to raise better opposition to your views than your opponents could. But where it is important to do so,

(a) consider which arguments to select, including those which apply to your major points only, and excluding any irrefutable ones;
(b) do not select the weakest possible opposing argument if it is obvious to your readers that it is too weak to be considered at all;
(c) exaggerate the follies of the opposition, or destroy their supporting evidence;
(d) divide your opponents by focusing on any disagreement among them and stressing its importance;
(e) if one of the opposition's arguments is very strong, take advantage of any badly expressed element in it and expose its weakness, and so try to show that the strong argument is built on weak foundations.

If it looks to be a very even contest between your arguments and those of your opponents, there are two other strategies that might work, but they are not always available for use: one is to build on your authority or status, if you have it, to override the weakness of your arguments; and the other is to put your case as if it is an act of information rather than argument, and hope that it will be seen as non-contentious.

Summing up

If your text is a long one and contains a good many different ideas, opinions, pieces of information, arguments, and so on, then it may need a summary of its main points to round it off.

An alternative ending might be to look to the future, beyond the text's proposition to its consequences (or the consequences of not accepting it). If it is suitable, you could show how the proposition fits into your reader's world. It can make it more easily acceptable if you save the reader trouble by showing how he or she might accommodate the proposition if it were approved.

STYLE

The style in which you write reveals much about the quality of your mind, your personality and your interests. It is therefore worth careful attention in the writing process.

It is certainly true that the earlier matters dealt with in this chapter are of greater significance to the success of the writing than style is; to most readers seeking to read it as part of a negotiation of some sort, a well designed text with an awkward style is more acceptable than a poorly designed text with a clear style. But it is most important to understand that the style of a text is not just a matter of a few elaborations of language superimposed on a text. It was shown in Chapters 1 and 2 that there is a complex relationship between language, culture and discourse, and so the language formulations used (that is, the style) cannot be separated easily from the other elements of composition. So, style should be a constant preoccupation throughout the writing process.

The main considerations when choosing a style of writing are:

(a) the genre of text – that is, whether it is a report, policy statement, letter, account of proceedings, or whatever. Each has different stylistic features;
(b) any precedents set by earlier examples of this kind of text;
(c) the relationship between writer and reader;
(d) your personal qualities, interests and so on.

When examining your text to see how best to use style to your negotiating advantage, the following features need attention.

Choice of diction

Ask whether you have used the correct level of diction for your purpose, which may be anything from providing technical information to persuading someone to do some task. Choices include terms which are:

(a) technical or lay;
(b) rational or emotive;
(c) general or specific;
(d) abstract or concrete;
(e) vague or precise;
(f) formal or informal.

Consider each one in the light of your previous experience of interactions with your reader. Did any set of terms or one particular item of diction cause problems? Did your reader respond badly to any term? If so, avoid it and substitute another next time. Have you heard your reader offer a comment on any general aspect of diction? If so, take it into consideration. Do you dislike the use of any term when others use it? If so, avoid using it yourself.

Practice

Check your files of written texts for instances of diction problems. Analyse the cause of the problem and avoid it in future.

Choice of sentences

First, decide what speech act you wish to perform, like *ask*, *assert*, *refer* or *promise*, and produce it in writing so that your readers can clearly understand what act it is meant to be.

Second, consider what you feel to be an optimum length for a sentence when you read texts in the same genre as the one you are in the process of writing. Check that yours are neither all much longer nor much shorter. Check that there is some variety of sentence length. It can be useful to highlight a good point by putting it into a short sentence surrounded by rather longer ones.

Third, for all your sentences, but particularly the most important ones, for instance the propositional ones, consider whether you have used the right design:

- *simple*, like 'Bill approved the plan' and 'The company considers the report most useful'; or
- *compound*, that is, putting two clauses together where the ideas have equivalent value, like 'Bill approved the plan *and* the company proceeded to use it'; or
- *complex*, using introductory words or phrases like 'if . . . when', 'because', 'since', which relate the clauses in more complex ways, for example subordinating one to another, as in '*Although* the plan was completed on time, it was not accepted'; or declaring one idea is the cause of another, as in '*Because* we were late delivering the goods, we lost the sale', and so on.

When editing your work, consider the effect of moving a clause around its sentence: it may be possible to improve its location. Consider also whether you need a clause at all in some cases; some clauses could be better expressed as words, as in 'The plan, which was the initial one produced, was accepted' which could be edited to read 'The first plan was accepted.' Finally, consider how to control the linkage of your sentences. (See the section on topic control in Chapter 3, pp. 65–6.)

Paragraph design

(a) Check the length of paragraphs in texts of the same genre and use that as a guide.
(b) Put your proposition sentence for that paragraph in a prominent early position.
(c) When editing a paragraph, remove any matter which does not belong to the proposition and relocate it in the appropriate paragraph. If no such paragraph exists, then remove it as an irrelevance.

Text design editing

At a late stage in the composition process, go over the paragraphs to make sure they are in the most effective order both to present your proposition and to make it persuasive.

PRESENTATION

Nowadays there are so many convenient means of presenting texts in attractive ways that there is no excuse for a shoddy presentation. It affects the reader adversely, and so acts as 'noise', preventing the full power of the propositional content from being understood or given careful consideration. The safest advice is to use the best means of ensuring readability of the text: the most appropriate font, the best paper and the best quality of printing. Do not make the presentation too elaborate, for example by sparsity of words per line or page, or too many headings with too little substance, because this acts to inhibit readability.

TEXT DISTRIBUTION

Consider how speedily and widely the text should be circulated. Build up a distribution list, matching subject matter and interested people and adding to it whenever the opportunity arises. The name of each new person encountered in the course of your work should be put into a list and which should be circulated with any relevant materials. For every text produced, distribute it to its primary reader, but also see if others should be sent copies; this might assist you in some future negotiating encounter.

Part IV

Negotiating actions

Chapter 8

Specific speech actions

Speech is an event in itself, not an accompaniment to or a commentary on an event.

INTRODUCTION

A detailed account is given here of a set of specific speech acts, chosen to represent a range of possibilities, including some with significance for interpersonal relationships, or for the achievement of goals, and some with importance for accuracy of information and the representation and development of negotiating content. Some acts are treated here because they very often cause problems, others are here because they occur frequently. Some of the acts are difficult to use because they require careful placement in the negotiation.

In order to know what kind of speech act a particular instance is, there are two guides:

1 Check to see if a speech verb is expressly mentioned in it, as in 'Can I *ask* . . .?', 'I must *apologise*', or 'May I *refer* to . . .?' But be careful, 'ask', 'apologise', and 'refer' may not be accurate names for the acts being performed. Using the name may be just a face work strategy, as in 'May I *ask* you to close the door?', which is a request rather than an act of asking.
2 Think what name would be used in reporting the acts 'Mary asked an important question', or 'Bill argued cogently that . . .'

The aim of the chapter is to provide for both speakers and hearers an increased awareness and understanding of a particular set of speech acts, and to supply a model for the reader to adopt in analysing the other acts experienced in his or her work. Synonyms and antonyms are supplied where they can assist in understanding the precise significance of the choice of act, and some useful variants in phrasing are noted. Examples are also supplied, and they will be of most help if used not only as illustrations to the text, but also as stimulants to memory, reminding you of features of particular acts with which you have been concerned as either speaker or hearer.

The matters raised here have close links with the face work strategies examined in Chapter 4 (pp. 67–75) and the two sets of ideas should be used in conjunction. Perhaps the most important point to note from that chapter is that in order to assess face work accurately, that is, to know whether too little or too much face work is being used, there must be a standard of measurement. Such a standard can be created if you consider a particular speech act in the general terms supplied in this chapter, along with examples from your memory of the degree and kind of face work such an act usually attracts among your fellow negotiators.

The ideas presented here can be used while you are preparing for a negotiation, or considering the implications of one recently completed, and even during an encounter if they can be retained in your memory. The ideas will be remembered more easily if you focus on any point or feature, or whole act, that strikes a chord, makes particular sense, or sounds familiar. This will happen for some good reason; either it has produced problems for you in the past, or you have heard an important person use it with memorable consequences. Choosing which act to perform depends on knowing all the complex circumstances of a particular negotiation. It is up to you to adapt anything found useful here to your own situation. It is hoped that the sample of acts given will set you thinking about other kinds of act, and that you will consider them equally carefully.

General advice

Do not dismiss as insignificant those acts which occur in the bonding parts of an encounter: every act is part of the negotiation.

Though this chapter is about acts used in speech, they can also be performed in writing. The material is intended to be equally useful for the analysis of written acts, provided that you include consideration of the difference that the form may make.

To fit this material into the general socio-psychological aspects of negotiation activities, it is necessary to see each act as part of a broader set. So, for example, speech acts of agreeing, discussing, offering and accepting opinions can be categorised as tokens of the social act 'sharing views'; and accepting and confirming can be seen as part of 'making concessions', and so on. Combining the two kinds of analysis will lead to greater specificity in a socio-psychological account, and to a broadening of significance in a speech–act assessment.

ACCEPT

> **Definition 1:**   to take or receive something offered by another
> **synonyms:**   *receive, take*
> **antonym:**   *reject*

Definition 2:   to agree to some idea or proposal offered by
                     another
synonyms: *agree, consent to, give consent to, acknowledge,*
                   endorse, accede to, yield to
antonym: *reject*

Under both definitions, accepting and rejecting are responses to an offer by another (see OFFER, pp. 189–91), and how the response is managed could either aid or damage cooperation with the first speaker.

Once an offer is made, the rest of the encounter must take some account of it as an act: since it cannot be undone, it must either be accepted or, of course, rejected. A basic acceptance with a minimum of politeness ('Thank you') will have least effect on the status quo, but beyond that some kinds of acceptance can improve the situation while others can injure it. Rejection, whether minimal ('No, thank you'), or not, is always a face work problem, and needs delicate handling.

RESPONSE TYPES

No acceptance

Without acceptance an offer cannot play a further part in the negotiation; so if you wish to stop someone's offer you can do so by:

(a) simply not acknowledging it in any way at all – it may be possible to have an offer founder without either accepting or rejecting it in explicit terms; by simply passing over it you could stop consideration of it, though this may diminish the cooperative atmosphere of the negotiation;

(b) acknowledging it without acceptance, for example 'That's an idea worth considering, but we must first. . .';

(c) giving general acceptance only, for example 'We would be keen to do something along those lines one day' or 'We must see if we can do something about that soon';

(d) setting up a response from another person, for example 'That's OK, but I'm not sure Bill would agree. Bill, would you care to speak on this one?';

(e) setting up a response outside the negotiating group, for example 'I would be keen on the idea but the company could not accept it without . . .';

(f) voicing hesitation (which nevertheless clearly indicates rejection), for example 'Er, em, well OK but . . .'

Acceptance

Whether the offer concerns the giving of personal gifts, prizes or invitations, or, alternatively, the giving of business contracts or brochures, the act of accepting requires a proper demonstration of gratitude if it is to result in satisfactory cooperation. In this it differs from (a) *take*, which is merely a bald receipt of something, and (b) *receive*, which may include some formal acknowledgement. To perform an acceptance you need to provide a degree of acknowledgement commensurate with the giver's right to gratitude, while at the same time preserving your own face. Balancing these two factors can be difficult. On the one hand, displaying too much gratitude for a small thing can mean loss of face as you appear to humble yourself; on the other hand too little gratitude for a great thing can be read as either the absence of proper face recognition for the giver, or arrogance, since you appear to take as only your due what the giver thought was worth more than this.

If the giver reads the response as a mistaken valuation of his or her role, status or position, he or she could then waste time by correcting the mistake, and firmly restating his or her role, etc. Every participant hopes that the others will echo his or her self-valuation, and so a due acknowledgment of it by the others is fundamental to good negotiation. One response is to reciprocate with a gift of relatively equal value. But even if this can be done, and it may be that it can't (because for best results it should be done without delay), there is still a need for some kind of verbal acceptance.

Acceptance of personal gifts

If the act of giving is presented as personal then there should be something personal in the verbal act of accepting it. This could be done by referring to the social bond between giver and receiver. For example, you could give some sign of personal recognition of the other (particularly good are those references which show remembrance of some detail from a previous encounter), as in 'I appreciate the gift, particularly from such an expert on golf.'

Alternatively, you could respond with some personal details of your own, though these should be carefully chosen, since they could give away more than you wish, as in 'Thank you for the splendid diary. It should help me get myself better organised', which implies, jocularly but none the less overtly, that organising is a preoccupation or even a problem: this could be useful ammunition for your enemies. A safer personal touch might be simply to declare an appreciation of some feature of the diary.

In some cross-cultural negotiations the exchange of gifts is a necessary preliminary to business, and a good deal of face work is done through it. In these circumstances a negotiator should have checked with those familiar with the other culture as to the meaning and social value of gifts, so that a correctly formulated acceptance can be produced to match the expectations of the giver, while yet being something that you, as a receiver, can feel comfortable with. Mistakes across cultures may not always produce anger, but they will always reveal ignorance and emphasise differences.

Finally, the wording of the offer could give indications of intention, or attitude towards the ideas or towards the recipient, for example:

'Here is just a small token of our appreciation of your efforts. It cannot hope to compensate for all your work . . .'

This suggests the offerer is not sure about the quality of the gift as recompense. If you wish to accept graciously, your acceptance should support the idea that it is adequate recompense. If an offer is made in these words:

'We hope that you feel able to accept this gift as a token . . .',

this suggests that the offerer is concerned about the social conventions for accepting gifts. And if the offerer says:

'Please accept this gift in the hope that it will be seen as a gesture of our willingness to cooperate on the project',

this appears to hint at a problem about future cooperation, or perhaps an overanxiousness about it.

Acceptance of a business matter

If the thing given is, for example, an informative document, a report, or a contract, then it should be dealt with as a significant move in the negotiation, and examined as a strategy used by the giver. Though it may be a dull or worthless contribution, it may be the only means of joining the discussion for a giver who has few ideas to offer; on the other hand, it may be a tactic to distract or delay, or an attempt to alter some part of the agenda.

As an illustration, at a moment when very general policy matters are being discussed as preliminary to deciding the goals of an encounter, the presentation of a detailed account of some aspect of policy could be intended to thrust that aspect to the forefront of the agenda, for instance:

Chairman: 'Next we must decide whether we can do anything useful at this meeting to try to settle our forward planning with respect to the choice of a new production method, or whether we should leave it till our next meeting.'

Brown: 'Oh, Mr Chairman, if I could just submit the latest figures on the Smith production line, which has just come into my office? I have prepared copies for everyone here. I think they will be helpful in our deliberations.'

The Chairman raised two issues: first, whether it was timely to settle things at the meeting, and second, the issue of forward planning on production methods. He presumably wanted the discussion to deal with them in the order mentioned. Brown's response pre-empted the first issue and sought to move straight to the second; if taken up, it might well waste time causing the production issue to be discussed before members have realised that the discussion is too premature to be useful. Equally, it might well influence the meeting so that when the production methods are eventually dealt with the agenda gives priority either to Brown's ideas, or to his methods of proposing ideas.

A suitable response to Brown's offer, which accepts the giving but yet keeps it in its proper place might be:

Chairman: 'Thank you, Mr Brown, I'm sure that will be a great help; we could look at it when we get onto the study of comparative methods. John, perhaps you could take care of the copies for the moment.'

Acceptance of ideas *or* propositions

This requires even greater care, and in this case several important features of the way they are offered need to be noted in preparing a response, even before the content of the ideas is considered.

First, the offerer's immediately preceding speech behaviours may usefully reveal what gave rise to the idea's introduction at that moment, and show what should be responded to and in what way:

(a) It could be an avoidance strategy, avoiding either the last-mentioned idea or the anticipated next one.
(b) It could show the speaker's goals, or preferred modes of negotiation. So, for example, if he or she often offers a practical proposition after a theoretical discussion, it could indicate that the speaker wants an action-centred outcome. By noting the association of ideas in speakers' offers, your listener can evaluate their general negotiating stances, or changes in them.

Second, consider what kind of active contribution it is. For example, ask the following questions.

(a) Why has any act been performed at all by that person now, and why that particular one?
(b) Did the giver feel it necessary to make some kind of contribution at that point for ego reasons?

(c) Has he or she developed a habit of offering ideas (either generally or just in this interaction) and is it now part of a self-image which the speaker has to live up to?

(d) Has the giver become uncomfortable with the procedures of the negotiation, and is he or she seeking to interrupt or alter them with this offer?

Other responses

Both acceptances and rejections can focus on the act, the person, or the content of the gift. Each produces different results.

The act

Accepting an offer can be done in such a way as to show that it is the act alone which is being accepted, irrespective of its content or who is offering it, for example:

'That's an entirely appropriate suggestion. Are there any others that people wish to make at this point?'

where there is no mention of the person, and the acceptance passes on immediately to calling for other offers as competition for this one.

Another acceptance of similar kind is

'We have just heard the suggestion "that we examine the profit margins rather than the raw profits". I think we could take this point [note that it is not described as "Mary's point"] now.'

Giving only the gist of the offer in this way has the effect of taking the offer away from the original speaker and, by rephrasing it in the accepter's own words, making it seem to be his or her suggestion, with resultant loss of face by Mary.

Rejecting the *act* of offering alone, can be done in the name of ritual or procedure, by suggesting that it is a mistake, either of minor significance, for example:

'Sorry, Bill, but we can't have a new motion until we get rid of this amendment.'

or of some importance, for example:

'I thought I made it clear I would not accept a new idea until we have finished with the present one', or

'No, we must keep to our agreed procedure, otherwise the meeting will degenerate into chaos and we'll get nothing useful done', or

'No, Bill, you yourself proposed that we would leave those matters till our next meeting.'

The person

Accepting an offer can focus on the person who offers it, and can be done by phrasing which emphasises the offerer's role or position, but ignores him or her as an individual:

'An excellent suggestion from the management side' or

'That's a useful proposal from the accounts department. I suggest we adopt it straightaway.'

Alternatively it can focus on the individual:

'That sounds sensible, Mary. Why don't we consider that next?' or

'One of your better ideas, Bill. Let's do that.'

Practice

To decide which form might best please a giver, consider how people name themselves or address others – by role or person – and use this data in your response.

If you sense that the negotiation up to this point has unfairly treated some participant and so created face damage to that person, this could now be rectified in the process of accepting any offer he or she might make, by an appropriately worded focus on the aspect most badly treated.

The *role* of the giver can be rejected by responding with a question such as:

'Is that the view of the people most concerned [i.e. querying whether the speaker is one of these]?' or

'Are you speaking as a representative here?'

and the *person* may be rejected by something like:

'Come on, Bill, that's not one of your better ideas' or

'Are you being serious?'

The content

Focusing on content in the offer can be done by, for instance, saying:

'That's a very good idea. I'm sure we can incorporate that into our scheme, perhaps combining it with . . .'

Here no recognition is given to the person. This is made more obvious if no further speech is directly addressed to that person.

Rejection of content alone can be phrased, with more or less impact, by suggesting that the offer shows unfamiliarity with the topic:

'But that's rather off the point, isn't it? We are supposed to be examining . . .';

or ignorance of the focus of the discussion:

'Perhaps you don't quite understand the major features of this new model';

or a general lack of intellectual ability:

'No, that's just not technically feasible: the sums just don't add up.'

It is also, of course, possible to accept or reject all three aspects of the giving – act, person, and content – though this would be a very powerful response indeed, to be reserved for those situations which appear to need a strong injection of face support for or face rejection of the offerer's contribution. As acceptance one could say:

'That's a useful idea to raise at this point, a very handy contribution, Mary. We have rather neglected that possibility';

or as rejection:

'I said I would take no more production ideas at this point, Bill; we've moved past the preliminaries on methods to the substance of the forward estimates.'

ACCUSE

> **Definition:** to bring a claim of wrongdoing against someone
> **synonym:** *charge*
> **antonym:** *pardon, exonerate*

The act of accusing entails saying that someone has done something which you as an accuser feel to be wrong, that you would like the situation to be put right in some way, and you are taking the first step by making it known to others that the accused has done something wrong. *Accuse* is less formalised than *charge* which is performed in socio-legal formulae and is often accompanied by a written version, and concerns some act which violates some formally determined law or convention. Accusing is a more tentative judgment of wrongdoing, and because it can be found to be inaccurate, an accusation contrasts with the more final act of proving someone guilty.

With this element of informality about it, much will rest on the phrasing of the accusation, since this act allows more flexibility to the accused than does *charge*. It can be made less or more face-threatening, as in the following set of examples, which run from mild to strong:

(a) 'Somebody has not done his job properly.'

This is obliquely addressed, not specific, and not strong in feeling.

(b) 'Your marketing division has let us down badly over this.'

This is addressed to associates of the hearer not the hearer alone, is not specific, has some degree of feeling (in 'badly') and names a consequence of the wrongdoing.

(c) 'You promised to do this, yet I can see no sign of it having been done.'

This is directly addressed to the person and there is an explicit accusation of lack of commitment, but it allows a withdrawal if the accuser has made a mistake, through the loophole of 'no sign'.

(d) 'Your report is late.'

This is bald, direct, and specific.

(e) 'Where is your damned report? It was promised for yesterday. It's most inconvenient.'

This is direct, shows feeling at two points, and names the consequences of the wrongdoing.

(f) 'You are quite inadequate for the job. That's the second time you've failed to submit on time and you've also . . .'

This is strong in feeling, a sweeping accusation, is personally addressed, and mentions a series of wrongdoings.

An accusation presupposes evidence; you must have knowledge of the wrongdoing, of someone specific's involvement, and be able to judge whose responsibility it is. So in preparing an accusation consider the following:

1 Will the accused be specified, and what form of address will be used?
2 Will the deed be specified, and how will it be described?
3 What consequences will follow from the act itself?

4 Will you mention your goal in making the accusation?

If there is any doubt about the truth of the accusation, as you formulate the accusation, allow both the accused and yourself opportunity to save face; be tentative or non-specific about the wrongdoing or about who did it.

If after the accusation has been made you are proved wrong, you can try to put things right by:

(a) apologising;
(b) transferring the blame to the real culprit;
(c) accepting the other's version;
(d) allowing that the wrongdoing might have been less bad than you indicated;
(e) making excuses for your own mistake.

Each of these affects your face to a different extent.

Before making an accusation, you should consider the consequences that will arise for yourself as speaker, the alleged doer, and any specific matters mentioned in the accusation, not to mention the consequences for the negotiation as a whole.

Consequences for the speaker

When you accuse someone, you reveal several things about yourself, for example:

(a) that the matter is one which concerns you enough to speak up about it;
(b) that you are prepared to risk the personal bond with the accused for the sake of the issue;
(c) that you want action (which you may even specify, thus further revealing your attitude to the matter or the person involved);
(d) if the accusation condemns the person as well as the deed, that you disapprove of something about the accused. Any of these revelations might be inappropriate or disadvantageous for you, so consider well whether the accusation is worth the risk.

If the accusation is found to be inappropriate, then you could be seen as too judgmental, non-cooperative, perhaps arrogant, and, of course, wrong: a position from which it will be hard to recover to play a useful part in the negotiation. If on the other hand the accusation is acknowledged by the others to be reasonable, then as an accuser you have distinguished yourself from the group by saying what the others might have been thinking but did not say. This could mark you out as a leading figure in the encounter. However, some of those present may wish the accusation had remained unsaid because of the difficulties it causes; some of them may be affronted that you took it upon yourself to speak on their behalf; others may wish the matter to have been broached in a different way or at a different time. All of these possibilities make it unlikely that there will always be wholehearted or unanimous support for an accusation.

Consequences for the alleged doer

As far as the alleged doer is concerned, once an accusation has been made, he or she may feel forced into self-defence. If this can be easily done, it will not only show you to be wrong, but may cause the defendant to retaliate with his or her own accusations. If the defence is difficult it places the accused in an unwinnable situation; he or she is registered in the minds of those present as having (probably) done something wrong, an opinion which may be sustained well beyond the original matter. Before making such a strong accusation, you should decide whether it would be good tactics to weaken the person in question to such a considerable extent; it might produce sympathy for the accused among the others, so that they withdraw support from you. If the accused is thoroughly discredited, he or she may then feel free to act outrageously, and this could be bad for the whole encounter, and for you in particular as the one responsible.

> You only have power over people so long as you don't take everything away from them. But when you've robbed a man of everything he's no longer in your power – he's free again.
>
> (Solzhenitsyn)

Overall consequences

Once you have made an accusation, its subject matter will be the focus of attention for some period of time. Consider whether this would be appropriate for your own interests or for the interests of the group.

ADVISE

Definition: to give counsel to, to offer an opinion to, to indicate that something is good or bad
synonyms: *inform, suggest, caution*
antonym: *conceal*

Those who perform the act of advising assume (a) that the hearer needs to be advised about something, (b) what it is that the hearer needs to be advised about and (c) that they have the right to offer advice. Each element needs careful thought because a mistake could be badly received.
  The act of advising is a dominant act to perform. It is stronger than informing because of the increased degree of influence the speaker expects

to have over the hearer. Advice concerns, and is intended to direct, the hearer's future behaviour. It does this by recommending particular acts or by suggesting alternatives among possible acts, which, it implies, are good for the hearer. The position that the adviser adopts, therefore, is one of authority, experience, and knowledge, not only about a particular matter, but also about what would be most useful for the hearer to do with respect to it.

Here are some standard advising forms:

(a) 'If I were you, I would ask Bill to organise that',

which assumes a likeness between the speaker and the hearer as the basis for the advice.

(b) 'I always do X . . ., you might find it useful too',

which, first, reveals something of the speaker's own behaviour, and, second, suggests that there would be value for the hearer in a similar act. It does this without presuming too much, and offers the suggestion mildly 'you *might* find it useful'.

If either of these kinds of advice is rejected, then what will be demonstrated is difference between the two negotiators, proving the speaker's sense of likeness is wrong.

(c) 'Why don't you ask Bill . . .?'

This offers the advice freely, with a minimum of influence sought with respect to the matter mentioned, but in doing so it still constrains the hearer to put into words an acceptance or rejection; and this may put him or her into an unwelcome position, for example he may wish to say 'I think I know more than he does.' However, this kind of advice can be rejected in a mollified way because it invites discussion, and reasons can be found which pose no threat to either person's face.

Possible acceptances of the first three kinds would be: 'I already have that in mind. I thought I could do . . . what do you think?', 'I already have', or 'That's a good idea.'

(d) 'You should ask Bill to organise that: he's the expert.'

This example is the strongest demand that the hearer take the advice ('you should') and although it supplies a reason ('he's the expert'), the way this is phrased suggests an oblique criticism of the hearer ('you are not an expert'), and in effect makes it a twofold piece of advice: that the hearer perform the act of asking Bill, while at the same time recognising that Bill is an expert.

This fourth kind may well meet with rejection as too dominant, even if it is good advice, and may result in strong resistance to the speaker's influence as, for example, in:

'I can do it perfectly well [or 'I'd rather get Fred to help]; there's no need to call Bill in.'

The *placement* of the act of advising within the negotiation process must be carefully done; if it is produced too late, and the relevant matter has already been finalised, it will annoy the hearers by its ignorance of this, or be taken to be offering false advice as a form of criticism. The (generally good) advice, 'You should always buy the best equipment', is inappropriate just after the hearer has disclosed that his or her equipment has broken down. Such 'advice' sounds like an attempt to rub the hearer's nose into the mistake, and this is never welcome. Advice offered when the hearer has already decided on an action for the same reasons as those offered by the adviser can be irritating:

A: 'You ought to do X because it will cause Y and Z.'
B: 'I know, that's exactly why I've already done it.'

It can cause irritation in appearing to take away from the hearer his or her individual skill at making a good decision, by showing it to be the same decision another would also reach; or it can be good in showing that there is agreement between speaker and hearer about the act and the reasons for it.

Practice

Before offering advice, see if any clues exist as to what the result might be. If the other is showing signs of concern to save face, then it would be an inadvisable move.

Advising may be an initiating act, as in the examples above, or it may occur in response to a request by another. If it is a response, the speaker-to-be should note the terms in which the request was made, what exactly was required, what has already been done, and what remains to be done, so that the advice can be relevant, timely and useful. Some people appear to seek advice when what they really hope for is support for what they have done, so check whether there are any signals of this in the request.

Although a difficult act to get right, advising is worth doing because it can have two important effects. First, the advice may be accepted, and with it the adviser's thinking, and second, if it works well, it creates a situation in which (a) the speaker is granted a degree of authority, and (b) the hearer acts at the speaker's suggestion. If, however, it is performed badly the speaker could have his or her authority rejected along with the thoughts, and, if it happens often, could appear ineffectual. Bad advice can also create antagonism if it is superfluous, irrelevant or inappropriately timed. At the least the adviser will be seen as unable to read the situation correctly. Bad or unsuitable advice tends to be remembered, along with its speaker, while good advice, that is, an idea which accords with the views of the person advised, is likely to be subsumed without attribution into his or her own ideas, or just remembered as general agreement with them.

ADVICE IN WRITING

When writing the advice, the problem of timing is particularly difficult to get right because of the lapse in time between awareness that advice would be appropriate, the writing of it, and the reception of the written word. It may well be useful, therefore, to err on the side of tentativeness or acknowledge the timing problem explicitly as in some such phrasing as:

'If you have not already done so, perhaps you should consider asking Bill . . .'

ANSWER

There's a simple answer to every question, and it is always wrong.
(H.L. Mencken)

Definition:	to respond to something said by another (for example, a question, a remark that requires a response)
synonyms:	*retort*, *reply*
antonym:	*be silent*, *evade*

Note that *answer* is here taken to be not only the response to a question, but to other types of initiating moves too.

Because an answer is the second part of a speech act pair (see Chapter 3, pp. 47–53 on speech pairs), it forms a joint act with the first part. Such joint acts can demonstrate in miniature the state of a negotiating relationship at a particular time, and are subconsciously judged by participants as such, as well as being recognised as acts concerned with the content of the encounter. It is rarely enough, therefore, to answer with a simple 'Yes' or 'No', since a response has more work than this to perform.

THE WORK ANSWERS DO

The answer needs to take account somehow of the degree of face work in the first move, perhaps acknowledging or acceding to it, or copying it; even resisting it is better than ignoring it, since an imbalance in face work can cause problems for the whole encounter. If these micro-acts are performed badly, the whole negotiation can be put at risk. This is true whether the pair deals with matters of major negotiating importance or more trivial ones. For example, note the different politeness strategies expressed in the following initiating moves:

A: 'I didn't get a copy of the report' or
A: 'Surely I was supposed to get a copy of the report' or
A: 'Am I the only one not to have a copy?'

and in these answers:

B: 'Oh? Well there are copies over there. Help yourself' or
B: 'That's disappointing, I specially wanted you to have one in time' or
B: 'How odd, something must have gone wrong. I specifically asked Bill in your office to deal with this.'

SUCCESSFUL ANSWERS

To produce a successful answer, you must first understand that an answer is expected. This is not always clear: not every speech act requires an answer. The phrasing used may not sound as if it seeks a response, or it may not make clear to whom the remark is addressed, for example:

'We should decide on profit margins soon.'

This could be understood as just an act of information unless the first speaker produces some signal that a reply is needed. Without such a signal you could produce a non-answer like:

'Sorry, I didn't realise you were waiting for me to comment on that' or

'Sorry, did you want me to reply to that?'

Both of these, while giving a minimal apology, also contain recognisable criticism of the first speaker, which may strain future relations between the two.

The second thing to try to understand is the underlying *intention* of the first part of the pair. To do this, its face work should be noted for its kind and quantity, for any emphasis made, and for any focus on particular ideas or attitudes. Then you must decide what will be answered, what not, and the degree of responding politeness.

EVASIVE ANSWERS

While the pair must be related in content, the answer need not contain a response to every single matter raised in the first part. For example, given the question

'Have you got the date of the meeting so we can organise the venue?'

if it would produce problems for you to raise the matter of 'organisation', it could be sufficient to answer only 'It's June the fifteenth.'

Answers can be more completely evaded in various ways, for example, by throwing them back at the asker:

A: 'Have we got time to discuss this today?'
B: 'Do you think that would be a good idea?'

or by producing a response which sounds as if it is part of, or on the way to, an answer, but which may never be intended to get there:

A: 'Does this mean we need to increase the price for our overseas customers?'
B: 'What percentage profit did we estimate for the national customers . . . and how many did we estimate we'd sell at that price . . .?'

The Matarazzo Effect mentioned in Chapter 5 suggests that people produce short answers to short questions, and long ones where the questions are long; a similar effect applies also to many other speech pairs. Consider carefully whether the effect is influencing your answer's length adversely, and be careful not to get caught up in someone else's rhythm of exchanges.

Other aspects of responses seem also to be affected by the nature of the initiating move. For example, the degree of precision or the amount of detail in the initiating move sets up a pattern which can influence the answer, so a vague comment like 'I suppose we should also have a word about X' is likely to produce a vague answer like 'I suppose so', and this could happen even though you might have a more detailed response in mind. Strangely enough, one consequence might be that the vagueness of the answer is judged to be a consequence of some inadequacy on the part of the respondent rather than something set in train by the initiator, particularly if the answer is more crucial to the encounter than the first move was. Do not let the formal patterning of the first move have an undue effect on your response.

APOLOGISE

Definition 1: to express regret for one's own past actions or for those of someone for whom one has responsibility

Definition 2: to indicate one's reservation about an intended action which might adversely affect the hearer

In the first case, the act of apologising involves a face-threatening act for the speaker, because it acknowledges that he or she has performed an act which others (may) condemn. Since it aims to redress a situation involving the speaker's 'fault', it depends on a recognition that a regrettable event has occurred and that blame has been attributed. Speakers must be sensitive to the possibility of their being at fault, and must note the signals of condemnation in others if they are to be aware of the need to apologise. In a cross-cultural situation this may be problematic, since what is a fault in one culture may not be so regarded in another, and in many cases the signals may take a different form. The preferred forms of remedial activity may also differ, with apology as only one possibility, though it is the favoured act in most English-speaking communities.

In the second case, an apology acknowledges that a future act of the speaker is likely to attract blame. In many cases it is a pre-emptive attempt to reduce the personal aspects of the blame, often taking the form 'I'm sorry but I will have to . . .' or 'I'm sorry if it causes problems, but we must deal with . . .', where the tokens 'have to' and 'must' indicate necessity and suggest that some external force is prompting the action, rather than the personal whim of the speaker. These apologies give deference to others, and allow them the opportunity to prevent a troublesome act if they so wish. They can also deny the hearer the opportunity to complain.

Apologies may be performed in any of the following ways.

Showing deference

You may recognise, for example, that the status, role, or person of the other negotiator deserves acknowledgment, or that his or her time or work has been wasted. Deference can be shown by acknowledging that your lower status or lesser role rendered the act in question inappropriate. This is a less acceptable mode of apologising in those cultures or communities or groups which profess a strong commitment to equality, for example in North American, British and Australian communities. When it does occur, apologisers may be thought to present themselves as too humble or insecure; but note that self-deprecation is the preferred mode in China and Japan.

Admitting the offence

This can be done either specifically as in 'I've lost your pen' (where both the doer of the offence and the offence are named) or more generally (excluding perhaps both the doer of the offence and its details) as in 'There's a slight problem.' The offence can be accepted in whole, 'It was my fault entirely', or in part, 'I must accept some of the blame for that.'

Apologies can be purely formal, for example 'We deeply regret the inconvenience caused by the delay in shipment', or 'I must accept responsibility for the work done by my departmental officers.' These tokens manage to involve little loss of face, since in the first example the standardised formality of the expression distances the speaker from engagement with the act of 'delay in shipment', and in the second demands attention to the superior status of the speaker.

The apology can be made in such a way as to diminish the offence, either (a) by reducing its impact, or (b) by explaining that there were good reasons for the fault occurring. Such forms as these could be used:

(a) 'I've lost that old pen of yours, I'm afraid, but you'll be able to get a new one, no problem', or 'I've mislaid your pen for the moment, but it must be here somewhere. I'll find it for you later.' Neither of these may be acceptable to the hearer, since the former seeks to downgrade the value of his or her pen, and also leaves it to the hearer to make good the loss rather than the one who did the losing; and the latter pays scant regard to the hearer's immediate need for the pen.
(b) 'I've lost your pen, I'm afraid. We've had an office removal and several things have gone astray', or 'I'm afraid I've lost your pen; it was so like my own that I mixed them up and gave it to my son, and he broke it at school.'

On the whole this is much more acceptable as a strategy, though it may reveal that further faults have occurred (in the second case by not checking whose pen was given to the son).

Expressing an attitude of regret

Strong expressions of regret can be made using phrases such as: 'I am extremely sorry . . .' or 'It's been worrying me since last week that I lost your pen.' This is a favourite in many European countries. In Germany, for example it is common to use the form 'It gives me pain that I've . . .'

Asking pardon

This can be done in an attempt to restore the equilibrium of the encounter. It can take many forms in different cultures: 'Excuse me' in North America and France, 'I beg your pardon' in British English, and 'I ask for forgiveness' in Persian. The ultimate expression of asking pardon is to declare that there can be no excuse, or that the offence is too bad to pardon: 'I'm sorry, that was quite unpardonable of me.'

Offering to make restitution

This may be for damage caused, or to replace a loss: 'I'll buy you another pen just like it.'

In some cases, it may be clear that an apology is expected, but the person 'at fault' may disagree, or may feel unwilling to take the blame, in whole or in part. Fault, of course, may be in the eye of the beholder rather than performed by the doer, but in either case its presence is an important factor in the interaction, and needs to be dealt with if the negotiation is to have a successful outcome. A refusal to apologise, where one is requested explicitly or implicitly, is a very uncooperative act, and can stop the negotiation in its tracks. So the loss of cooperation involved in not apologising must be weighed against the loss of face in performing the apology. A good strategy may be to tender a formal apology, which can be done with relatively little face loss. It is also possible to apologise in such a way as to indicate that one is merely complying with the request of the other person, without in any way agreeing with the need for the request, or conceding that the blame is appropriately ascribed, for example by saying in the first case, 'Well, if you feel an apology is called for, then of course I apologise', and in the second case, 'I'm not sure what I am supposed to have done, but if you are feeling offended, then I regret it, and apologise.'

Recognising that an apology has occurred is not always easy, since some speakers may put such energy into not losing face, that they produce very oblique forms of the act. The tone of voice may be the only indication of how seriously the act is meant; some people can make 'sorry' into an insult.

The standard reactions to apologies each brings a different social value to the relationship between the apologiser and the offended. The forms used include:

(a) simple acceptance: 'That's OK';
(b) acknowledgement of the difficulties involved in apologising: 'Never mind', 'Don't mention it', 'Don't worry';
(c) concern for the loss of face of the apologiser: 'Not at all', 'It's nothing';
(d) maintaining equilibrium: 'There's no need to apologise';
(e) refusal: 'I don't think you should apologise', 'Why are you apologising? There's no need.'

ARGUE

The best argument is the one that seems to be merely an explanation.

> **Definition:**   to present reasons for or against something; to contend with another's reasons, to maintain a view with reasons
> **synonyms:**   *debate, discuss, quarrel*
> **antonym:**   *agree*

A typical beginning to an argument could be:

'We need to settle this point: I would want to argue that . . .'

This example encodes the most important factors in the definition of argument as an activity, namely:

(a) that it is a joint activity;
(b) that it could end in settlement (rather than just in winning and losing);
(c) that it is about 'points' made and responded to; and,
(d) that there can be both a personal element in argument, and a distancing from the personal, as shown in the apparently (but not really) hypothetical use of the word 'would' in the phrase 'I would want to argue'.

Arguments place speakers in positions and roles, and raise subjects which can be good or bad for the negotiation seen as a whole, so they should be treated warily.

WHY ARGUE?

What is the point of arguing when there can be no guarantee that the outcome will be a resolution of differences? Fortunately, its virtues are many, so it may be worth risking. For example, it can produce an acknowledgement among the group that judgments on a particular matter are relative, and that differences have to be accepted (which may prove a useful negotiating move). And it can bring to notice aspects of the matter which one or other of the negotiators has not considered previously, and so deepen the complexity of the negotiation and render it a more comprehensive event.

A speaker can either start an argument or join in one set up by another.

STARTING AN ARGUMENT

In starting an argument, you make the assumption that there is actual or potential disagreement, or difference of opinion, about some aspect of the negotiation, and you choose the act of arguing to solve the problem, on the assumption that this can be done through the exchange of reasons.

You must be certain that there is disagreement, because if wrong about this, you will be seen as misinterpreting the situation, or as being argumentative, that is, preferring conflict to cooperation.

Because introducing an argumentative speech act creates the possibility of a sustained set of speech acts (if other participants take up the points raised), you should consider whether this is a suitable development for the time and place.

To make certain that a difference of opinion will come to a satisfactory end, it is important not to be so forceful in expressing your opinion or in rejecting the other's that it would make it hard to end in agreement. In an oppositional argument potential face loss is always a major factor, so you should phrase your acts to ensure that face loss is minimised. One way to do this, if you appear to be winning, is to make it unnecessary for the other to have to make a final statement of capitulation like

'OK, I think you have convincingly won this one.'

You can prevent this by anticipating your win and ending the matter yourself, with some such phrase as

'I'm sure I've said enough on this matter. If we are agreed on it, we should move on to the next item on the agenda.'

This requires the loser only to give a minimal agreement signal, or even say nothing at all.

If another starts the argument, then you should consider whether to take it up or not; it takes two to have an argument. You should think whether the matter is of sufficient concern to everyone to spend time on. (If just a few of a large gathering engage in an argument, it can isolate them and hinder the majority from getting on with its business, and hence be resented.) Injudicious arguments can be ignored, or met with silence (which indicates rejection without specifying any reasons), or postponed, either neutrally or with some judgment incorporated:

'We can't really argue about that without more data.'

'That's not relevant now; we've moved to Item 7 of the Agenda.'

'Good idea, but let's leave it till . . .'

By listening carefully to the act by means of which an argument is started, you can learn:

(a) what subject the speaker thinks is important enough to argue about;
(b) from what position the argument is launched; and
(c) what the speaker's attitude is towards the subject or towards the act of arguing itself.

This may be useful information to know, whether or not the argument is taken up. Note whether fellow negotiators have certain subjects they are prepared to argue about whenever they happen to come up. Consider whether their attitudes are common to all their arguments and see whether they constantly use the same strategies. All of these could be important clues to their major concerns, attitudes, or goals.

LOSING AN ARGUMENT

When losing an argument yourself, you should accept any face-saving tactics offered by others, or bow to the inevitable as gracefully as possible. A touch of humour may work well, or an act which makes the moment as productive as possible, for example:

'Well, I seem to be on my own on this one. Perhaps we had better leave it and stick to what we can agree on. As I understand it, we agree on . . .'

Though you have lost the battle, you are trying to win the war by influencing the next part of the agenda.

Whether starting an argument or responding to one, you may be able to influence the agenda of the whole negotiation by carefully selecting which aspects of the argument to deal with. You can justify your selection in such forms as:

'*In my view* the most important matter to be decided is . . .'

'That [idea of yours] is *merely a detail*, but what we *really* need to consider is . . .'

As the argument progresses the participants may become more or less personally engaged or emotionally involved, and you would be wise to keep a close eye on variations in others' involvement, monitoring them for their usefulness to your goals.

Arguing differs from the roughly synonymous acts of debating, discussing and quarrelling in the following ways: it is less structured than *debate* – less polarised – and does not involve formalised turntaking; it is less free-ranging than *discuss* and it differs from *quarrel* in being less personal, and less emotional. Arguing should be conducted from within a negotiating position rather than with a strong personal emotion, for example:

'As representative of the group I feel I must take issue on this one',

rather than

'I can't stand people who do not fulfil their promises.'

Emotion need not be excluded, but it should very seldom be directly expressed; it is better to introduce it in reported form, as in

'I should be extremely annoyed if we did not come to a decision on this now'.

which would be better received than

'For heaven's sake, come on, let's get this damned decision made.'

ASK

Definition 1:	to seek to be informed about, to put a question to
synonyms:	*inquire, question, query, interrogate*
Definition 2:	to seek through words to have something done
synonym:	*request*

ASKING FOR INFORMATION

Asking as a speech act is an exploratory act, which could lead the interaction in as many directions as the answerer wants to go. It can be used for several purposes:

(a) To produce new information.
(b) To seek clarification of given information.
(c) To check that something said in the negotiation has been understood.
(d) To require evidence from others, which supports their opinions, and so on.

Ask differs from its synonyms in that it is a directly interpersonal act which calls upon another to speak in response, setting up a speech pair. It is therefore unlike *inquire*, which is a more formal and impersonal act, often part of a routine set of speech activities, which people use when they wish to activate a standard communication procedure. It is therefore a less specific imposition on the hearer at a personal level, since he or she is required only to perform a routine behaviour as his or her role dictates. In the following example the respondent quite routinely passes the imposition on to another:

Bill: 'Madam Chair, I'd like to inquire what has happened in the matter we discussed last week.'
Mary: 'Fred, that's your department.'
Fred: 'It is currently being implemented by my staff.'

Questioning and querying imply disagreement with or reservation about the point at issue, while asking is quite neutral in attitude towards the point. Asking differs from interrogation which is a purposeful series of blunt questions, often performed by an official to a lay person, as in court. The choice of *ask* as the speech act to be performed is therefore appropriate where what is required is an informal, personal act of addressing a single question to a particular hearer.

Asking introduces several factors into the negotiation. First, it assumes that the hearer would not volunteer information without being required to by the speaker. This may be a false assumption, and if so, you run the risk of annoying the hearer. Second, asking can strongly influence the answers that may be given in response to it, and can establish a set of constraints to produce the preferred response, thus impinging upon the hearer's freedom of action and his or her negative face to varying degrees, depending upon the type of question asked.

Open questions

Completely open questions like

'Should we do X?' or
'Did you say X?'

allow a full range of responses because they are framed very broadly, and use few words which the response needs to take up.

There are also partially open questions, which focus the response more narrowly by asking about the how, who, what, when, where or why of something, and so constrain the response to deal at least with that, though it may go on to other aspects of the 'something'.

Closed questions

There are different types of 'closed' questions. Some constrict the possibilities for responding by mentioning so many things that are to be responded to that there is little room for manoeuvre, for example:

'Do you want to consult with your accounts section on this?',

which uses the words 'want', 'consult', 'accounts section' and 'this', each of which requires some kind of recognition from the respondent, leaving little room for new possibilities.

There are also closed questions which set up a *yes* or *no* answer, and force the respondent to produce one or the other, when he or she may not wish to do either, for example:

'Do we have a letter from them on this?'

Another type of closed question expects only one response and makes it difficult for the respondent to deviate, for example:

'It's X, isn't it?'

'Most people think X, do you?'

'It's obvious this is the only reasonable thing to do, don't you think?'

Finally, there are other, less obvious forms of closed questions, such as:

'What problems did your marketing division find with this one?', that is there must have been *some* problems.

'Do you have a policy on this?', that is you should have one.

'Can we discuss . . .?', that is I want to, or we must.

'Do you mean that?', that is you should not mean that.

Rhetorical questions

Some acts which resemble acts of asking are not real questions at all, but empty 'rhetorical questions' to which no answer is sought:

'Is it any wonder the product was faulty?'

'What difference does it make?'

A negotiator might wish to produce one of these because they provide opportunities to bring into the encounter such things as self-praise, or to register a strong personal emotion which would normally need to be omitted from negotiation, but which could be inserted by means of such forms as:

'Didn't I tell you that would happen?' or

'For heaven's sake, what difference would it make?'

ASKING FOR SOMETHING TO BE DONE

Asking also has a second meaning, that of seeking to get something done, and it is often used as a polite form of requesting. Where such a form is required, the speaker could use some of the indirect face work strategies mentioned in Chapter 4, pp. 74–5, for example:

'Should we discuss the problem now?', which is a command to discuss, or

'Can we ask you to reconsider that?', which is a command to reconsider.

As a hearer you should explore what politeness strategies the act incorporates, in order to judge the degree of authority taken by the speaker, the degree of the request's imposition, and the face work involved.

Asking can also be a problematic speech act because it can introduce subject matter that the respondent finds awkward, difficult, or embarrassing to handle. Yet such is the force of the asking move that some response must be forthcoming. It could be face-threatening to ask such questions as 'How did the promotion go?' to someone who has just failed to get promotion, and who would prefer not to have the subject raised at all, but once it has been asked he or she must answer. An asking act, like any other speech act, is virtually inescapable, because whatever the respondent does, from falling silent, to joking lightly, or changing the subject, will be read as a response. Thus the avoidance of a 'straight' answer in this case will be understood as meaning a failure to get promotion. So think carefully before introducing a topic in this way, because of its potential for social trouble and damage to relationships.

ASSERT

In England it is bad manners to be clever, to assert something confidently. It may be your personal view that two and two make four, but you must not state it in a self-assured way, because this is a democratic country and others may be of a different opinion.

(George Mikes)

Definition: to state as true what others could see as debatable
synonyms: *inform, affirm, defend*
antonymns: *deny, question, be negative about*

SIGNALS OF ASSERTION

Assertion is an act which provides information for agreement by others; it tells of something the speaker thinks is true and wishes the hearer to accept. It can be recognised by the presence of one or more strong signals of attitude, as in the following examples:

(a) 'Obviously, as you know, the X is . . .'

Here *obviously* and *as you know* imply it is within the knowledge of the hearer, and hence already agreed. If the hearers do not know it or are not in a position to know it, the phrase could be a strategy to make them appear small. A sensible response in this kind of situation might be:

'How could I know that? Only an expert on the matter could, and you know that I'm not required to be that kind of expert.'

(b) 'In my mind I am utterly convinced that X is so.'

The implication here is that the speaker has been absolutely convinced by some (unmentioned) proof, and that the hearer should take the speaker's word on the matter. The token *utterly* may be worth particular study. Compared to synonymous alternatives such as *absolutely* or *thoroughly*, it has a mild note of personal emotion. The speaker is, then, investing something of his or her emotion in the assertion, and will therefore be very unlikely to adjust it in the face of argument or criticism, because personal attachment to an opinion is harder to alter than logical attachment.

(c) 'There is no question but that X is the right way to proceed.'

There is no question but means 'Do not question my assertion', and acts as a covert command not to ask a question. Contrarily enough, however, the very presence of the word in the assertion raises the possibility that a question could be asked; perhaps the speaker is seeking to prevent questioning precisely because it is likely to occur.

(d) 'The most crucial factor in this business is . . .'

Here *most crucial* means 'my assessment of the factors leads me to judge this one to be the most crucial', though no discussion, arguments, or proofs are offered.

(e) 'Smith is a very important client of ours so you should agree . . .'

The assertion *very important* rests on the 'argument' that because Smith is involved with the speaker's firm he must be worth agreeing with.

(f) 'The technical details provide no problem at all and can safely be left to us. What we need to consider now is . . .'

This makes three extremely confident assertions: there is no problem; details can safely be left to us; and we need to do something now. Among the multiplicity of issues, one or other may be left unresisted by the hearers, and it will then appear that the speaker has had that assertion accepted.

(g) 'Bill produced an excellent report on this, in which he says . . .'

This assumes that the speaker knows the person concerned well enough to call him 'Bill', and that his work is 'excellent'. In effect, when people say such things, they imply that their own reputations are so good that those of their close colleagues must be good too. The use of 'excellent' here is worth particular study. It may be being used as a loose assertion about the quality of Bill's work in general, with no particular application to the 'report', or it may be specifically applied only to the report. If the latter is the case, the statement leaves vague what is actually excellent about the report, and is typical of the way assertions differ from arguments. An argument would need to supply some reasons for the judgment of 'excellence'.

Asserting differs from informing as an act by containing extra force because the speaker anticipates that the hearer may need to be persuaded to accept what is asserted. Informing, where the speaker is less concerned with the hearer's reactions, is produced with less attempt at persuasion. Assertions differ from affirmations because they relate to matters which are susceptible of proof, while affirmations declare a belief in some generally accepted matter which is to be taken on faith, as, for example, 'People are basically good if they are given the chance to be.' Asserting an opinion is stronger than defending one, which occurs as a response to disagreement, or appears to expect it; if an opinion is defended too strongly, it may in fact *create* disagreement because it is in effect anticipating it.

SOCIAL IMPLICATIONS OF ASSERTION

Using an assertion will have certain social implications for the negotiation. The speaker is usually revealed as having a strong commitment to the view asserted. However, if it has been already raised as a matter of concern to all, then the assertion may only be a sign that the speaker shares the general view and wishes this to be known.

Alternatively, if the assertion is one which deals with a potential outcome of the negotiation, like 'It is *absolutely definite* that we will be able to produce them on time', it can indicate either that the speaker expects doubt in others and is seeking to remove it, or that he or she has a sense of doubt about the timing of production. It would obviously be important for a hearer to try to determine which is the prime meaning.

In general, because an assertion is an act which does not bring any proof to bear upon the matter it expresses, it assumes that the word of the speaker will be enough. This bespeaks a self-confidence which is worth noting. A hearer would have to judge whether the confidence is warranted. If not much proof is needed, the assertion could display a reasonable confidence; but if a good deal of proof is needed, and little or none offered, it could demonstrate arrogance. A hearer can use the tone of voice to distinguish the kind of confidence being displayed; different tones can differentiate assertion, aggression, the statement of an agreed commonplace, and the expression of individual particularity. Whatever the eventual judgment, an assertion should certainly not be allowed to pass without consideration of what it reveals of the speaker's sense of self and his or her attitude towards others in the negotiation.

The proof that is not supplied in an assertion can be of several kinds, and the difference between these kinds can provide clues as to what meaning to attribute to the assertion.

(a) The proof may be something that is quite obvious to the speaker who is (known by the others to be) an expert in the matter, and therefore the assertion is quite acceptable without explanation. If the others are experts in the matter too, it is unnecessary to detail proofs; this kind of assertion is simply an efficient way of registering a view that will meet with a reasonable hearing – it need not be developed further than that.

(b) The proof may however be quite wrongly assumed to be known by the others; they may in fact be ignorant of it. This situation may simply arise because the speaker does not know them well, but it is also possible that the speaker may make a deliberately false assumption of their knowledge for some tactical purpose, for example to have them appeal to his or her own superior knowledge for an explanation.

(c) The speaker may assume that the others could easily supply the proof if they thought a little about it because it is a matter of general knowledge, in which case the speaker is only asking them to do a little work instead of doing it for them. But, equally, the speaker could be pretending to expect the hearers to know (while in reality being aware that they are ignorant) in order that they should accept the assertion rather than reveal their ignorance and in the process lose face.

GOALS OF ASSERTION

The main goal of an assertion is to have the view that is expressed accepted without discussion or question. Therefore hearers should consider whether they are willing to concede it. If they think that it is inappropriate or even unacceptable, it is worth asking whether it needs questioning, and whether this can be done immediately or should be left till later. Although an immediate resistance to an assertion may lead to a lengthy argument or discussion at a time when this would sidetrack the negotiation, the alternative of returning to it later is often difficult. As matters move on, it is often hard to return to an earlier topic, and, in any case, the speaker may well resist any attempt to return to it, on the quite reasonable grounds that the assertion has already been accepted without debate, and therefore the objectors are going back on their word – an important criticism of a negotiator.

COMPLAIN

> **Definition:** to express unease, dissatisfaction, or censure; to find fault in something or somebody
> **synonyms:** *grumble, deplore*
> **antonyms:** *praise, approve*

Complaining presents a difference in attitude from grumbling, which has a surly ill-tempered tone. It also differs from deploring, which includes signs of deep concern. The act of complaining itself may indicate relative indifference towards the matter complained of, but there must have been enough feeling to cause the speaker to speak at all about the matter:

'It is far too late to settle this now. It should have been done earlier.'

'Surely it is too late to consider this now . . .'

Many complaints, because of the personal element involved, occur in the bonding parts of the encounter, where they can provide useful tactical information for the negotiation proper.

Some complaints are generalised expressions of unease, as in:

'We really need to get on faster than this',

where the speaker's aim may simply be to have the complaint registered, so that the hearers know how negatively the speaker feels.

On the other hand, because a complaint concerns the speaker's lack of ease or satisfaction, it is always informative about some personal aspect of the speaker. In the example above, we learn that he or she wants negotiations to be conducted at a fastish pace. In presenting this feeling the speaker may be seeking sympathy ('This is how I feel: share my feelings') or be requiring some act from the hearers to improve his or her emotional state. If the purpose appears to be to get sympathy, it at once puts the speaker on an unequal footing with the others, who have no such complaint. In the giving and receiving of sympathy there is always an inequality, as one without a problem offers support to one who has a problem. By expressing a complaint the speaker *causes* this inequality, and it is often a difficult one for both parties to handle. Requests for sympathy are often badly received because many people feel that their sympathy should be freely offered, rather than required of them.

The complaint made may be of very minor significance, as in:

'The traffic today is impossible',

which can mean 'I had a bad time getting here. Acknowledge this, or make allowances for me', or of more importance, as in:

'It is just impossible to rely on any supplier these days',

which may just mean 'My work is difficult to do successfully. Sympathise with me', but which can also indicate that 'relying on suppliers' may be a problem in the negotiation. In any event the content of the complaint should be noted for future reference.

A speaker who offers too many complaints, of whatever kind, will be perceived as unpleasant, because the acts put the hearers into a position which they may feel is unjustified and unproductive, particularly if the hearers feel that they are the ones who should be receiving sympathy, not giving it to others. If the complaint is seen by its hearers as wrong, there is not much that they can do; to defend the matter may be to sidetrack from the main part of the negotiation, while to explain that the speaker is mistaken may cause antagonism. If the reponse to the first example about the traffic is

'Oh surely it is not as bad as that',

this questions whether the speaker has the right attitude to the situation; while in this response to the second example,

'But it wasn't a matter of the suppliers being at fault, it was . . .',

the speaker's judgment is called into question. Neither act will produce a good result for cooperation. Yet by leaving a weak or false complaint unchallenged, the hearer could begin to feel a sense of antagonism towards the speaker.

Practice

Consider, if you can, your own complaints, their subjects, the attitudes they reveal, and what they require from others. Consider what your usual response is to each type of complaint by others. To what particular aspects do you address yourself? Are you aware of any one who is an expert at handling complaints? Could you copy any of his or her responses to improve your own response acts?

In some cases the complaint produces an agreement with what the speaker has said, in order to show that there are shared feelings (whether this is true or false) or experiences (with or without shared feelings), as in

'Yes, I know, we had the same problem.'

As in question and answer speech pairs, there appears to be a power in complaints that leads the second speaker to use the same terms, or to speak in the same pattern of words as the first. It may be important to guard against doing this, because of your response's implications. For example, if you reply as above, you are firstly admitting to a problem, and secondly saying that it is the same as that experienced (and perhaps handled badly?) by the first speaker. Though you are simply being supportive, if you were to use the same words as the first speaker, this quite different interpretation could be made by others listening.

Generally speaking, in Western cultures, there is little of positive value in making a complaint unless it is one of those for which the hearer can supply a practical remedy. But in cross-cultural negotiation remember that the expression of an emotional or personal complaint may be an acceptable or even a required element. In some cultures a speaker who does not volunteer to share something about his or her feelings, both good and, as here, bad, may be considered to be hiding them for some possibly underhand purpose. More specifically, some cultures, for example Polish, use different forms of complaint according to whether the focus is on the intent of whoever caused the damage, or on the possibility of repairing the damage.

CONFIRM

Definition:	to corroborate or verify, to make valid or binding, to make certain
synonyms:	*testify, answer*
antonym:	*deny*

To confirm is to add the weight of one's views in support of an idea which has been communicated earlier. It differs from testifying, which is an extremely formal act involving the production of proofs as corroboration. Confirming is a more personal act, and only corroborates through speech; it may not supply proofs at all. Confirming differs from answering because it is always in support of the prior act to which it is linked, whereas answers can vary.

There are several features of confirming which have social significance. A confirming act is a response to another speech act or set of acts, or to non-spoken behaviours, either within a negotiation or not. A speaker can confirm his or her own earlier acts or confirm those of another. To confirm one's own earlier view is to register it very clearly at that moment in the negotiation and to bring it back to people's notice. You may wish to do this to show that any problems or uncertainties about the view have now gone:

'I am now in a position to confirm that the problem of supply that I mentioned earlier has been solved . . .'

Also, confirmation can demonstrate commonality between the first speaker and the one who confirms. Someone who asks for confirmation may wish only for this, without needing explanations or proofs. Occasionally corroborations are sought for what appear to be trivial matters; this may be a signal that the seeker needs some indication that his or her view is shared at that point in the negotiation.

Practice

It would be worth thinking why this need for confirmation of a shared viewpoint arises. Is it a sign of some sensed disagreement which should be put right? Is the disagreement about something other than the matter raised for confirmation, i.e. is the confirmation displaced from its proper focus for some reason?

A confirmation may be a voluntary response or one demanded by another. Demanding a confirmation suggests an uncertainty in the first speaker about his or her views. This may arise from a due modesty in the person, or be a reasonable acknowledgement of another's superior knowledge. It may indicate some hesitation about a detail of the matter being discussed. If you are asked for confirmation you should note carefully the focus and emphasis of the request to see what exactly is required of you. In a request such as:

'Remember we were discussing this last week – that's OK with you isn't it?',

there is only a very vague statement to confirm, and there could be unwelcome consequences if, for example, you have forgotten an item which you do not wish to confirm. Check what exactly was 'discussed' and what would be entailed by a confirmation; for instance, will there be some action required of you? The example implies that some matter was settled; perhaps this is not true, but the speaker is trying to have it taken for granted. If in doubt do not confirm. All likely possibilities should be examined before producing the required response.

Confirmation is always an imposition, whether accompanied by verbal, moral or personal pressure, so you should think carefully before requiring it of others. How much of an imposition would a particular instance be? Is an involuntary confirmation worth the trouble? Can a forced confirmation be relied on, if the request is put like these?:

'You must agree with that, for goodness sake!'

'Surely you cannot disagree with that. It's just common sense!'

If you as hearer are asked for confirmation, and are prepared only to agree in part, you should tread carefully, noting that a refusal to confirm can bring into the open a degree of disagreement which would be counter-productive. At the very least it could involve face loss for the one seeking confirmation.

The following are examples of useful responses which reduce disagreement as far as possible.

(a) 'We wouldn't be prepared to say that at this point.'

In this example 'we' reduces the personal aspect of the refusal, making it that of an unspecified group 'we'. This could be damaging, however, if it is taken to mean a large number disagrees, or, worse, everyone present in the negotiation. 'Prepared to say' is less oppositional than 'say' alone; while 'at this point' allows the possibility that confirmation is only postponed and may be given later.

(b) 'That sounds reasonable but I just have one small problem with it.'

Here, partial confirmation is suggested, and the difficulty is declared to be of minor importance.

(c) 'Not exactly, though I'd agree up to a point.'

Here, only a low degree of confirmation is given, as well as a negative response, with no specificity about what is being confirmed and refused.

(d) 'I couldn't commit myself to that without more consideration.'

Here confirmation is postponed until some unspecified matters have been dealt with. All four examples allow the one asking for confirmation to save face.

There is one situation in which an agreement reached through a confirmation between speaker and hearer can produce unwelcome consequences. This is when a declaration of common ground between two people runs counter to the views of others present. It may not be an astute move to align yourself with someone specific in the group instead of remaining on the same terms with all. So ask what effect you would achieve by linking yourself with that particular person. (How powerful is he or she, or how out of step with the others?) Equally, it may be bad tactics not to confirm something which all the others agree to.

Confirming has another part to its meaning, namely 'to validate or make binding' a matter, as in:

'I wish now to confirm details of the terms of the provisional contract we discussed earlier.'

When a speaker offers such an act, it may perform an act of binding by being spoken at all, or it may have a very different meaning. It may mean that the speaker wishes to have the matter of the contract raised for discussion at this time in order to have it eventually confirmed (or not) by all concerned. A listener to the confirmation should consider which result is intended, and make the appropriate response: either agreeing at once (or raising disagreement at once), or setting off upon the discussion now knowing exactly what goal the speaker has in mind.

DIRECT

Definition 1: to command, manage, control, guide another with advice

synonyms: *order, command*

Definition 2: to give directions to, show how to do something

synonym: *instruct*

The first kind of act of directing is one of telling another what to do, either generally or in specific detail. It assumes authority in the speaker, but does not stress this, as the acts of ordering or commanding do. To order someone to do something also suggests that the speaker anticipates some resistance in the hearer, while to command is to expect unquestioning obedience. When directing someone the speaker assumes that the hearer will obey, but saves his or her face by supplying some explanation or information which could lead the hearer to be willing to comply.

The authority to direct may derive from one of several sources. It may be an institutionalised authority, set by the organisation or profession to which the negotiator belongs, or by society at large which sets up hierarchies of importance in status and roles. It may be, of course, that a speaker will assume the authority without a legitimate right to it. This is possible because any negotiation involves complex movements of status and roles and, as these vary throughout the encounter, mistakes can be made. Occasionally a negotiator may try deliberately to direct in order to see whether the authority is granted to him or her, perhaps without the others noticing. If the direction involves only a small imposition on the others they may well accept it, but each time they do so that person's right to direct is solidified. So, for example, someone who says

'Could someone get us some extra copies of this document?'

is producing a mild directive, and thereby exercising a mild authority, though its power is concealed because the person who must get the copies is not specified, and because the thing required is something that all present can see as useful. It is as if the directive is issued on everyone's behalf. But it is nonetheless a directing act. As are:

'Well now, I think you'll agree we've covered that sufficiently? We must move on now to the legal implications' and

'I think we should think about setting ourselves a time limit on this discussion, OK?',

both of which seek to direct a movement in the agenda, and thereby control the behaviours of all present. In each case the directive is put in mild terms, with mollification through the use of a question form, but it still involves major effects upon the negotiation agenda if accepted, and can set up a precedent for that speaker's future authority.

Because of the broad range of ways in which directives can be offered, they tell hearers a good deal about the speaker. Modest speakers can use heavily mollified forms like:

'Perhaps you could see to someone organising this' or

'It's probably about time we thought of doing X, Bill?',

while assertive ones can use bald forms like:

'You need to do something about this at once' or

'Somebody is going to have to do something.'

(Note that the term 'somebody', when directly addressed to a particular person, can appear insulting, because the person is not given a proper name.)

If you receive a directive which is about a small matter, or which has been mollified to recognise your face rights, you may be willing to accept it rather than cause trouble by resistance. This may well be the best way to handle it. What you should always do, however, is note what kind of directions are being issued. What are they about? In what terms are they couched? How are the directees being treated? This will allow you to get as much information about the speaker's negotiation position as possible, which you can then use in planning tactics for this and future encounters.

Directives can be aimed at having you act in person, or at getting you to set the actions of others in motion to achieve an end; this latter kind can leave the hearer a degree of flexibility, and provides an avenue for saving face which reduces the imposition. So, for example, the directive

'Mary, you can get that organised, can't you?'

could produce the response:

'OK, I'll do that, but it may be better to leave it for a day or so for maximum effect.'

Here the respondent takes part herself in deciding what the direction should be, almost joining with the first speaker in doing the directing. This also happens in:

'OK, I'll see to that. My secretary is extremely efficient and he'll get it done in no time.'

Here she passes on the direction to another, and so indicates that she is too important to do the thing herself.

A hearer can also interrupt the directive in mid-flow and finish it off, so saving face by producing a kind of self-direction, rather than a direction by another:

A: 'It would be useful if you could organise the . . .'
B: 'The conference. Yes, I know. I can do that easily.'

If the hearer wishes to resist a directive absolutely, this also can be done. For example, to the directive

'You'll organise the report, Bill',

Bill could point out a flaw in the direction:

'You've got the wrong person. Fred handles our reports'

or in the action required:

'We can't do that till we've settled the budget'

or in the purpose of the proposed action:

'We could produce a report, I suppose, but it wouldn't tell us much without the latest figures'

or in the circumstances surrounding the proposed action:

'I don't think that would be very useful now, because. . ., but it might be worth doing later, when we come to do X.'

Before trying to direct others, you should check on the degree of power you hold at that moment, on the imposition involved in the projected act, and its likely consequences. Does the direction assume that the others can do something they might not be able to do? This could either cause a loss of face if you have to admit to this, or could cause problems of non-compliance if they conceal it. What degree of informative guidance should you give to make sure the action is correctly performed? Are there other things you might like to direct later, which this present directive might prejudice in some way?

The second kind of direction – showing someone how to do something – requires the speaker to consider whether the other already knows, or already thinks he or she knows, how to do it. It is annoying to be given instruction on something already known, and it is nearly as annoying to be given instruction on something that is half known. Therefore, since the directing act very often involves the expression of a good many details, for example describing a process to be undertaken by the hearer, and can be a long act to listen to, it would be advisable to see if time and patience, as well as face, could be saved by using some kind of preliminary question about the hearer's knowledge of the matter before issuing an instruction.

DISCUSS

Definition: to examine a matter through reasoned talk
synonyms: *talk over, debate, argue, negotiate, chat*

Discussing is more purposive and involves more progress in thought than talking something over; talking over tends to involve the simple reiteration of thoughts already put into words on previous occasions. Debating is a more formalised exchange of talk, and both it and arguing can have as an outcome someone winning and someone losing. Negotiating suggests (among other things) that obstacles to agreement have to be overcome by talk. Chatting suggests that the matters raised, and the approach to them in talk, are light-hearted and fairly insignificant. The most important feature of this set of synonyms is that each is a multiple act, performed by two or more people. (Though it is possible to hold a debate or discussion with oneself, this assumes that one speaks with at least two 'voices', and expresses two different views.)

Discussions occur when two or more speakers are unsure about what they should think about a topic. It is a process of thinking aloud, each producing ideas in a rational way, and on the assumption that the other will accept an idea if the reasons are good enough, and will thereupon consider altering his or her own view with the aim of settling on some agreed view. Though this is not always the case, all involved with the discussion should assume that it could happen and behave accordingly. If it did not result in agreement, it would not indicate that the discussion had failed in any way; what is essential to a discussion is that participants speak rationally on a common matter, and hear and understand the others' views.

Discussion assumes that the way to examine a topic, and be able to hold a view on it, is to speak aloud with another, and listen to what the other thinks. It assumes that no-one holds the only 'right' view, but that each can make a useful contribution to a joint understanding. The ideas raised stand partly on their own merits and partly on the authority of the speaker, and both may have to be established. So if ideas are well expressed, are well argued for, and aim to have the other person understand and sympathise with them (even if he or she cannot ultimately agree with them), then the discussion is a good one.

In order to have a really productive discussion, the participants must display certain qualities.

(a) They must have trust in each other, since the process involves revealing the workings of their minds, as they produce thoughts perhaps not previously put into words, and which therefore may be in badly constructed language. They have to feel confident that no adverse judgment will be made as they produce hesitations and reformulations, and make criticisms or even revisions of their own ideas. It can mean risking being revealed to others as somewhat illogical or careless at times.

(b) They must know how to correct or sharpen the thought processes of others, criticising their speech for misuse of terms, lack of clarity, lack of coherence, and so on, but with minimum face loss to the ones criticised.

(c) They must be able to listen constructively to criticism, and be prepared to defend a thought which perhaps they have never before had questioned.

Since trust is the essential foundation for a good discussion, this is what has to be established first. Where some or all of the negotiators do not know each other and a sense of trust has to be built up from scratch, the initial bonding phase of the encounter will prove useful for this purpose. Even if it has been established on earlier occasions, it must be renewed on each occasion of meeting, since it is so fundamental to a good encounter.

Since a discussion involves such face risk, and does not always bring about agreement, what it can and will achieve should be carefully considered before it is entered into. It is valuable for a person to speak his or her thoughts on a topic out loud to another, since in the process they can often be clarified or even altered: 'How can I know what I think till I see what I say?' (Wallas). If a successful discussion can be well managed, the trust it generates may continue beyond the encounter and be of use for other shared activities between the participants. It also gives useful information to help predict others' behaviours in the future, which can aid the efficiency of later negotation processes.

Most topics are suitable for discussion, but some, like the establishment of facts, or the presentation of very simple ideas, are better dealt with in ways less time-consuming than discussion. (The *meaning* of facts, however, is a very important and frequently used topic.) It is worth thinking in advance of the parameters of the topics to be explored. Their causes and effects, the how and why, the when and where of them, and so on, could be usefully considered while preparing for discussion, so that a reasonable spread of the topic's aspects are dealt with, some of which might otherwise be neglected once the discussion starts. (For a full range of possibilities, see Chapter 7, pp. 121–4 on topic coverage.)

To achieve a successful discussion, negotiators should set its goals, and set limits to its content and timescale to ensure it does not stretch beyond its usefulness. These limits would, of course, need to be agreed either by those present or by some kind of written agenda before the talking began; to seek to impose limits on a discussion once it has started seems to be a very authoritarian act, as in:

> 'We've discussed this now for twenty minutes: that's enough, let's move on' or

> 'This has become irrelevant. Let's get back to the point.'

DISMISS

Definition 1:	to direct to go, to remove from office, to give permission to depart
synonym:	*discharge*
antonyms:	*appoint, permit*
Definition 2:	to refuse to accept an idea, argument or suggestion
synonyms:	*reject, refuse*
antonyms:	*accept*

DISMISSAL OF AN EMPLOYEE

To dismiss in official terms is to end the appointment or contract of employment of someone. Its occurrence in negotiation should be infrequent, but it may occur as a result of a failed negotiation. Because of its social consequences it requires care, and because of possible legal ramifications any formal dismissal procedures laid down for particular circumstances must be fully complied with, and there should be no deviation from them. (It may be wise to have a colleague as witness if you are having to dismiss someone. It is certainly important to rehearse, and to take notes afterwards. In some circumstances it may be possible to record the occasion.)

The following comments will deal only with the social aspects of the act.

The speaker who has to carry out the dismissal is acting in an official capacity, and it is important for the sake of the hearer's face that he or she is actually empowered to perform the act, and indicate clearly that he or she is acting officially. It must always be a situation in which face loss is great, but this can be reduced if the act is performed in an official manner. The speaker may need to declare his or her authority to perform the act, and to be sure that this right will be accepted by the dismissed person. This is because for the hearer there is less face loss in being dismissed by one who is recognised as having a clear right to do that than there is in being dismissed by someone whose authority is questionable.

> 'You can't do that. Only the Managing Director can do that'

can be a legitimate objection from someone who is threatened with loss of employment.

The utterance itself should be put in formulaic terms – ones selected from written language could be suitable, as for example:

'The company regrets that it must dispense with your services', or

'The company has reluctantly been forced to make a cutback in staff, and hence must require you to give up your position.'

The virtue of such formulae is that they reduce the personal element on both sides, reducing the speaker's degree of personal imposition on the one hand and the hearer's face loss on the other. It appears to put the matter at one remove from the two people concerned. In the first example, this is achieved by using not 'I' but 'the company', not 'you' but 'your services', not 'sack' or 'dismiss' but 'dispense with'; while even the note of 'regret' is put in less immediately personal terms. It is wise to use any terms supplied in the formal dismissal procedures if these exist.

The official mode should remain the only one used in the encounter; it is safer not to branch into the personal. If, for example, the speaker were to reveal a personal response to the dismissal which in any way undermined the act, it could be picked up and used by the other, either to create an argument then or to save it for ammunition later in an appeal against dismissal. So no personal regret should be expressed without also giving a clear signal of agreement with the dismissal; there should be no praise without a similar amount of dispraise.

A well prepared encounter can also reduce the face problems. Signalling in advance that there is to be a formal interview, and hinting at dismissal, has the advantage of absorbing the first shock, which might otherwise cause the dismissee to display emotional responses in the encounter which he or she would afterwards regret. It also sets the stamp on the formality of the occasion by making the first move in the dismissal process a written one.

DISMISSAL OF AN IDEA

When dismissal is rejection of an idea or opinion, it obviously occurs more frequently in negotiation. In this kind of dismissal the speaker declares that he or she will not think of some idea any more, and calls for the removal of the idea from its place on the agenda. It implies that the idea is not worthy of a place in the discussion. Reasons are not necessary, since it is assumed that the authority of a speaker who dismisses is force enough to have the matter removed, but reasons may be given in an attempt to soften the absolutism of the act (or to reinforce an authority which may be in doubt). The dismissal is not a request to postpone the topic, or an argument to relocate it; it seeks to have it completely removed from consideration.

Consequently it is a very strong act, and will badly affect relations with any who hold the idea which is being dismissed, or who are in partial agreement with it, or who disapprove of so absolute an act. It can therefore isolate the speaker if performed too harshly.

Dismissing an idea

As a speaker, note that a dismissal can address various aspects of the thing dismissed. It can focus on only the poor quality of the idea (without criticism of the person holding it), as in:

'I don't think we can consider the costs without settling X first . . .',

which could be less damaging than the personal criticism:

'That's rather an illogical position to hold, and it's out of place here.'

In the following examples:

'Your idea is a quite typical mistake, and shows you know little about . . .', and

'Well, Bill, I am surprised at someone of your experience falling for that notion . . .',

the speaker tempers the criticism by suggesting in the first example that others have made it too, and in the second by including a compliment.

A speaker might choose to emphasise some aspect of his or her authority, to establish it more solidly in the whole encounter, as in:

'We don't want to waste time on trivialities like that. As Production Manager, I need to know . . .' or

'New marketing strategies of the kind I mentioned in my report have made that kind of idea irrelevant.'

The dismissal could suggest that another, opposed, idea is better:

'No, no, what we need is something more forward-looking, like the idea of . . .',

or that the negotiation is the wrong forum for consideration of the idea:

'This meeting has a limited brief, and that idea is simply beyond its scope.'

It is not easy to see how best to rank such dismissals from least to most damaging, because much rests on the context in which they might occur, but it is reasonable to suggest that the worst ones are those that attack the quality of mind of the one being dismissed, since these constitute a criticism which extends far beyond the particular occasion, and which cannot be rectified.

To prevent, as far as possible, any damage that will accrue from such acts of dismissal, it is advisable that they be mollified by politeness phrases and tokens. For example:

'That seems a *fairly* foolish idea'
'*I may be wrong but* to me that is just foolish . . .'
'*As far as I am aware*, that is not a viable possibility'
'*Correct me if I'm wrong*, but that is just not possible'
'*My reading of the facts* suggests that is impossible'
'*My company could* not accept that without serious emendation'
'That has *surely* been dismissed *already* as too idealistic'.

Another strategy is to imply that the idea being dismissed is a common one, and that therefore its speaker is just one of a group who are all wrong, as in:

'Many people hold that view, I know, but it is of no use here'

A dismisser may try to conceal the absolutism of the dismissal:

'That is reasonable as far as it goes, but you'll find it won't work here.'

Here the implication is that if the other gives it more thought he or she would reject the idea him or herself, and reduce the need for the speaker to do so. And in

'That may be OK in the marketing division, but it won't work in personnel',

the implication is that the other has expertise, but not in the area in question. A dismisser could combine the dismissal with a demonstratively face-saving act, such as apology:

'I'm sorry to have to disagree, but that simply won't work.'

Or he or she could employ praise:

'That's not workable, Bill. Can't you come up with something as good as your idea that . . . ?'

Having an idea dismissed

To be on the receiving end of a dismissive act is obviously a position with little dignity. If it happens to you, try and survive with as little loss of face as possible. The following ideas may be of assistance.

First, consider whether the act should be taken at face value, or is an oblique attack on some other event or person in the negotiation. The attack may be directed at you since the real target is more difficult to tackle. Signs of this obliqueness could include allusions to the connection between you and the target, as in:

'That's not a very useful idea. I'm surprised that wasn't noticed when *your group* was preparing for today', or

'That's not a very good idea to put forward. I thought you *were appointed* because you could handle such things', or

'Those figures are wrong. I would have thought *your company* could do better than that.'

If you think you are not the real target, leave the response to those who are, or ignore the attack, since it is clear your role is perceived as a subsidiary one, and consequently your 'fault' is subsidiary too.

Second, consider whether the problem concerns some small detail of your idea and not the whole thing. If so, perhaps this detail can be jettisoned or expressed differently in order to save the rest of the idea.

Third, the problem could be with the *expression* of the idea. If so, consider how to restate the idea more satisfactorily.

Finally, perhaps the idea was badly timed, placed either too late or too early within the overall framework of the negotiation procedure. If too late it may well have to be lost, but if too soon, watch for a more opportune time, and put it again, perhaps in different words, and taking account of any criticism which was useful.

If, however, the dismissal is really directed at your idea and you strongly feel that the dismisser is wrong, then you must consider whether to object to the dismissal and fight for your idea. In determining whether this is a useful strategy, note the responses of others to your dismissal, and judge whether you have any support for a fight. Also, consider what damage such a struggle might cause. Then decide on your tactics.

INFORM

Definition 1: to provide oneself with knowledge on some matter

Definition 2: to impart knowledge to others
synonyms: *notify*, *report*
antonym: *conceal*

INFORMING ONESELF

The act of informing oneself as preparation for a negotiation would require considering the following:

(a) what matters are likely to be raised, which will be major focuses of attention and which just ancillary concerns;

(b) what background sources and references might be required knowledge for the negotiation;
(c) what degree of detail at what level of specialisation is likely to be needed;
(d) what degree of clarity and relevance would be most useful;
(e) how often you should make a contribution, and how long any particular contribution should be.

Negotiations can be centred on practical details, requiring accurate and up-to-date figures, tables and statistics, or they can be occasions of policy discussion, requiring members to have ideas, opinions and suggestions. To both kinds of information a negotiator should add whatever seems important given his or her attitudes to the matter, any ethical or moral concerns, and whatever might be usefully brought in from an unexpected or unusual source to add full value to the occasion. A negotiation is only as good as the ideas that inform it; and it is sometimes helpful to think laterally about the agenda items in order to ensure that the outcome incorporates everything that might usefully contribute to it.

For each item of information that could play a major part in the encounter, you should check that all its aspects have been covered. Use Chapter 7, pp. 121–5 on coverage, as a guide, asking the questions given there of any matter you think needs it.

Part of the early skirmishing in a negotiation involves the establishment of an agreed level of ideas, as well as a jockeying for positions of authority. If the members of the group are strangers this may continue throughout the whole encounter. While it continues there are two major considerations to bear in mind.

1   Matters will arise on which you are not well informed. If this happens, make no commitment to anything until you have ascertained exactly what it entails.
2   Once the negotiation begins, information will be supplied by others which should be added to your store. It may be the case, however, that there is little of use, and much to correct in what is said. Do not let a lower level of knowledge in others affect you so that you neglect to use your own higher level; your only problem will be the question of how best to introduce your knowledge and impart it to others without threatening their face or damaging relations between you.

INFORMING OTHERS

Informing others acceptably is strongly influenced by the relationship of speaker and hearer, the role the information can play in the encounter, and the subject matter involved.

Relationship

There is an important convention in human relationships which bears upon the act of informing. In some degrees of relationship we have a serious social obligation to provide information to others, and our freedom not to do so is severely restricted.

The strongest obligations concern the most important information and the closest relationships. For example, you must inform a boss that you wish to take leave or to resign – it is antisocial just to go – just as you should inform a parent that you are getting married, and do so before telling a more remote relative.

Within less close relationships, as among colleagues, there are also obligations, though perhaps less strong. For example, if Bill knows that Mary is writing a report on a particular topic, and she knows that he knows, then if any relevant information on that topic comes to Bill's attention, he should pass it on. If later she finds out that he knew and did not inform her, then she will be properly displeased. The obligation among colleagues, as within the family, varies with the situational factors; in this case these would be the value of the knowledge to Mary, the degree of relationship between Mary and Bill, the degree of effort required from Bill to inform Mary, and so on.

In the case of reasonably remote associates, who meet infrequently, little information may be obligatory, and, precisely because this is so, the act of informing can be used as a way of improving the bonding they have. An example might be:

'I remembered you were interested in this topic, so here's a copy of my new report on it.'

Degrees of relationship can exclude some information acts. If a stranger who comes to the negotiation were to say

'I am feeling very unhealthy these days [laughs]',

it is both to mistake the tone and the degree of relationship to produce as an earnest response the information:

'There's a good gym near here, and it has a good dietician too.'

Information which implies an excessive interest in another's private life is rarely acceptable.

Practice

On entering a negotiation ask yourself:

1 *What relationship do you have, or expect to have in the future, with those who are present?*
2 *Will this involve you in any obligations to inform them of anything?*

Role

The role the information can play in the encounter must also be taken into account. If it is crucial, it needs the most careful preparation, and should be given the fullest expression, with all elements covered.

Occasionally, however, it may be useful to offer a lower grade of information, for example a rumour or a not yet clearly formed perception. This could be worthwhile since knowledge of the very fact that the rumour or perception exists might be useful to the negotiation.

The only kind of information that is quite unacceptable is that which is vague, as in:

'I heard something about that the other day, but I can't remember what.'

This is worse than silence because it is so tantalising, whereas

'Someone in one of the departments at Smithson's was working on that, but I can't remember who. Probably it was someone in the legal department'

supplies sufficient precision for the hearer to decide whether it is worth following up, and sufficient detail to follow it up, should he or she wish to.

In some cases, the best tactic might be not to inform at all: to remain silent or to claim ignorance. This might be sensible, for example, as a means of escaping from some onerous task:

'Bill, you know about this. Could you do a report on it tonight?

should perhaps be answered by:

'Unfortunately my knowledge doesn't extend that far.'

If the possession of certain knowledge gives you a tactical advantage of some kind, or if others would lose too much face if you supplied it, or it would attract an adverse judgment of some kind, some other avoidance strategy should be used.

Subject matter

It may happen that information you have prepared in advance is made valueless because the negotiation has taken an unexpected turn, or it may be that you have it available in inappropriately excessive detail, or have not yet fully digested it. In such a situation it would be both distracting and unproductive to bring it into the discussion. If it is not in a state to be produced with the needs of that particular meeting as its organising principle, it should be concealed; to produce it in the wrong way would only have a harmful effect, and would probably lead to its rejection, and that of its speaker too. You can give too much information as well as too little.

Most of the time, however, it is useful to inform others, provided it is done properly. To achieve a successful act of informing, it is important to know enough about the hearer to know what kind of information would be most appropriate, helpful and well-received. You must ask yourself the following questions.

(a) What does the hearer know already?
(b) What degree of expertise does the hearer have, and on what subjects, and so how technically should this information be presented?
(c) How acceptable does the hearer find the receipt of information? Does he or she perhaps see it as an insult, or as an attack?
(d) What kind of face risk would be involved for the hearer? Can this be avoided or minimised, for example by a tentative offer of information before actually providing it:

'I heard something about the sales figures the other day. *Have you seen them?*'

The first two questions concern *what* information should be given, while the second two concern *how* it should be given. With regard to the former the speaker needs to make an assessment of the hearer's knowledge, and this involves recognising to what groups in society he or she belongs. Consider whether the hearer is a member of a profession, to what degree he or she is educated, whether they're local or new to the district, how old they are, of what political or religious persuasion, and so on, since any of these factors could affect what he or she knows, and how new information might be received. Use the bonding moments of interaction to find such things out. What this information does is to enable a speaker to know what 'scripts' of life that are within his or her repertoire are also known to the hearer.

SCRIPTS

A 'script' is the unwritten knowledge we have of the routine behaviours of our daily life, ranging, for instance, from getting to work each day, or ordering a meal in a restaurant, to knowing the procedural rules of a committee meeting. Much of life is routine in essence, that is 'scripted', though it may differ in details, so although eating in McDonald's is very different to eating in the most elegant restaurant in town, there are some routines in common between them, such as knowing what a menu is, how to read it, how to order the food and how to pay for it. The more routines we share with another person, the easier it is to talk with him or her; so much can be left unsaid. Think how much one needs to know in order to understand why the following speech pair makes full and perfect sense:

A: 'The Candlelight Room has a new dish.'
B: 'As entrée or main course?',

and why the following makes no sense:

A: 'McDonald's has a new dish.'
B: 'As entrée or main course?'

With the shared knowledge of a script behind us, we can talk with others about such matters without having to spell out every item. So you can provide the information 'My train was late this morning' in the sure knowledge that your hearer knows you were a traveller on the train and not the driver, that you were on your way to work, and that lateness is bad, because being late for work is frowned upon, and that therefore you are seeking sympathy. The hearer is unlikely to think that you own the train (though you call it 'my') or that you were delighted with its lateness, though you have offered no information one way or the other which would clarify the matter. Someone who shared the script, that is, knew what lay behind this minimal statement, could easily respond, and perhaps might reply 'That's a nuisance. I hope you didn't get into trouble', whereas a person without the script knowledge, say from a remote region of an underdeveloped country, could be left very confused. Whenever we give information we should make considered assumptions about the shared script knowledge of our hearers. It is very rare that we have to produce information which is unable to rely on shared knowledge. It could occur in cases of negotiation where one speaker is an expert in an esoteric subject and the other is entirely ignorant of it, or when dealing with someone from a different culture (in fact, a simple definition of the difference between cultures is that they do not share many scripts), but usually we can rely on some shared scripting. If information does not match with the script understanding of the hearer, it may miss its target and be misunderstood or dismissed.

When providing information to members of another culture there is another matter to consider: some subjects are taboo, and therefore information on them will be poorly received, while others are impolite and may cause offence. For example, in a very formally polite culture, like the Japanese, personal information, perhaps meant to indicate friendliness and calling for reciprocal items of personal information, like

'This rain is dreadful, isn't it? I got soaked to the skin just getting from the car to the office today',

could simply make the Japanese hearer uncomfortable at a personal revelation of a physical condition. It could also be misinterpreted as having more interactive significance than it has, and result in the hearer feeling awkward because he or she can make no useful response.

NEGOTIATE

Let us never negotiate out of fear. But let us never fear to negotiate.

(J.F. Kennedy)

Definition: to confer with another to bring about a result, to arrange to bring some result about by discussion and the settlement of terms
synonyms: *discuss, deal, bargain, mediate, consult*
antonym: *quarrel*

Negotiation begins with the assumption that negotiators need each other's agreement to proceed on some matter, and cannot manage it alone. Therefore the goal of a negotiation is to reduce any differences between the positions of the participants to a manageable number and to find points of agreement, so that finally a settlement can be made which those present can accept. Matters must be assessed to see which are essential to the business and therefore must be decided, and which are peripheral and can remain in contention; this may be the most important part of the encounter. An early consideration must be to check what the structure of the interaction will be, for example to note what conventions of speaking turns apply, to establish an agenda for the business, and to decide on any matters of role or hierarchy either of people or topics.

So the central speech acts of negotiation are those which:

(a) call for agreement,
(b) give reasons why there should be agreement,
(c) compare and contrast options,
(d) judge or evaluate ideas and opinions,
(e) clarify and test views expressed,
(f) assess the strength of feelings and concerns, or
(g) establish and reiterate goals.

These can to some degree be achieved by non-linguistic behaviours, perhaps by research or experiment, but talk will play a major part in any negotiation. Inappropriate negotiating acts are those which bring conflict, obstruction, and obstinacy to the encounter.

The speech activities most likely to be in demand in a negotiation are those which:

(a) can adjust the talk to a practical purpose,
(b) can produce accommodation between differing points of view,

(c) can introduce new ideas and reject existing ones without threatening the face of others,

(d) can allocate tasks and responsibilities, or

(e) can prioritise and categorise suggestions and opinions.

All require good listening skills (see Chapter 3, pp. 57–60), to note useful contributions, and to build on the speech of others to achieve the desired goals. Some participants will have as their goal the achievement of a practical purpose, such as signing a contract, or allocating work; others will primarily want only their self-interest to be served; and some will accept a range of outcomes provided that the approach taken in the negotiation process allows them a degree of individual freedom or makes clear the chain of responsibility. The goals of the other participants are often signalled linguistically in one of two ways.

1 They may be stated directly as in 'We must aim at . . .', or 'The most important thing we must do today is . . .' (Notice the different ways in which the statement can be put: these two examples use the words 'we' and 'must', which demonstrate that the speaker sees it as a joint activity with an urgent purpose, where another set of examples would show a very different sense of the activity, for instance: 'I want', 'You should', or 'It is essential that X be done.')

2 The goals may be suggested obliquely. For example, a speaker who frequently makes comments like 'That's OK, but it doesn't help us sort out our priorities', and 'But that can only be done after we've done X' is indicating that his or her goal must involve a set of priorities; while another speaker might have in mind a rather different way of evaluating the goal, saying, for instance, 'But would the *community* accept that?' and 'That's the sort of thing *people* really like.' The first speaker wants a tidily arranged outcome; the second wants the outcome to be a popular one.

Listen for the signs of agreement, and of concession and compromise, which can be built on to form a good conclusion. The following are promising signs to varying degrees.

(a) A speaker may accept and use another's words. For example, after one speaker says:

'What we need here is not so much a specialist as a generalist',

another might respond with:

'Well OK, I'm in favour of a generalist provided he or she can . . .'

(b) A speaker may accept and use words roughly synonymous with those of another speaker.

(c) A speaker may use, though not accept, another's words, which could indicate that something which has a link to the other's words may be acceptable. A speaker may also pick up on another's words by producing their antithesis or some variant on them which relates to his or her own goals. For example, if a speaker responds to:

> 'We've got three priorities in this matter: what we do, how we do it, and who is to be in charge'

with

> 'Well, we've certainly got to settle who is to do the groundwork, and it's got to be someone very efficient at X, or it will not get done',

then it is clear that it is the third priority which reflects what he or she perceives to be the central issue.

(d) A speaker may use another's term giving it a different meaning, as, for example, taking up and appearing to accept the word 'generalist' but using it for someone who only has two specialisations – which could constitute a far narrower meaning than the first speaker intended.

(e) A speaker may reject the connotations, rather than the essential meaning, of another's term. This could perhaps be addressed by categorising the connotations into those which are inevitable and those which are less closely tied to the term, and then substituting an alternative term which fits these better.

Others' negotiating positions can be read through various language signals. First, listen for the recurrence of words, phrases, particular ideas or attitudes; reiteration, whether it is in the same terms or not, indicates a high degree of interest in something.

Second, note the linking strategies used, since these provide evidence of the relative weighting given to the things linked, for example:

> 'X is very good on the whole, however, it is also bad in that it . . .',

where the second quality of X is a drawback to the first, but the first is the one that matters. Contrast the difference in emphasis achieved by reversing the order

> 'X is bad on the whole in that it . . ., however it is also very good . . .'

The first example wants the 'bad' thing discussed and sorted out, while the second wants the 'good' thing discussed. Both of these speech acts, despite their differences, divide the subject of X into good and bad aspects. They are making a cut and dried opposition, where someone else might wish to discuss degrees of practicality, or appropriateness, and so on.

Finally, listen for the use of qualitative assessment contained in a speech act, as in such word choices as:

(a) (revealing personal attitude) *excellent, clever, poor, expert, boring, special*;

(b) (addressed to some quality of a thing) *poor quality, accurate, disorganised, strong, shoddy*;

(c) (addressed to some specific concern of the negotiation) *useful, inappropriate, sensible, unsuitable*.

Note

The participants of a negotiation come to it with a sense of what their role is and what they have a right to expect of the event; they will undoubtedly expect to express a view, to be given a fair hearing, and to register a vote, in the final decision-making part of the encounter. The more unlikely it is that a particular speaker will get the outcome he or she wants, the more that person may wish to talk, both as a kind of substitute for success and as a face-saving exercise; it will be particularly important if the speaker represents others and has an obligation to be heard on their behalf. If denied proper opportunities to speak, he or she may well seek to make another kind of impression, by disagreeing with the majority, and end up having to be placated or accommodated.

OFFER

Definition: to present something to another's notice for his or
                  her consideration, acceptance or rejection
synonyms: *give, proffer, tender*
antonyms: *withhold, withdraw*

(See ACCEPT (pp. 139–45) in conjunction with OFFER: they are closely linked.)

In order to offer something, the thing offered must be something with which the speaker is linked; he or she either owns it or has discovered it or has formed it in the mind. To offer it, the speaker must be willing to share it or give it away, or to have it taken up, adopted, or made the focus of attention by others. If the thing is a concrete object the speaker must be willing to lose possession of it, but if it is an idea or opinion it will be retained, though others will have the use of it.

A speaker may be willing to do this because it is useful to another, or to the self, or to both. It is done in the expectation that others present will make the same kinds of offer, and that everyone will benefit; if some only take from others and offer nothing in return, it will be remarked on as poor negotiating behaviour. It may be better therefore to offer a weak idea than to offer nothing. Some people habitually make 'rhetorical' offers to act, that is, ones they can be sure no-one will take up, because they know someone else has already been allocated to do them.

How the speaker registers 'ownership' will have a strong influence on the response the offer gets. For example, a speaker could choose one of the following.

1 'My view is that we should . . . What do you think?'
2 'In my view it needs a report. I am willing to do one if you like.'
3 'I've just had an idea. Why don't we do . . .?'
4 'I heard this useful idea last week . . . why don't we . . .?'
5 'What do you think of the idea of doing . . .?'

The first has the strongest declaration of ownership – 'my view is that . . .' (interestingly stronger than 'in my view') – and means that acceptance will give authority to the speaker. The second makes two offers, and so requires two acceptances (or rejections) and therefore extra effort from the hearers. The third loosens the grip on the idea; it is no longer 'mine', it is 'an' idea, and I have 'just had' it, (which sounds as if it may only recently have arrived and is easier to accept without face loss to hearers). The fourth is reported, and therefore the possession is second-hand and is easier to reject. The fifth makes no mention of ownership, and emphasises the question form, thus reducing it from a firm offer to a tentative one and allowing the freest range of actions to the hearers.

To avoid any bad effects from making offers,

(a) make only a reasonable number of offers: too many and it may appear as though you have a sense of inferiority and are trying too hard to be helpful, or, strangely enough, have a sense of superiority and are being too domineering;
(b) check the likelihood of acceptance first;
(c) be tentative, not about the quality of the idea or its value, but about whether it will be accepted, and so leave room to avoid face loss; and
(d) separate yourself from ownership enough to make sure that if the offer is rejected you are not yourself being rejected.

If it is crucial to you that an idea is given importance in the negotiation, do not introduce it as an offer, but rather make it a statement, or an answer to someone's question. Remember that if an offer is made and not accepted the matter will end there and be extremely hard to resuscitate.

Once the idea has been offered, various results are possible.

(a) The speaker may be seen as one who has special knowledge, or opinions or ideas. Others will then decide whether these are worth considering. If they are found to be foolish, they will understand that the speaker is unable to read correctly either the negotiation or the other participants' needs, or the topic boundaries.
(b) The thing that is offered may exert some influence on the proceedings, and affect the acts of others.

(c) The speaker may be seen as the owner of the thing offered. Where the thing offered is an idea or a point of view, it may just be a matter of luck who manages to offer it first, and so the credit for owning it may be unfairly allocated. Nonetheless it will happen, and this credit is worth trying for, even though sometimes an offer receives an adverse reaction.

(d) The recipients of the offer may learn what the speaker thinks of them (a shoddy offer may mean a mean giver, but it may also mean the giver has a low opinion of the recipient).

(e) Face loss may result if the offer is refused in terms which make it clear that the speaker is seen as incompetent.

PROMISE

Definition: to declare a commitment to undertake (or not undertake) some action
synonyms: *assure*, *pledge*
antonym: *threaten*

The act of promising is more than a statement of intention to do or not to do something, it is a commitment which encourages in the hearer the certainty that the thing will occur. One of its goals is indeed to reduce the hearer's uncertainty about the thing's occurrence. Therefore it is important that the terms of the promise are made clear; a vague promise is no promise at all.

It differs from an assurance in being a much stronger commitment, and from a pledge in being a more personal undertaking by the speaker.

Promising as an act makes several assumptions. First, it assumes that the thing to be done is one the hearer would be pleased to have happen. If this is a completely mistaken assumption, the speaker is not promising but threatening. A mistaken promise is difficult to deal with because the hearer has simultaneously to correct the false assumption while applauding the good intentions of the speaker:

A: 'Don't worry, I give you my word that I will draft the report by Tuesday.'
B: 'Er, thank you, but in fact we've already asked someone else to do it.'

or

A: 'I'll deliver the goods directly to the new warehouse myself to make sure nothing goes wrong.'
B: 'Well, as a matter of fact, we want to collect them ourselves, and anyway we want to leave delivery till a later date.'

Second, a promise assumes there is doubt either that the speaker can or will do the thing, or that the thing can be done at all, and the act of promising is meant to remove the doubt.

Third, it assumes that the speaker will only do the thing if the hearer wants it done; that the speaker is only doing it because the other has either requested it or is likely to request it. There is a sense that what is promised is not to the speaker's advantage, probably because it often involves effort. Its value is that it meets some need of the hearer:

A: 'I will definitely ask the manager for your extra funding today.'
B: 'Is that a promise?'
A: 'Yes.'

is a typical promise exchange, whereas

'I promise to leave the office early today'

could only be a promise to oneself since only the speaker is advantaged by it.

An act of promising may be made in response to earlier actions by the hearer, or perhaps in response to doubts already expressed about the possibility of something being done either by the speaker or at all. It could also be made as an initial move, when it indicates that for the speaker as well as the hearer there is some doubt about the thing being done. A speaker only promises to do something that he or she might otherwise not do, and which might therefore not get done. This could mean that where a promise is volunteered as an initiating move it is only the speaker who has a doubt. This may be a useful thing to know.

A promise can indicate either that the speaker will personally do the thing, or will take steps to cause others to do it:

'I'll make sure that it is organised on time.'

In this case it must be regarded as a weaker promise, partly because others are involved (and they might not be as malleable as the speaker hopes), and partly because the hearer cannot know precisely what actions the speaker will take. This could cause miscommunication if the speaker and the hearer each wrongly assume that the other has in mind exactly the same process of achieving the thing. In such cases, that is, where the promise leads to a complex series of actions that involve others, the hearer should ask for details of who is to do what.

It is generally assumed that people are able to recognise how much work a promise entails for them, and hence to know how important it is to resist committing themselves to results they will be unable to achieve. However, at times, a good deal of pressure can be put on someone to promise, and so some promises are forced. This pressure can take the form of flattery, or a reminder of a sense of obligation. But whether it is forced or freely offered, it still remains true that the promise is a commitment which will redound badly on the promiser's credibility if it fails. 'But you promised!' is a serious accusation to make of a fellow negotiator.

REFER

Definition 1: to direct attention to or point to, to report on or make mention of

Definition 2: to make reference to something

The act of referring involves using words or phrases which represent in some way the thing referred to: this can be done either (a) by using *deictic* terms (i.e. pointing words), or (b) by *specification*. For example:

- **time** reference can be made by using deictics like *today*, *next week*, *soon*, *some time ago*, or by specification like *on 21 September 1984*;
- **place** reference can be made by using deictics like *here*, *there*, *in this place*, or by specification like *at 1 High Street, Anytown*;
- **speaker/reader** reference can be made by using deictics like *I*, *my*, *we*, *us*, *you*, *your*, *yourselves* or by specification like *as Personnel Officer*;
- **object** reference can be made by using deictics like *this*, *that*, *these*, *those*, *the-ones-you-know*, or by specification like *the arrangement to meet . . .*;
- *reference to* **previous discourse** can be made by using such deictic phrases as *the-latter*, *as-I-said*, *my-earlier-letter* or by specification as *in the 1984 Annual Report*.

Deictics can be unclear, primarily because most of them take as their base point the time and occasion of their use; so, for example, 'last week' means the week before the phrase is used, and this may get lost or be unclear if, for instance, it comes on the third page of a letter and is far removed from the letter's date. Others are vague or relative in meaning, depending on such factors as the attitude or wishes or goals of the speaker, and these may not be clear to the reader; so, for example, 'soon' can mean 'in an hour', 'in a day', 'in a week or so' or 'within a year'; 'we' can mean 'my company', 'my department', or can refer to speaker and reader together.

Reference by specification can cause different problems according as it refers to people, events, objects or texts. When a *person* is referred to, methods of reference are: by name, position, relationship to speaker or a combination of these.

Names can be given in various ways. For example, as an employee of a company you can refer to your Senior Executive by such variants as 'Mary', or 'Smith', or 'Mary Smith', or 'Dr Smith', or 'Dr Mary', or 'MS', or 'The Black Widow'. Each has a different value, both in itself and for what it reveals of your attitude to her and to the negotiation. They all bring a note of personality or individuality to your evaluations of her, and of the hierarchical power involved in her position. The significance can vary according to whether you and your hearer are members of the same company or belong to different companies.

If you refer to the Senior Executive in the hearer's company as 'John', or 'Brown', or 'The Boss', each choice of term will reveal a different attitude: 'John' suggests an intimacy with the hearer's employer, perhaps over the other's head; 'Brown' may indicate a downgrading of the other's employer, or of his or her company; while 'the Boss' suggests a companionship with the hearer, and one which is mildly anti-authoritarian.

If you both belong to one company and use different names to refer to the same person, the choice will highlight any difference in your relationship, or position. Take, for example, the following exchange in a committee room before a meeting, where reference is being made to the Chairman:

A: 'Is Mr Smith coming today?'
B: 'Oh, Bill's always late.'

The implications of all these choices should be considered. First, consider the case from your point of view.

1 What do you wish to reveal of (a) the named person, (b) your status, (c) your relationship to him or her and (d) your attitude to the negotiation and the other negotiators?
2 Do you wish to exclude your hearer from a group by being deliberately non-specific, or to include your hearer in the group by using a more casual or intimate term?

Then consider the case from the point of view of your hearer.

1 Is your hearer in your company, or in another?
2 Does he or she know the person or not?
3 What term does he or she use?

If the hearer's term differs from yours, consider whether you should use his or her term or keep to your own and allow the difference to have whatever impact it might. If you are both in the same firm, the shared term would suggest a sense of bond, while a difference in term would indicate differential status or familiarity with the person referred to. If you are in different firms, the shared term may be inappropriate, while the difference in term could be a simple recognition of the situation.

A person can be referred to not by name but by position. When this is done, it emphasises status or power (whether powerful or powerless), and the relationship of the speaker or hearer to the person referred to. It excludes the personal or individual. It declares the organisation to have structure, hierarchy, and different responsibility loadings. This may or may not be the most valuable focus to give to the information that is being imparted. Also, where the hearer will need not only an indication of position for future use but also a name, the absence of this can lead to the hearer having to ask for the information. This at once puts him or her into an inferior position, dependent on the speaker for an answer. The hearer is then open to such comments as 'Oh sorry, I thought you knew', which (in certain tones of voice) stresses the hearer's ignorance, or 'Oh sorry, I forgot you would not know' or 'Oh sorry, I forgot I wasn't talking to you last week when I mentioned it.' (The word 'forgot' certainly could imply that the speaker has a bad memory, but it could equally mean that to the speaker the hearer is eminently forgettable.)

A person can be referred to by his or her relationship to the speaker. One possible value of this is to emphasise the speaker's sense of loyalty or commitment to the company, for example, '*our* Personnel Officer' rather than '*the* Personnel Officer'. It can also be used to hint at the speaker's high status as in 'my assistant', 'my secretary', or low status as in 'my boss', 'my supervisor'.

Using a combination of these types of reference brings an extra value to the communication. So, for example, in 'our Personnel Officer, Susan Jones', the extra detail of name could be helpful if the hearer has to contact her, though it also acts to exclude the hearer by assuming that he or she does not know that Susan Jones is the Personnel Officer. So, if the hearer *does* know her name, he or she may feel mildly insulted that the speaker assumes ignorance, or that the speaker has forgotten a previous encounter at which such information was exchanged.

When an *event* is referred to, you must decide whether the hearer was present, and whether he or she views the event in the same way as you, or has the same level of interest in it. You can choose to reveal or conceal your part in it, for example by such a form of words as 'We had a meeting about this' (which does not indicate whether you were present, because 'we' could either include yourself or be a reference to the group to which you belong), or by using a phrase like 'That item was discussed last week' (which leaves unspecified the agents in the discussion and whether or not you were one of them).

When an *entity* is referred to, you must decide whether your hearers know it, whether they would consider it in the same way you would, and whether they have the same attitude to it as you. Take, for example, a new kind of plastic tubing made by your firm. This you may know quite technically, while its features may not be understood by all your hearers; they may see it as an expensive way to deal with a problem, while you see it as a cheap product, and one which would ensure profits to your company.

When a *text* is referred to, you must assume that you and your hearer will have differences in interpretation. No two readings of a text are the same. So give your sense of the text, showing what you would focus on, and then ask your hearer for his or her interpretation and focus. Decide whether your hearer has easy access to the text or is unfamiliar with it, and whether an assumption of his or her familiarity with it is advantageous to you, or not.

Note

Naming the event, object or text bestows a particular meaning on it, and this can be used to advantage in referring to it. So, for example, a document can be named as 'a preliminary draft', 'a draft incorporating your [hearer's] objections raised at the last meeting', 'a proposal', 'a position paper', 'some thoughts on the matter for consideration', or 'a firm basis for discussion'. Each has a different value, and brings something different to the negotiation.

(a) 'a preliminary draft' indicates a high level of tentativeness about the matter;
(b) 'a draft incorporating your objections raised at the last meeting' might deal with only those objections the speaker thought useful, and might neglect others, hoping that the former become the focus of the present discussion rather than the latter;
(c) 'a proposal' is probably the most neutral term;
(d) 'a position paper' may indicate that a striking initiative is being declared, or suggest that a firm stand is being taken, and this may lead to an adversarial clash if it is in any way provocative;
(e) 'some thoughts on the matter for consideration' implies a lack of structure which in turn suggests that all aspects of the matter are open for discussion, with not even a framework settled;
(f) 'a firm basis for discussion' indicates a firm commitment by the speaker to the proposal and a hope that it will be agreed.

Choose which term would suit your purposes best, and use that one; your hearers may follow suit.

If your name for a thing (whether person, event, object, or text) is accepted, your interpretation of the thing is halfway to acceptance by the others.

REPORT

> **Definition:**   to repeat as a message, to relate what has been
> learnt, to give a formal account of something
> **synonyms:**   *testify, state, announce*
> **antonym:**   *conceal*

Reporting is a particular kind of informing; it may be a restatement of others' information or a truthful account of a personally experienced event. It should be capable of verification, and demonstrate that the speaker is trying to act simply as a conduit through which the information is passed. It differs from testifying which requires that the reporter prove the honesty of the report; and it differs from stating which gives information which originates with the speaker. If the information is notable for its newness to the hearers, the act may be that of announcing.

Reports can form much of the groundwork of a negotiation, providing the material base from which the discussion will proceed. They are not only the kind of formalised reports that a committee or working party calls for to assist its deliberations, but can be much more casually introduced. For instance, whenever a speaker gives a set of figures on a subject, or else asserts, assumes or proposes something, there may be a report embedded in that act.

Reports of events can deal with matters either outside or inside the negotiation. In the first case, a speaker can research a report, check its accuracy and rehearse it before a meeting. In the second, a report must be given at the meeting, while all the other actions of the event are occupying the reporter's mind. In both cases, however, the following skills are required.

(a) The reporter should be accurate in observing detail. If reporting an event, questions about the who, what, when, where, and how of the thing reported need to be addressed, and verification prepared. A broad vocabulary will be necessary if the reporter is to have a good range of paradigm choices from which to select the best term for the thing to be reported, and a specialist vocabulary may be needed to deal with matters of technical significance.

(b) The reporter should be able to summarise: to select important features and to rephrase them briefly and without distortion. A standard report might be an account given by a manager on staffing needs. This could be based on a variety of sources: a set of documents, personal observations, discussions with various people, a knowledge of the funding possibilities for staffing in the future, and so on. All of this would need to be distilled into a few sentences – as a report on the present situation.

(c) When reporting on a communication, the reporter should be skilled in seeing through rhetorical strategies to the basic points made. It also helps to be able to note what aspects of a topic were dealt with and which were omitted – these are often crucial and should be chased up for what they can tell of the speaker's concerns. It is important to distinguish those matters which were of major value to the reported event and those which were incidental. An assessment then needs to be made as to whether these values remain the same for the negotiation in progress, or whether any matters that were peripheral in the earlier account are more important now.

(d) The reporter should be able to perform high-level categorisation, pulling together matters with little superficial resemblance but some deep connection, and separating matters which were joined together in the original event for some purpose which is no longer pertinent.

A report can either be solicited or unsolicited. Before attending a negotiation consider whether any report might be asked of you, and be prepared. Ascertain from others, or from your experience of reporting or of hearing others' reports in like circumstances, what requirements will have to be met. If you are thinking of offering a report of your own volition, make sure that you have a solid knowledge of the matter and be certain that the hearers need or want it. Then consider when it might best be given in order to provide the most help and least hindrance to the process of negotiation.

Be prepared to explain why you feel the role of reporter is right for you, and to justify your assumption of that role. You should, for example, be able to show your connections with the reported event, your relations with the actors reported on, your specialised knowledge of reporting itself, and your role in the current encounter. It is a general rule that the weaker the link is perceived to be between the reporter and the event the less the report is credited. Thus your hearers might criticise in these terms:

'Why is Fred telling us this? What has it to do with him? What does he know about it?'

So always consider whether any credit will accrue to you and, if so, whether you can increase it in any way, or whether indeed the best move might not be to keep silent.

The mechanisms for verbalising a report of a communication are of three kinds: it can be done through direct speech, indirect speech, or free indirect speech. Each has different procedures, and leads to different consequences.

Direct speech

Direct speech requires that the reporter make clear the exact words used by any actors in the reported event. Several forms of words can introduce this kind of report:

'He *said* "I am unable to name the precise figure."'

'The report *said, and I quote* "Our business is. . ."'

'"I am sure we can" were *his exact words*.'

'*If memory serves me correctly, he said* "I am delighted with . . ."'

The first three indicate that the process of reporting has introduced minimal interference with the events mentioned; while the last offers a loophole in case someone else objects, and has a better (or different) memory of what was said.

Hearers of such direct reportage must feel that they have the speech exactly as delivered on the reported occasion. They might well repeat it elsewhere as the gospel truth about what the actor said, and attribute it to you. If your report has been inaccurate even in a small detail, it could lead to unfortunate consequences. This is because if the detail was important enough it could change the whole sense of what the actor said, and the actor concerned could rightly be concerned about this.

Indirect speech

Indirect speech is reported through the operation of a set of grammatical rules. These are shown here, using the following as the example of direct speech to be reported:

'I will not be available today at any time.'

(a) Any first-person words such as 'I' (or 'we' meaning the speaker) must be turned into third-person words such as 'he', 'she', or 'they', or, if the original speaker's identity is unclear to the new hearers, his or her name, title, or position should be given.

(b) Any indications of present time in the original speech should be changed to a time further away in the past; this means not only changing the tense of any verbs used, but also altering any adverbs of time, like 'today', 'tomorrow', 'then', 'last Tuesday', 'now', and so on.

(c) A verb which accurately records the general quality of the original speech act should be chosen to introduce the reported words; for example, one or other of such verbs as 'said', 'agreed', 'proposed', and 'complained' might be appropriate.

Any of the following, therefore, could serve as a suitable report of the sentence given above:

'He said that he would not be available at any time on Monday.'

'Bill complained that he was not available all that day.'

'She argued that she wouldn't be available at all then.'

'Ms Smith agreed she wouldn't be available on the 15th.'

If the set of rules is understood, the second hearer (as it were) should have little difficulty in re-constituting the original words spoken.

The act of reporting speech in the indirect mode does more than this, however. Choosing indirect reportage allows the reporter to incorporate something of his or her opinion of the original speech act in ways that are more or less surreptitious, and hence influence the response that the reported matter will receive from the new hearers. This is done particularly through the verb of speech action that is chosen. 'Said' as in the first example is the most neutral verb possible, but the choice of 'complain' in the second example adds an element of interpretation. It may be hard for new hearers to know whether this is a rhetorically strategic choice, or an accurate record. Here are two examples which could be more than simple reports:

'He claimed that he would not be available',

where the word *claim* implies that the statement may not be true, and

'He declared that he would not be available',

where the word *declare* implies either a sense of making a public statement, or an extra dimension of affirmation.

Interpretation plays an even larger role in the third way in which reports can be given.

Free indirect speech

As a means of reporting, free indirect speech is a combination of direct and indirect reporting. To see the comparison, note the differences in the following set of examples:

Direct speech – 'I heard him exclaim "Is that the only problem today?"'

Indirect speech – 'He asked me if that was the only problem that day.'

Free indirect speech – 'I heard him say Good Heavens, was that the only problem today?'

As a hybrid form, the last gains something vivid and dramatic by directly supplying some of the words used in the original speech, while yet retaining something of the objectivity and distancing found in indirect reportage. What it keeps in direct form and what it alters by indirect reporting is an important rhetorical choice, and will affect the hearers' understanding of what took place, and their response to it. It can be a very persuasive strategy to produce this kind of reportage, since it leaves ambiguous what belongs to the original speaker and what to the reporter.

The following is an example of a report which modulates from direct to indirect to free indirect speech:

'He was arguing angrily, "Your delays have caused us far too much trouble." I was trying to explain that the shippers were at fault, but he was not listening, and next thing we were making an appointment to settle new delivery dates. Thursday? All right? Well as long as you don't let us down again, or we'll sue.'

Although it is a little confusing to hear, its complexity could produce very useful information; it selects accuracy where the reporter feels this is essential, gives a condensed indirect report of argument and explanation, and decides to display depth of feeling to make a point.

As a reporter you can choose to use the form most appropriate to your aims. As a hearer, however, your options are different. If accuracy of reporting is what you want, then you may need to ask questions and test the choice of word use, or even do some further investigating, perhaps seeking a second version from someone else who was present.

REPRIMAND

Definition: to offer formally an adverse judgment to another about a serious matter

synonyms: *reprove, rebuke, reproach*

antonyms: *praise*

A reprimand is a formal or official speech act which declares a negative judgment about someone, usually face to face, but occasionally by other means of communication. It is among the most face-threatening acts to offer to another because its goal is to bring the hearer down a peg or two, and, if done inefficiently, is capable of causing humiliation or resentment in the hearer. This could occur if one of the necessary elements of the act's performance is missing.

In order for a reprimand to be made, the following are essential conditions on the speaker's part.

(a) Since reprimanding is an official act the speaker must have some authority in relation to the hearer. This could be generally by virtue of his or her hierarchical position, or could be granted in a particular case by others involved. It can also occasionally happen that the person to be reprimanded provides authorisation to another to perform the act, saying 'You have a right to be annoyed with me over this.'

(b) The speaker must be able to take the high moral ground in the matter; if the matter is one on which the speaker has at other times been at fault, then the hearer is entitled to feel angry at the injustice of the act.

(c) The speaker must have accurate knowledge of the issues involved in the reprimand; if details are wrong, or even the whole reprimand (perhaps because it should have been addressed to another person), then the speaker could be justifiably criticised, and the relationship involved could be severely damaged.

(d) The reprimand must be acceptable to any others who are witnesses. If the wrong people are present, it makes it even worse for the hearer to have them see his or her humiliation. Moreover, the people themselves may be most unwilling to observe the act, and if forced to do so may attempt to soften the reprimand in order to reduce their own awkwardness, thus spoiling its effect.

For the hearer to accept a reprimand as proper, the following conditions should be met.

(a) The reprimander must be an acceptable person to perform the act.
(b) The hearer must have done something deserving of reprimand, and there must be some evidence of this available.
(c) The thing for which the reprimand is delivered must be taking place at the time, or have been done in the fairly recent past. (There is an unwritten 'statute of limitations' about such things. For example, a reprimand at one meeting for something done at the preceding meeting could be quite reasonable, even if the meetings take place only once a year, but a reprimand for something done six months previously, when the speaker and hearer meet every day, could be seen as unreasonable, unless the something has just been discovered, or was extremely serious and has had continuing repercussions into the present.)

A reprimand is a punishment: it may be the whole of the punishment or only the first part, but since its effect should be to provide (at least) discomfort to the hearer, it must be done with punishment in mind. The severity of the reprimand, therefore, must match the gravity of the act. If a very severe reprimand were offered for a minor misdemeanour, it would fail in its effect, with the hearer able to mount an argument against it; if a serious act received a mild reprimand this too would miss its effect of punishment. If unsure that the hearer's interpretation of the offence is the same as his or hers, the reprimander should spell out the features of the offence, and mention those consequences that are most serious. Be prepared for the hearer to raise objections to any of these features as untrue, invalid or unfair.

Since the act of reprimand is an official one, its power is strongest if there is a strongly impersonal quality in it, as in:

> (to Bill, the Personnel Officer) 'Personnel Officers should not behave in ways quite contrary to professional rules and company policy.'

Here neither the speaker nor the hearer are personalised, and the offence is not specified. Its power may well be reduced the more personalised it becomes and the more particulars are given; for example, the following is an extremely weak reprimand:

> 'Bill, I was extremely annoyed that you called that secretary a "girl", you should know better in your job, and particularly when we are trying to stop sexist remarks in the office.'

Its weakness arises from a number of features.

1 The use of 'Bill' shows that the personal relationship between the two has not been affected by the act for which Bill is being reprimanded, which

suggests that it was not serious, or perhaps that the reprimander wants the reprimand to have little 'personal' effect.

2 The personal 'I' could suggest that the offence only affected the speaker.

3 Since the phrase 'extremely annoyed' represents just a personal emotional state (and is used rather than, say, a phrase which might indicate the speaker's concern with more formal, even legal, consequences of sexual discrimination), the effect of the fault is minimised.

4 The specificity of the act – 'called that secretary a girl' – means that Bill could deny it happened, or claim that it was not serious.

5 'You should know better' is weaker than 'you must do better' or 'you must stop that' because it leaves any improvement to Bill himself, and only requires that he somehow improve his knowledge, 'know better', with no mention of how this might result in different and better acts.

6 The company's policy is not stated firmly as a positive general goal, despite the reference to 'the elimination of sexist practices', to which Bill's act runs counter. But in the form of words used here his act takes place within a state of 'trying to stop sexist remarks' in which failures may occur during the period of 'trying', and so Bill has done little out of the ordinary.

If the act were offered in an even more personal way than this, for example:

'Bill, you were quite wrong to speak to that secretary in that way. You knew I was trying to stop that kind of thing; I trusted you, and you let me down',

it would cease to be an official reprimand at all, and become a reproach or a rebuke. Both of these are more informal and personal acts than that of reprimand, and have influence only as far as the authority and status of the speaker are strong; otherwise, they can be easily dismissed.

TELL

What I tell you three times is true.

(Lewis Carroll)

'You must not tell us what the soldier, or any other man, said, sir,' interposed the judge; 'it's not evidence.'

(Dickens)

Definition: to give an account of, to make known through speech or writing, to express in words
   synonyms: *utter, mention*
   antonym: *conceal*

The act of telling, of producing a 'tale' (which should not be taken as referring only to fairy tales or fictions), is one of the most common speech acts, in both formal and informal, personal and business negotiations, from the most casual to the most rigorously formalised. At the casual extreme it can be introduced by 'Let me tell you . . .', or invited by 'Tell us what happened to you . . .', while at the formal extreme it could begin with 'May we call upon the staff representative to tell us what was decided . . .', or 'Madam Chairman, I would like, if I may, to tell the meeting . . .'

Telling resembles reporting since both are accounts of happenings and persons. The two acts have a quality in common which makes them powerful persuaders in negotiation: they both take for granted that a single event can easily be isolated from the complex of interrelated happenings in the world and put into language. Tales and reports are therefore always personal selections, involving simplification, and revealing the speaker's interpretation of the world. They differ markedly, however, in several respects.

While reports are concerned with accuracy, rationality, and verifiability, tales seek to have hearers acknowledge their 'truth', which means only that the thing told is recognisable and familiar to others from their own general knowledge. Reporting activates the hearer's mind to go through the routines of reasoning on the data supplied, in order to assess the accuracy of the report. Telling is more likely to discourage hearers from thinking rationally; so familiar is the narrative patterning of tales that, as the story begins, hearers let themselves relax, and offer their minds into the control of the teller. So a hearer asks him- or herself not about accuracy, but about whether the patterning of the events, or the narrative line through which the events are told, 'makes sense'. And the judgment of 'sense' rests almost entirely on the tale's capacity to match previously heard tales. A new tale is therefore likely to have its material believed and accepted if it fits the 'scripts' of other tales known to the hearer. Provided that it does not clash strongly with what is already known and understood about the world outside tales, it may well be found to be 'true'.

The standard patterns of tales, which appear to apply universally across cultures, are:

(a) calm exists, is disturbed, and the disturbance is resolved;
(b) a person meets another person, they disagree but finally reach agreement;
(c) a person goes on a journey, has adventures, and reaches safe harbour;
(d) one person tries a test and fails, a second person tries the test and fails, and a third person tries and succeeds and is rewarded;
(e) one person has a small adventure, a second person has a bigger adventure, and a third person has the biggest adventure of all.

Tales which use one of these tried and true patterns are only likely to be queried, resisted or rejected if they do not support or reinforce the status quo, or if they tell of new, strange, and therefore not readily acceptable, things.

Reporting should be chosen as the speech act when your main goal is to leave your hearers freedom to make what sense they can of the material; telling should be chosen when you wish to have the material accepted, and with it your interpretation unquestioned, or perhaps even unnoticed. Using a tale to speak of some happening disguises the degree and kind of interpretation being wrought upon it for two reasons: first, because the manipulation is at such a deep level, and, second, because the hearers are conditioned from earliest childhood to accept the authority of tales.

The act of telling has other consequences. As the hearers experience the speaker telling the tale, this demonstrates the speaker's authority as one who can analyse and communicate the simplicity that lies behind the world's complexity; and also they may be influenced by the liveliness of the telling to ignore the full implications of the story's content and its basic assumptions.

HOW BEST TO USE THE NARRATIVE FORM

The narrative form arranges the material of the happening into agents, actions and results; it judges the agents, actions, and results to be of main or secondary value; and it omits and emphasises aspects of the happening. It also matches events to the standard patterns of narrative.

There are a number of elements that are essential to a good narration. First, selection and omission of matters must be made carefully. There is no need to tell of something which happened just because it did, if its absence would improve the chances of the tale's being accepted. (It may not necessarily be a distortion of the event's meaning to omit some element; it may just make the telling more focused, or easier to understand, because it has been edited.)

Second, the choice of what to foreground as the main event and what to treat as of secondary value is critical. This choice can often work subconsciously to impose the speaker's valuation of the matters being treated.

Third, language strategies should be selected to bring about acceptance of the tale. These should include:

(a) changes in tone of voice – acting out the characters to brings vividness and memorability to the tale;
(b) changes in vocabulary (for example, fitting the language to the character as appropriate);
(c) the use of attitudinal words, like 'unfortunately' (as in 'Unfortunately the boss came in just at that point', where the speaker places the hearer with him or herself on the side of the workers against the boss, seeing bosses as people whose sudden appearance is 'unfortunate'); these may

not be noticed by a hearer, but nonetheless could help to bring about acceptance of the view expressed.

Fourth, structuring of the material, both at the broadest, speech-interaction, level and at the micro-level of word and grammatical choice, should take into account the effect that is intended, the events to be related, and the repertoire of narrative structures that are available. One standard narrative form shapes the material in three phases 'first, then second, then third'; another signals the priorities of its material by labelling one part as 'most important' or one event as being 'primarily' something or another; such simple and familiar structures will incline hearers to understand and possibly, therefore, to accept this (interpretative) ordering of the event.

Structuring accomplished through such words as the following is very powerful in persuading hearers to accept the teller's judgment of the relations between elements in the event: 'because', 'consequently', 'on the one hand . . . and on the other', 'although', 'if . . . then', 'therefore', and so on.

Fifth, the teller should choose a suitable point of view to adopt, that is, he or she should decide what role to play, for example whether to appear as a participant in the matters related or as a bystander.

Finally, some means of connecting the event told and the present event should be found, because any resemblance of patterning between the two events will make it easier for hearers to absorb the tale's information (there will be less new matter to take in) and may influence them to accept the narrated event because they accept the present event. So the narrated event could be represented as having the same structure as the present one, 'It was an occasion much like this', or the same location, 'It was in this very building that . . .', or the same personnel, 'Mary was there then, and Bill, you were there too, but you two were absent that day', or the same goals, 'It was another meeting trying to decide on this matter . . .', and so on. Such resemblances could cause the two events, one narrated and one experienced, to become somewhat fused in the hearers' memories, and hence remembered (and accepted) together.

Hearers of tales should note that while telling is a very common activity, and a useful one, it is not without hazards for those trying to understand, as well as extract the truth from, the matter narrated. As a hearer of tales concerned to interpret the event fairly, it is important to consider the various elements of it that have been manipulated in order to produce the tale. This will require:

(a) discovering the propositions which underlie the events of the tale;
(b) noting the basic elements of the event behind the mode of telling, and assessing their validity according to your general knowledge;
(c) estimating the goals of the teller, to determine what the manipulation might have been;

(d) using any previous experience of the teller by which you could measure the accuracy of the tale, judging what to trust and what to doubt;

(e) noticing signs of the teller's personal evaluation. This can be achieved by the use of a paradigmatic analysis, which would show both what other choices were possible and what were the specific implications of the choices that had been made.

Further, consider what influence the very act of telling – its form and content – will have on your next act in the negotiation. There are conventions connected with the hearing of tales which could produce an undesirable result. For example, there is a convention that hearers agree with tales if possible, and even that they seek to cap them with similar tales, often more exaggerated in some aspect: 'Yes, well, I had a much worse experience myself . . .', or 'Oh, that's nothing, I did . . .' The tale might be told with just this result in mind, so before producing your own tale, ask yourself what it will reveal, what effect the act of trying to cap the first narrator will have on the relationship between you and the others present, as well as on the negotiation itself, and then decide whether or not to proceed.

If as a hearer you wish to object to the tale, there are several polite options open to you, which could be acceptable to the speaker and to any third parties present as face-saving, and which yet act to engage with the debatable elements of the tale.

1 Acknowledge the positive values of the tale as a preliminary to criticising it: 'that's interesting, but . . .'
2 Question the applicability of the events of the tale to those aspects of the current negotiation to which the teller has linked them: that is, check their relevance.
3 Question the ordering and choice of elements: 'Did nothing else happen next?' 'Are you sure you haven't missed something out?'
4 Take up the specific terms used and query them: 'What do you mean by saying they were *similar*?'
5 Ask for further details on any matter where you think distortion may have occurred.
6 Check causal connections for validity.
7 Check for any significant omissions.

Part V

Wrap-up –
language after the event

Chapter 9

Completing the negotiation

REMEMBERING AND RECALLING

INTRODUCTION

There are two processes involved in memory: *remembering*, that is, putting into memory storage, and *recalling*, that is, retrieving from memory storage. Some remembering requires almost immediate recall, as in noting a phone number and then straightaway dialling it; some remembering needs longer-term storage since recall will not be required for days, weeks or years.

There are two very important points to note about the processes of memory. The first is that very little is remembered. Research has shown that people remember only half of what they hear, even immediately after hearing it. After a day the percentage of information retained drops to 35 per cent, and by a month later only some 25 per cent remains. What is vital in these circumstances is to ensure that what is remembered is the most important information, and that it is minor matters that are lost. This can be achieved by taking time immediately after an event to decide on what deserves to be remembered and focusing attention on it. The very process of selecting and deciding to remember can mean that more is remembered. The paucity of what is recallable is not as bad as it sounds, for two reasons: first, your general impressions of the participants and of the event usually last longer than details of the matters discussed; and second, the rate of the information flow received may be such that only about 25 per cent was ever meant to be remembered.

The second point is that the storage ability of participants in an event is restricted. Social psychologists have discovered that most subjects can only remember approximately four things from an event. So a hearer could remember four topics, ideas or opinions from a meeting, but, without the assistance of memory strategies to improve this rate, would forget or retain only a minimal memory trace of any other matters. One strategy which most people use naturally to circumvent this problem is to cluster matters together in their understanding of an event; such clusters then 'count' as one storage item. Clustering involves perceiving close connections between matters, for example between an idea offered by a speaker, his or her attitude to it, and the kind and degree of the hearer's own response to it. These may all be remembered together.

Given these two general facts about memory, a negotiator can choose to work within their restrictions, or else try to reach beyond them to other possibilities.

If a hearer accepts them, he or she should concentrate on those matters which are of sufficient importance to form the four that he or she will remember. The process involved in deliberately selecting memorable items is a useful one, since it requires the negotiator to maintain a sufficient critical distance from the event to make running decisions about the degrees of importance of the matters as they occur, and to search the ongoing event for significance or lack of it. The cognitive effort involved in doing this automatically assists in the storage of memory.

The negotiator can, however, refuse to be bound by memory limits, and work to improve the remembering and recall processes.

The data which is to be remembered differs: negotiators may need to store ideas, facts, opinions, perceptions of attitudes, or a sense of physical happenings; and the significance of the material may be social or cognitive. But while the nature of the material has some impact on the ease or difficulty with which it can be remembered (some people have good memories for facts, others for attitudes), rather more important influences are the kind of context in which the material is received by the hearer, and the mode of its presentation.

Context

Memory storage does not take place in a vacuum, but occurs in response to a particular event. Each event has features which can make remembering easier or harder. Those events which resemble ones which the participant has previously experienced come, as it were, already scripted for memorising, because he or she already has similar events in storage, and so can guess what occurrences will take place, what matters will be raised, what speaker A is likely to say and do, and so on. This recurrent patterning means that little cognitive effort is required either to remember the detail of a new event, or to recall it, because it simply slots into place as another instance of some matter already present in memory. Such a familiar event might be reported later, by a participant saying 'Well, it was the kind of meeting we always have: Bill did his usual stuff, Mary raised her favourite scheme again, and I can't remember what Fred and Susan said exactly but I think it was much the same as usual.' In this way previous memories are brought to the aid of the current one.

Presentation

This kind of memorability would apply equally, however, in an event where a speaker broke dramatically with his or her previous behaviours, and produced speech in an unexpected fashion. This would be relatively easily remembered as a marked contrast to his or her norm. (In such circumstances, however, it is possible that only the unexpected will be remembered, and this may be undesirable as a fair account of the event.) Where every participant behaves unexpectedly, or where the kind of event is new to a participant, or all the speakers are strangers, and each makes an unforeseen contribution, there is too much data for the average memory to store, and only the minimal four items may be processed.

What actually takes place in memory is not a matter of rote learning, or of parroting in exact terms what was said and done in an event, but rather a reconstruction of the meaning of the event. What is remembered is not usually a speaker's exact words (unless there is a crucial reason to do just this) but a construction of the gist of his or her words, an interpretation (in line with previous experience of the speaker) of the words used, of the event, and so on. That is why an entirely new kind of event is so problematic for memory: there is no previous experience to use to interpret this one. It is also why memories differ between people: they have different experiences to use for interpretation.

STRATEGIES FOR REMEMBERING

Memory is helped if you have a strong impetus to remember; so prepare for an event which you wish to remember by being clear about your goals.

Where a matter is connectable with prior matters it will be remembered better, so seek to link an important matter with previous knowledge, and other similar matters.

Do not seek to memorise parrot-fashion (except where detail is crucial), but rather, while trying to remember, elaborate on the matter to be stored. For example, think what its antecedents were, consider and judge the words and phrases that the speaker used (try a paradigmatic analysis), think about the speaker's tone of voice, estimate his or her intentions, and consider your own response and that of the others present. These things will be remembered better if you rehearse all of them in speech or writing; this will fix them more firmly in your memory than just vaguely or indirectly thinking about them. The more cognitive work there is involved in this elaboration, the more securely the matter will be fixed in memory storage.

Do not expect to be able to store discrete items easily, but rather seek to remember them in relation to elements around them: to previous speech, to any antecedent matters of relevance, or to any post-sequence words used or issues raised. In particular, try to place the matter to be stored in the hierarchy of the structures in which it occurs. If an item appears to be worth remembering, then note, for example, within what grammatical structure it occurred; in what frame of reference it happened, or at what point in the interaction or during what phase of behaviour; whether the speaker chose to foreground it; or whether it was the first or last sentence in the speech, or the fourth point in a list of six. The more data you have with which to reconstruct the meaning that you wish to remember the more you will in fact remember it and the more accurate the memory is likely to be.

Which matters are easily remembered can vary according to whether you are a participant or an observer in the event. While it is not always possible to change from one of these positions to the other, it is worth knowing the difference and preventing it from being too incapacitating.

Participants are more likely to remember not only the speech acts of an event, but also the situational factors, since they themselves are affected by these factors. They are also more likely to attend to the broad thematic concerns of the encounter. Participants may find the matters dealt with easier to remember because someone who addresses them may mobilise knowledge they are familiar with in order to take full account of their presence. As a result, hearers are personally involved, and that means that their prior memories are activated, and can assist storage of the current event.

Observers, that is, outsiders or those present who take no active part in the proceedings, have less awareness of the situational factors since they have not had to take them into account to the same extent as full participants. As a consequence, they have to read the situation with less data than is available to the participants. Also, less of their own personal prior knowledge has been activated (as it is when one is in dialogue and has to speak in turn), and so less is available to assist memory. On the other hand, observers may be better placed to remember details in opinionated or heated debate than participants, who may be more involved and less distanced from the event.

So, the strategy should be: if it is crucial to remember a matter together with all the factors that accompany its presentation, then become actively involved in the encounter. If only specific details are to be remembered, then be an observer.

STRATEGIES FOR RECALLING

While the remembering process is being activated, consider that recall will one day be necessary; therefore, judge what form this will take, and for what purposes the recall will be needed, and this will assist the memory to store the matter in a usefully recallable form.

Where the matter to be recalled is primarily abstract or general in nature, then seek to make it concrete while storing it; find an illustrative example, or convert the abstract into an action or a story illustrating the principles involved. This is useful because most people can more easily recall concrete memories than abstract ones.

Between the time of the original storage and the likely time when there will be a need for recall, repeat the matter, rehearse responses to it, reorganise it, search it for key ideas and investigate it for alternative meanings. That is, use any opportunity to do cognitive work on the matter; this will keep it in memory, and moreover to the front of the memory data-store. It may be useful to support your understanding of it through discussion with others, and by exchanging memories with them.

Supplement your memory store capacity by using other storage methods, for example putting the matter into an oral or written record. Write notes immediately after the event, or do a tape-recording of your version of the event. Then file it in a way useful for recall.

Devise a personal strategy for recalling matters – some people remember words well, others remember facial expressions, or tones of voice, or locations. Think what comes most easily to your mind about occasions when you try to recall them. Focus on what triggers these easy memories, and try to systematise your skills by practising recall, using your triggers more consciously, and seeking to add others.

STRATEGIES FOR BEING REMEMBERED

Speakers who hope that their hearers will remember and be able to recall their ideas need to produce them in ways that are memorable.

Connect your current ideas with your earlier ideas and messages, to make it easier for hearers to make connections, and to store the incoming data with those earlier examples. For example, make references to related prior messages by yourself or others and repeat your terminology when repeating your ideas. Indicate to your hearers how the present message should be seen in relation to the others, for instance as a development or an exception.

If your most important contributions are abstract or general, then provide concrete examples to assist others to store them.

Repeat your main points, either during the negotiation, or in writing before or after it. One of the greatest helps to hearers' memories is a prior signal of what subject matter will be raised, or an indication of its importance, so that cognitive effort can be focused on it and the memory storing mechanisms can be activated in advance. So produce a written or oral outline of the points to be made, or explicitly signal their value (for example, 'And now I come to my most important point') and, if they are in your view essential matters, follow them up with a written record after the meeting.

Utilise the hearers' awareness of the 'scripts' of negotiation by doing the expected, or at least recognise that in doing the unexpected you run the risk either of not being understood and remembered or, if it is marked enough, of having the unexpected remembered to the exclusion of all else.

Get the rate of speech right, neither too fast nor too slow for assimilation.

Do not overload the speech with information; produce a steady information flow by using devices such as repetition or exemplification, or by putting in work on the social aspects of the encounter to slow down the flow to one that your hearers seem comfortable with.

Use language which assists memory retention, for example:

(a) use similar grammatical patterns for similar ideas;
(b) whenever possible use the most easily memorised grammatical pattern, which is the simple statement form – subject, verb, object;
(c) distinguish main and subordinate points by using main clauses for the one and subordinate clauses for the other.

RECORDING

To establish a proper record of the events of a negotiation, it is necessary to prepare in advance.

Use any signs you have by way of agendas, notices of meeting, or memos, to determine what will take place, what topics will be raised, what purposes will be addressed, and so on.

Use any prior knowledge you have of the people who will be present to assess how they will approach the negotiation, what issues they will raise, what activities they will perform, and so on. With these clues, prepare a recording document – either sheets in a small looseleaf notebook, or a set of cards – and label it according to the matters to be dealt with. (Use a separate sheet or card for each matter; it would be a false economy to put several items on one card if they might need to be separated later.)

Consider what filing system you will adopt for easy reference. Cards could be filed as chronological accounts, or by topic, or by the person presenting the topics.

Prepare your own contribution as far as you can, so that you have some spare time during the meeting to take notes.

The object of the exercise is to retain a summary account of the event, therefore the parameters of your notetaking should include the following.

(a) Note the propositions discussed, any crisis points or points which created dissension or achieved easy agreement. Note any absences or omissions you think are of significance, and in particular highlight any matters left outstanding to be dealt with at another meeting. Observe the kind and quantity of data used to support propositions and note its sources accurately, especially if it meets with general approval, for similar material could assist your case in a later meeting.

(b) Note the order of events, along with any prioritising of matters. If the meeting considers a matter to be of importance it is worth noting.

(c) Note the contribution of each participant, whether it was of ideas or opinions, whether it was strongly initiating or simply responsive to others' initiations. Note who supported whom, who opposed whom, and for what reasons. Note the names and other details of any new people, and any key facts about them. Note how people voted.

(d) If any tasks are allocated during the event, note whose responsibility they are. If you are asked to perform some task, make sure you understand it exactly, highlight it, and make it a priority in your notes. Note particularly any success or failure your contribution met with and analyse why this happened.

FOLLOW-UP

There are three important aspects to this last part of the negotiation: that you follow up any ideas that interest you or are useful to your work; that you build relationships with fellow negotiators; and that you perform any tasks allocated to you.

If the ideas raised and the propositions discussed strike you as being useful to develop further, highlight them in your notes and as soon as possible begin work on them. If you can anticipate some development by others from the meeting, prepare your response to it: if it is one you approve of, anticipate your defence of it; if it is one you disapprove of, prepare a case against it.

If a useful, budding relationship needs support, consider how best to do this. If social damage is done, try to repair it. If you form a useful alliance, try to take early advantage of it.

As far as tasks are concerned, some will arise in the negotiation for you to do, but there are also those suggested in this book. Try gradually to incorporate any lessons you can from them into your negotiating behaviour. Take notes on how best to do this, and record any successes and failures you have. This book has been written on the assumption that better knowledge of the language elements of discourse can help to improve your skills in all aspects of the negotiating process.

Bibliography

Anderson, James A. and Meyer, Timothy P. (1988) *Mediated Communication*, Newbury Park: Sage.

Antaki, Charles (1988) 'Explanations, communication and social cognition', in Charles Antaki (ed.) *Analysing Everyday Explanation*, London: Sage.

Beattie, Geoffrey (1983) *Talk: An Analysis of Speech and Non-Verbal Behaviour in Conversation*, Milton Keynes: Open University Press.

Bolinger, Dwight and Sears, Donald A. (1968) *Aspects of Language*, New York: Harcourt Brace Jovanovich.

Broughton, Irv (1981) *The Art of Interviewing for TV, Radio and Film*, Blue Ridge Summit PA: Tab Books.

Brown, Penelope and Levinson, Stephen, C. (1987) *Politeness: Some Universals in Language Use*, Cambridge: Cambridge University Press.

Casey, Edward S. (1987) *Remembering: A Phenomenological Study*, Bloomington: Indiana University Press.

Clark, H.H. and French, J. Wade (1981) 'Telephone Goodbyes', *Language in Society* 10: 1–19.

Cohen, Akiba A. (1987) *The Television News Interview*, Newbury Park: Sage.

Corbett, Edward P.J. (1971) *Classical Rhetoric for the Modern Student*, New York: Oxford University Press.

Corbett, Edward P.J. (1977) *The Little Rhetoric*, New York: John Wiley.

Crystal, David and Davy, Derek (1969) *Investigating English Style*, London: Longman.

Dillon, George L. (1981) *Constructing Texts*, Bloomington: Indiana University Press.

Draper, Stephen W. (1988) 'What's going on in everyday explanation?', in Charles Antaki (ed.) *Analysing Everyday Explanation*, London: Sage.

Fielding, Guy and Hartley, Peter (1987) 'The telephone: a neglected medium', in Asher Cashdan and Martin Jordin (eds) *Studies in Communication*, Oxford: Basil Blackwell.

Fisher, R. and Ury, W. (1981) *Getting to Yes: Negotiating Agreement without Giving In*, Boston: Houghton Mifflin.

Fiske, John (1982) *Introduction to Communication Studies*, London: Methuen.

Flower, Linda (1981) *Problem-solving Strategies for Writing*, New York: Harcourt Brace Jovanovich.

Foucault, M. (1970) *The Archaeology of Knowledge*, London: Tavistock.

Fowler, H.W. (1983) *A Dictionary of Modern English Usage*, 2nd edn, Oxford: Oxford University Press.

Galtung, Johan and Ruge, Mari Holmboe (1970) 'The Structure of Foreign News', in Jeremy Tunstall (ed.) *Media Sociology*, London: Constable.

Godard, D. (1977) 'Phone call beginnings in France and the United States', *Language in Society* 6: 209–19.

Goffman, Erving (1978) *The Presentation of Self in Everyday Life*, Harmondsworth: Penguin.

Goodwin, Charles (1987) 'Unilateral Departure', in Graham Button and John R.E. Lee (eds) *Talk and Social Organisation*, Clevedon: Multilingual Matters.

Gumperz, John J. (1982) *Discourse Strategies*, Cambridge: Cambridge University Press.

Halliday, M. (1983) 'Language structure and language function', in Bob Hodge (ed.) *Readings in Language and Communication for Teachers*, Melbourne: Longman Cheshire.

Halliday, M.A.K. (1979) *Language as Social Semiotic*, London: Edward Arnold.

Halliday, M.A.K. and Hasan, R. (1976) *Cohesion in English*, London: Longman.

Harris, S. (1983) 'Rules of interpersonal communication', in Bob Hodge (ed.) *Readings in Language and Communication for Teachers*, Melbourne: Longman Cheshire.

Hayakawa, S.I. (ed.) (1987) *Penguin Modern Guide to Synonyms and Related Words*, revised by P.J. Fletcher, Harmondsworth: Penguin.

Hayakawa, S.I. (1978) *Language in Thought and Action*, 4th edn, New York: Harcourt Brace Jovanovich.

Heritage, John (1988) 'Explanations as accounts: a conversation analytic perspective', in Charles Antaki (ed.) *Analysing Everyday Explanation*, London: Sage.

Jordan, Michael P. (1984) *Rhetoric of Everyday English Texts*, London: George Allen & Unwin.

Jucker, Andreas H. (1986) *News Interviews: A Pragmalinguistic Analysis*, Amsterdam: John Benjamins.

Kniveton, Bromley and Towers, Brian (1978) *Training for Negotiating: A Guide for Management and Employee Negotiators*, London: Business Books.

Kress, G. (1983) 'The social values of speech and writing', in Bob Hodge (ed.) *Readings in Language and Communication for Teachers*, Melbourne: Longman Cheshire.

Kress, Gunther and Hodge, Robert (1979) *Language as Ideology*, London: Routledge & Kegan Paul.

Lakoff, George and Johnson, Mark (1980) *Metaphors We Live By*, Chicago: University of Chicago Press.

Larson, Richard L. (1968) 'Discovery through questioning', *College English* XXX: 126–34.

Leech, G.N. (1983) *Principles of Pragmatics*, London: Longman.

Leech, Geoffrey and Svartvik, Jan (1975) *A Communicative Grammar of English*, London: Longman.

Lyons, John (1981) *Language, Meaning and Context*, London: Fontana.

McCarthy, Paul (1989) *Developing Negotiating Skills and Behaviour*, Sydney: CCH Australia.

Miller, Gerald R. and Burgoon, Michael (1973) *New Techniques of Persuasion*, New York: Harper & Row.

Montgomery, Martin (1986) *An Introduction to Language and Society*, London: Methuen.

Nash, Walter (1980) *Designs in Prose*, London: Longman.

Pool, I. de Sola (ed.) (1977) *The Social Impact of the Telephone*, Cambridge, Mass.: MIT Press.

Rutter, D.R. (1984) *Looking and Seeing*, New York: Wiley.

Scott, W.P. (1981) *The Skills of Negotiating*, London: Gower.

Schank, Roger C. (1982) *Dynamic Memory*, Cambridge: Cambridge University Press.

Schramm, W. (1983) 'How communication works', in Bob Hodge (ed.) *Readings in Language and Communication for Teachers*, Melbourne: Longman Cheshire.

Tennison, Patrick (1985) *Mastering the Interview*, Melbourne: Information Australia.

Wall, James A. (1985) *Negotiation: Theory and Practice*, Glenview, Ill.: Scott, Foresman.

Walton, R.E. and McKersie, R.B. (1965) *A Behavioural Theory of Labor Negotiations*, New York: McGraw-Hill.

Whorf, B.L. (1956) *Language, Thought and Reality*, ed. J.C. Carroll, Cambridge, Mass.: MIT Press.

Wierzbicka, Anna (1987) *English Speech Act Verbs: A Semantic Dictionary*, Sydney: Academic.

Index